OFFENDERS
AND
CORRECTIONS

OFFENDERS
AND
CORRECTIONS

edited by
Denis Szabo
Susan Katzenelson

PRAEGER PUBLISHERS
Praeger Special Studies

New York • London • Sydney • Toronto

Library of Congress Cataloging in Publication Data

Main entry under title:

Offenders and corrections.

   1.   Prisoners--Addresses, essays, lectures. 2. Cor-
rections--Addresses, essays, lectures. 3. Crime and
criminals--Addresses, essays, lectures. I. Szabo, Denis,
1929-   II. Katzenelson, Susan.
HV8665.033   1978   365'.6   78-8399
ISBN 0-03-044236-2

**Published in cooperation with
the American Society of Criminology.
General Editor: Arnold S. Trebach**

PRAEGER SPECIAL STUDIES
383 Madison Avenue, New York, N.Y. 10017, U.S.A.

Published in the United States of America in 1978
by Praeger Publishers,
A Division of Holt, Rinehart and Winston, CBS, Inc.

89   038   987654321

Printed in the United States of America

CONTENTS

LIST OF TABLES

LIST OF FIGURES

Criminology is an expanding discipline, encompassing a wide range of human behavior--from the conforming to the deviant to the criminal to the sinful, the methods of social control, and processes of change on the personal/psychological as well as on the social/ normative level related to modes of deviance and their control.

This volume of papers, presented in Toronto at the 1975 Annual Meeting of the American Society of Criminology, covers only a small portion of this universe. It focuses on the incarcerated offender, prison attitudes and behavior, and some general issues concerning corrections.

The first chapter, by Susan Katzenelson, gives a background description of a large defendant population. It compares male and female defendants, their social characteristics, their offense patterns, and differential treatment by the criminal justice system. The chapter by Handler and Schuett is demographic in nature. It analyzes some of the implications of inmate marital status for correctional policy.

The following chapters explore various aspects of existence in prison and the different styles of "doing time" behind bars. Johnson and Dorin describe the "black revolutionary" in prison, and they question the frequency of this style of adjustment as well as its functionalistic value for the black offender. Wilson compares some masculine and feminine alternatives of doing time and concludes that preprison and felonious identities are more significant in shaping prison behavior and attitudes than sexual identity.

Akers, Hayner, and Gruninger test in two chapters the relative significance of two sets of variables in the prisonization process. Their findings are not conclusive, but they point to the fact that intervening variables such as the inmate's being a first or a repeat offender might be at work in determining the normative alienation of inmates and their future attitudes and behavior. In the United States and four other countries evidence was gathered to support the hypothesis that an intricate net of "functional" and "importation" processes take place in determining the degree of prisonization.

The next three chapters discuss some of the economic phenomena created by prisons. Meyer relates that prisoners are used without the benefit of financial reward for pharmaceutical experiments, with some undesirable correctional results. Miller describes the illegal market situation created by economic deprivation in prison, and its contribution to the creation of the inmate subculture. Finally, Wickman examines the alternative of paid prison work, describing the work system in Sweden and Finland.

In a Canadian study, Kasinsky questions the underlying social motivations and the political implications of the therapeutic model, using the example of the mentally disordered offender held captive by the state.

The therapeutic labeling of defendants is brought into focus in the chapter by Steadman and Cocozza. They point out the problems in the psychiatric assessment and in the prediction of the relative criminal dangerousness of these defendants.

Scharf, concerned with the problems following incarceration, proposes a process of attitude change in prison, through the "just community approach," in order to help inmates adjust to society upon their release.

A review chapter by Gottfredson surveys the much-analyzed field of parole. It singles out some positive changes in this area, such as the development of a national parole analysis data base, the articulation and examination of parole policies, and the evidence for the effectiveness of parole in comparison to other modes of release.

Finally, Roll takes the issue of corrections to the community and discusses the resistance raised by the concept of "community-based corrections."

1

THE FEMALE DEFENDANT
IN WASHINGTON, D.C.
Susan Katzenelson

INTRODUCTION

"Female crime" is largely an understudied area of criminology, principally because of the belief that it is less serious and less frequent. Although some classical theories address the problem of female criminality, * there are very few empirical studies to substantiate them, or even to describe in detail the phenomenon under study.

The purpose of this chapter is to utilize a large, available data base† to describe female offenses, to test some hypotheses, and to try to gain useful insights into criminal behavior in Washington, D.C., and its handling by the criminal justice system.

THEORETICAL BACKGROUND

Most studies of female crime compare it to male crime and point to its relatively less serious nature and low frequency. Two

---

*For a discussion of some of the classical theories by Lombroso, Thomas, Freud, Davis, and others, see Klein (1973).

†The Prosecutor's Management Information System (PROMIS), U.S. Attorney's Office, Washington, D.C., as described in Hamilton and Work (1973).

This project was supported by Grant No. 74-NI-99-0008-G awarded by the Law Enforcement Assistance Administration, U.S. Department of Justice, under the Omnibus Crime Control and Safe Streets Act of 1968, as amended. Points of view or opinions stated in this chapter are those of the author and do not necessarily represent the official position or policies of the U.S. Department of Justice.

1

distinct lines of reasoning can be distinguished: one accepts female
crime as being truly less frequent and serious[*] and explains that
women are basically different from men, biologically, psychologically, and socially; the other questions the validity of the known ratios
between male and female crime[†] and argues that female crime ap-
proximates its male counterpart at least in frequency, if not in form.
In the latter, the emphasis is on cultural, social, and psychological
variables characterizing female behavior and the male response to
it as an explanation for the hidden nature of female crimes. Both
approaches agree that female crimes are less serious, less violent,
less professional and that they involve mainly larceny, shoplifting,
forgery, fraud, drug- and alcohol-related offenses, prostitution,
and vice.

In terms of its etiology, female crime is still viewed as partially determined by the feminine physique and personality, but increasing importance is assigned to social variables that reflect the
differential roles women have in our society (Konopka 1966; Payak
1963; Landis, Scarpitti 1964; Reckless and Kay 1967; Bertrand 1969).

Another major issue is the treatment of the female offender in
the criminal justice system. A variety of studies (Giallombardo
1966; Canadian Correctional Association 1968; Singer 1973; Chesney-
Lind 1973; Schenerman and Kratowski 1974) points to the differential
treatment of the female offender all through the criminal justice system, from her chances of being discovered, reported, arrested,
charged, and prosecuted to the probability of her being convicted
and incarcerated. As summed up by Reckless and Kay (1967: 13),
a large part of the involvement of women in crime that is not officially acted upon "can be traced to the masking effect of women's
roles, effective practice on the part of women of deceit and indirec-
tion, the instigation of men to commit their crimes (the Lady
Macbeth factor), the willingness of men to 'cover up' for them and
the unwillingness of the public and the law enforcement personnel to
hold women accountable for their deeds (the chivalry factor)." Yet
many studies argue that women--viewed as property by men, and
tied to them by obligations of personal morality--are more severely
punished for violations regulating "proper" feminine behavior.

---

[*]A review of biological, psychological, and sociological theories explaining the lower female crime rate is found in Pollak (1961).

[†]See Pollak (1961) or Radzinowicz (1937). In questioning the
known ratios, they argue that the "fictitious" nature of criminal
statistics, or the "masked" behavior of women, explains why a
higher proportion of female crime remains hidden, compared to
male crime.

Thomas, in a colorfully written and classical analysis, searches into the sociocultural reasons for this doubly differential treatment and concludes that morality is an "adult and male system, and men are intelligent enough to realize that neither women nor children have passed through this school. It is on this account that man is merciless to woman from the standpoint of personal behavior, yet he exempts her from anything in the way of contractual morality, or views her defections with allowance and even with amusement" (Thomas 1907: 234). These assumptions seem to indicate that "at each stage in the procedure women are treated either more harshly, or more leniently, depending on the special value threatened by the crime (Adler 1971: 22).

In view of the literature, with its limited scope and lack of empirical findings, the main task of this chapter is to present a statistical description of female crime in a major urban area. Because of the tremendous increase in known serious female crime,* an intriguing question is: What are the projections for the future, given the social changes affecting women's status and functions in today's society?

An interesting insight might be gained by viewing black women as a predictive group.[†] Considering their relatively high and authoritative position within the black subculture, as breadwinners and heads of family, they might resemble the future status of all women who are becoming more independent. Thus, their present criminal behavior might serve as an indicator for the "future shape of things to come." Especially in regard to violent behavior, one might argue that it "depends more on cultural differences, than on sex differences. In a more matriarchal role than that of her white counterpart, the Negro female both enjoys and suffers more of the male role [and] this imposed role makes her more aggressive, more male-like, more willing and more likely to respond violently" (Wolfgang, Ferracuti 1967: 154). Based on available statistics,

---

*See, for example, the <u>Uniform Crime Report</u> (UCR) for 1973. Based on 2,378 agencies, with an estimated population of 94,251,000, the UCR lists the following increases between 1960 and 1973 for selected offenses, by sex: all crimes--27.8 percent for males, 95.3 for females; violent crimes--131.5 percent for males, 134.1 percent for females; property crimes--77.1 percent for males, 315.7 percent for females. The differential increase is even stronger when comparing male and female juvenile delinquents.

[†]See the hypothesis advanced by Freda Adler (1971) on the criminal "halo" effect accompanying the black female's masculine status as head of household.

black women, with the assumption of male roles and responsibilities,
seem to approximate the male crime pattern (Sutherland, Cressey
1974: chaps. 6, 7; Moses 1970: 430-39).

The social changes in sex roles affect not only female behavior
but also male values, attitudes, and behavior. Most likely, this
will also change the handling of female offenders by a so far
predominantly male system. In general, one would hypothesize
an increase over time in the frequency and seriousness of known
female offenses and a trend toward their more equalized treatment
in the criminal justice system.

THE WASHINGTON, D.C., STUDY

The source material for this empirical study is the Prosecutor's Management Information System (PROMIS) of the U.S. Attorney's Office in Washington, D.C. PROMIS records all known adult
offenses resulting in an arrest in Washington, D.C., except federal
and traffic offenses, drunkenness, disorderly conduct, and municipal
violations. The information included is collected from forms filled
out by the police and the prosecutor for all the 1973 cases. Out of
a total of 15,460 arrests, 16.4 percent (or 2,537) were of females.

The study uses descriptive statistics to analyze female crime
internally and, in comparison with male crime, controls for a
series of independent variables. Due to the size of the sample, all
differences reported are statistically significant.

A Profile of the Female Offender in Washington, D.C.

The background variables of age, race, employment, and residence were studied to describe District of Columbia offenders by sex.

Age

Most offenses were charged to young people, ages 16 to 25.
The median age for male offenders was 25, for females slightly over
24. Over 85 percent of all offenses were charged to persons aged
40 years and younger. Female crime peaked at age 23 (9.3 percent
of all female crimes), considerably later than the peak for males at
age 19 (8.2 percent of all male crimes). The overall percentage of
offenses charged to females was 16.4 percent. Only two age groups,
around 23 and 43, exceeded this mean. The two peaks were accounted for by different offenses: prostitution for the 21-to-25-year-
old group and aggravated assault for the 41-to-45-year-old group.

These variations in crime patterns by age might be related to changes in the female role and identity throughout life.

Race

Most arrests in the District of Columbia were accounted for by blacks--79 percent of the female offenses and 88 percent of the male offenses. In comparing the sexes, 25 percent of all white offenses, but only 15 percent of all black offenses, involved females. This finding might be accounted for by the fact that a much higher percentage of prostitution cases was charged to white females than to black females. (Viewing these figures, one should keep in mind that approximately 75 percent of the District of Columbia population is black.)

Employment

For the purpose of computing employment rates, only cases with a definite response (86.5 percent of the total) were included. Significantly more (54 percent) male offenders were employed at the time of their arrest than female offenders (31 percent). Women constituted only 10 percent of the employed offenders but 33 percent of the unemployed ones. This finding is not surprising, however, in light of the differential distribution of employment in the general population by sex.*

Length of Residence in the District of Columbia

The female offender seems to be slightly more mobile geographically than her male counterpart: 44 percent of the females, as compared to 41 percent of the males, were nonresidents. Only 36 percent of the females, compared to 43 percent of the males, have resided over five years in the District of Columbia. This fact might be related to race: with respect to the racial mix of the residential population, proportionately more female offenders arrested in the city were white; and these white female offenders were more likely to reside outside the District of Columbia.

---

*The Statistical Abstract of the United States (1974: 337), in its figures on labor force and participation rates for the period 1960-73, quotes the employment rates in 1973 as 78.7 percent for males and 44.5 percent for females, out of the total labor force.

Criminal History

Offenders having histories of previous arrests made up 56 percent of the total arrested--88 percent male, 12 percent female. Of all males, 58.7 percent had a record, compared to only 41.2 percent females. This gap grew even larger if the category of victimless crimes (in which males and females had the same proportion of recidivists--52 percent) was not considered: the male recidivism rate was then 61 percent; female, 33 percent. Of the most persistent recidivists, those with four or more previous arrests, over 90 percent were male.

For offenders with previous arrests, females tended to have their most recent arrest nearer in time to their present crime than males. This might indicate that females were committing their crimes more frequently, but only within a limited time period, and that males, who were more recidivistic, seemed to have their offenses spread out more. Indirect evidence of this might be found in the fact that female crime peaked at age 23, only slightly before the median age of 24 for female crime, while for male offenses there existed a larger time gap between 19, the age at which male crime peaked, and 25, the median age for male crime.

Characteristics of Female Offenses

The type and seriousness of the offense and the victim involved were used to describe the cases brought against females in 1973.

Type of Offense

One of the questions this study aimed to answer was, what were the types of crimes committed by females? About 44 percent of all the cases were felonies; but females were charged with only 10.2 percent of them (compared to their 16.4 percent share in all crimes), while they accounted for 21.2 percent of the misdemeanors. The male/female ratio for felonies was 8.8:1, for misdemeanors 3.7:1. Looking at it another way, of all female offenses, only 27 percent were felonies, compared to 47 percent for males.

In viewing a detailed listing of the various crime categories (see Table 1.1), it appears that females commit only a small percentage of most of the crimes. Only in the categories of aggravated assault, personal and business fraud and embezzlement, arson, business larceny, gambling, consensual sex offenses, and unclassified offenses did the proportion of crimes accounted for by women exceed their overall mean of 16.4 percent.

TABLE 1.1

Distribution of Offenses by Felony/Misdemeanor, Offense Type, and the
Percent of the Total Charged to Females
(N = 15,400)

Offense Type	Misdemeanors Percent	Misdemeanors Number	Felonies Percent	Felonies Number	Total Percent	Total Number
Crimes involving a victim						
Murder	--	--	15.5	200	15.5	200
Manslaughter	--	--	10.2	49	10.2	49
Negligent homicide	10.0	10	--	--	10.0	10
Aggravated assault	14.6	609	18.7	1,393	17.5	2,002
Simple assault	9.1	678	0.0	6	9.0	684
Assault on a police officer	9.7	31	13.3	173	12.7	204
Forcible sex--victim 16 years and over	0.0	17	0.0	340	0.0	357
Forcible sex--victim under 16 years	0.0	3	1.4	69	1.4	72
Forcible sex--male victim	0.0	2	0.0	19	0.0	21
Armed robbery	9.0	11	5.0	714	5.1	725
Robbery	15.4	26	10.0	688	10.2	714
Personal victimization without violence						
Larceny	17.3	986	8.0	350	14.9	1,336
Auto theft	0.0	41	7.8	331	7.0	372
Fraud	27.6	58	20.8	130	22.9	188
Crimes against residences or households						
Burglary	12.3	495	2.5	679	6.6	1,174
Property destruction	9.5	158	33.3	6	10.4	164
Arson	16.7	6	26.9	26	25.0	32
Crimes against business or institutions						
Robbery	0.0	4	2.3	213	2.3	217
Burglary	17.0	199	2.3	173	10.2	372
Larceny	31.9	913	6.8	146	28.4	1,059
Embezzlement and fraud	31.0	129	28.4	176	29.5	305
Auto theft	33.3	3	4.2	71	5.4	74
Arson	100.0	1	14.3	7	25.0	8
Property destruction	8.9	56	0.0	8	7.8	64
Crimes without identifiable victims						
Weapons offenses--gun	8.9	664	4.9	163	8.1	827
Weapons offenses--other	9.0	177	11.1	36	9.4	213
Gambling	15.8	215	19.7	157	17.5	372
Consensual sex offenses	80.7	795	2.4	41	76.9	836
Drug offenses	10.1	1,804	4.4	68	9.9	1,872
Bail violations and prison breach	18.8	420	11.2	215	16.2	635
Crimes that could not be classified	19.5	179	12.6	103	17.0	282
Total	21.2	8,690	10.2	6,750	16.4	15,440

Note: The 20 cases that were not classified as either a misdemeanor or a felony were excluded from the distribution.

Source: Compiled by the author.

When breaking down the various crime categories to felonies and misdemeanors, relatively more of the female offenses were charged as misdemeanors. This might indicate that female crime is not only less frequent but, within the same offense type, also less serious. (One of the interesting exceptions is aggravated assault: 14.6 percent of the misdemeanor assaults, but 18.7 percent of the felonious assaults, were charged to women.)

A breakdown by different crime categories revealed that women were charged with a small percentage of violent crimes and an increasing proportion of property and victimless crimes. Of the 5,049 violent offenses, 11.6 percent were charged to females. But if rape cases (448) were excluded, women accounted for 12.7 percent of violent crime. Of the 5,367 property offenses, 15.2 percent were charged to women. They were responsible for 22.8 percent of the 4,756 victimless crimes.

The largest proportion, 43 percent, of all female crimes was victimless (25 percent of all female offenses was prostitution); another 23 percent was violent (17 percent assaults), 32 percent against property (20 percent was larceny), and 2 percent all other offenses. This compares to a distribution of all male crimes as 28 percent victimless, 35 percent violent crimes, 35 percent crimes against property, and 2 percent other offenses.

Several interesting findings resulted from looking at the offense patterns of males and females, controlling for age. For women, victimless crimes peaked at the earliest age (21-25 years), followed by property crimes (31-35 years) and finally violent crimes (41-45 years) (see Figure 1.1).

As mentioned earlier, these different types of criminal behavior may very well be linked to women's changing social roles and functions in their life cycle. For men, the order was different: property crime peaked first (16-20 years) followed by violent and victimless crimes, both reaching their highest share in all male offenses at the age of 46 and over. In terms of specific crime categories, prostitution was the most frequent crime for all women between the ages of 16 to 30, and aggravated assault for all women over 30. For males, the single highest category was drug offenses up to age 30, and aggravated assault over 30.

The relative frequency of different crime categories for men and women varied considerably with age. Between the ages of 36 and 45, the percent of female crime that was violent was higher than the percent of male crime that was violent (48 percent and 38 percent, respectively). Similarly, property crime was relatively more prevalent among females than males between the ages of 31 to 40 (37 percent and 30 percent, respectively), and victimless crimes were relatively more frequent for females compared to males in the younger age group of 16 to 30 (constituting 50 percent of all female crime, but only 27 percent of all male crime for that age group).

FIGURE 1.1

The Relative Frequency of Female Offenses, by
Offense Type and Offender's Age

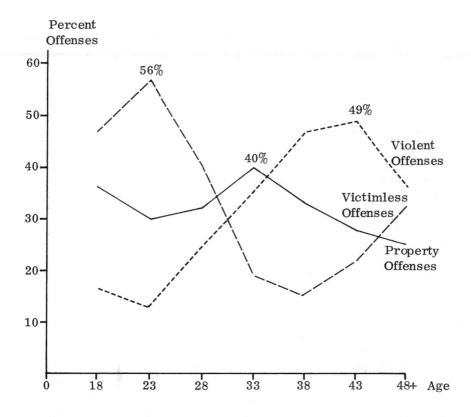

Source: Compiled by the author.

Although the District of Columbia is not typical in the race composition of its residents, offense types of the two sexes were further analyzed by race, in order to obtain some insights into criminal behavior patterns. In general, both for males and females, the white offender seemed more involved in victimless crimes, the black offender in violent and property crimes. When comparing the internal distribution of offenses within each race/sex group, black female offenses seemed to resemble that of the black male to a greater extent than that of the white female (see Figure 1.2). The most striking race difference for women was in the "violent crime" category: it constituted only 9 percent of white female offenses, but almost 26 percent of black female offenses. The same gap held true for property crimes. On the other hand, victimless crimes accounted for 64 percent of white female arrests, compared to only 40 percent for black females.

The findings might support the hypothesis mentioned previously (Wolfgang, Ferracuti 1967; Adler 1971) and might serve as a possible prediction for future changes in female crime patterns. If black women can indeed be viewed as forerunners of a future increase in economic participation* and social position for all women, one can expect a relative increase in violent and property crimes and a corresponding decrease in victimless crimes. This, in turn, might eventually change the prevailing social values and expectations concerning the perception of certain types of deviant behavior as being more "masculine" or "feminine," and social and economic factors, rather than sex, may be recognized as determinants of crime patterns.

There seems to be a positive relationship between unemployment and offense type. Violent offenders had relatively lower rates of unemployment than property offenders, with victimless crimes situated between these two categories, although the relationship appears to hold stronger for males than for females. (In terms of

---

*The Statistical Abstract of the United States (1974: 337), in its analysis of employment trends, points to some interesting race differences. In 1973, 79 percent of the white male labor force was employed, as compared to 72.3 percent of the black male labor force, while only 43.6 percent of the white female labor force worked, compared to 48.5 percent of the black female labor force. When comparing 1960 and 1973 figures, black female rates changed only slightly from 47.2 percent to 48.5 percent, while the largest gain in employment was by white females from 36 percent to 43.6 percent. Male participation dropped for both races: from 82.6 to 79 percent for white males, from 80.1 to 72.3 percent for black males. This might indicate a trend toward closing the gap in economic status between the sexes and might have an effect on future patterns of crime.

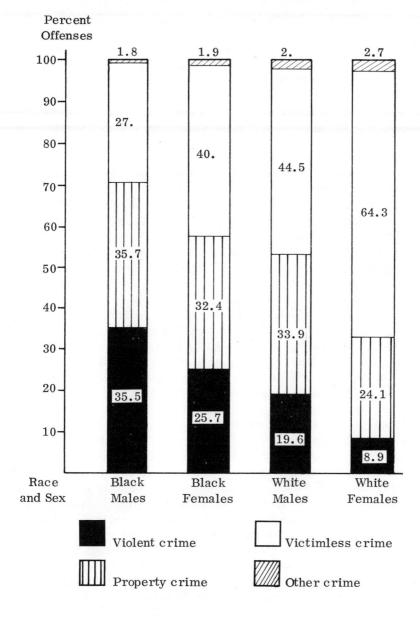

FIGURE 1.2

Distribution of Offenses within the Four
Race/Sex Groups of Offenders

Percent
Offenses

Source: Compiled by the author.

motivation, prostitution is usually considered a property offense;
and for that reason, it was added to property rather than victimless
crimes.)

The same general picture emerges when looking at specific
offense categories with the highest and lowest percentages of unemployed offenders. Males committing assaults, forcible sex, and
gun offenses had the lowest rates (between 29 and 33 percent) of
unemployment, compared to the property-motivated offenses of
robbery, burglary, and auto theft committed by males with high unemployment rates (between 56 and 68 percent). Again, for women
the findings are less consistent and point to the possibility of employment being a less significant explanatory variable. While
women with the highest rate of unemployment (80-89 percent) con-
formed to the male pattern and were charged with crimes seemingly
property-motivated, like robbery and prostitution, the offenses
charged to women with low unemployment rates (between 40 and 57
percent) followed no specific pattern.

As was previously shown, over half of the offenders handled
by the criminal justice system had at least one previous arrest.
Recidivism was evaluated based on rearrest, not necessarily for
the same crime. For both sex groups, black offenders were more
recidivistic, although the gap was larger for males than females.
Recidivists also were not equally distributed by type crime among
those charged with various offenses. For males, robbery was the
offense charged to the highest proportion of recidivists (66.4 percent), followed by homicide and property crimes against residence
and business. For females, the pattern was different: most of the
recidivists were found in victimless crimes, followed by robbery
and homicide. Victimless crime was the only category in which the
percentage of female recidivists was as high as that of the male
recidivists--52 percent. Given the current concern with recidivism,
a further look at this most recidivistic female group, the one committing victimless crimes, is warranted. Among the female
recidivists committing victimless crimes, 65 percent had their
current arrest for prostitution, another 11 percent for drug offenses, 5 percent for weapon offenses, 3 percent for gambling, and
16 percent for bail violations. Of all the females arrested in the
District of Columbia in 1973, 18 percent were prostitutes and addicts with previous arrest records. The literature indicates that,
for a majority of these recidivists, their prior arrests were also
for victimless crimes (Clinard 1974: 507, 522). Some indication
to the same effect can be found from the PROMIS data based on
offenders rather than offenses. The 2,537 female offenses in 1973
were accounted for by 2,031 female offenders. In other words, 402
or 16 percent of the female offenses were charged to women who

were arrested more than once within a year. And 41 percent or 261 of the 643 prostitution cases were charged to women recidivating within 1973, but it may be that many of these were the same women going through the "revolving" doors of justice, paying their dues, and returning to the streets without any change or rehabilitation.

Although prostitution and drug addiction constitute illegal and, in the opinion of some, immoral behavior, the women being arrested time and again for these offenses probably do not fit the intended definition of the "career criminal," who causes serious harm to society and justifies concentrated efforts for punishment. By nature, prostitution and addiction are status offenses, embracing not only the offender's actions but his whole being. And indeed, if this status is viewed as undesirable morally or otherwise, a better and more effective way to deal with it may be outside of the criminal justice system so that the resources of the criminal justice system could be more successfully focused on the serious offender, male or female.

Seriousness of the Offense

The most frequent form of female crime, as measured by the revised Sellin-Wolfgang seriousness scale, has a 0 score of seriousness compared to a 1 to 9 score for male crime.

Females also scored lower on the loss involved in property crimes: in only 30 percent of the female crimes (compared to 38 percent for males) was there any theft, damage, or destruction of property.

Victim-Offender Relationship

The original question concerning victim-offender relationships covered the following alternatives: family, friend or acquaintance, complete stranger, and unknown. However, the category "unknown" lacked consistency and reliability due to different interpretations on the part of the policemen-respondents filling it out. For that reason, the following analysis is based only on the first three alternatives and covers a total of 8,000 cases.

Females were charged with relatively more crimes against family, while males were charged with relatively more crimes against friends, acquaintances, or strangers. This finding is consistent with the different offense patterns of the two sexes and with their respective social behavior. Women's activity tends to be concentrated around the home, while men generally spend more time on the street, with groups of friends, or at work.

When subdividing victim type by offense, further evidence of this differential pattern emerges. Female offenses against friends and family tended to be more violent than male offenses (see Figure 1.3). Both in the violent and property crime categories, women victimize family, friends, and acquaintances more than men.

FIGURE 1.3

Percent Violent Crimes Committed by Male and Female Offenders against Various Victim Types

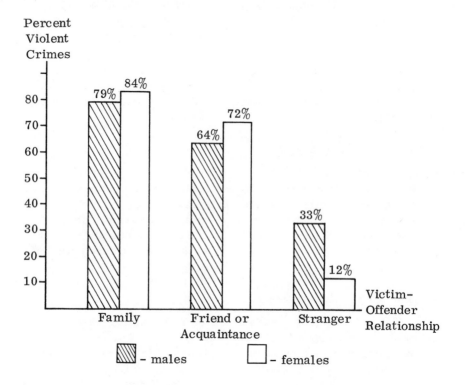

Note: Rape was excluded.
Source: Compiled by the author.

Handling of Female Offenses by the
Criminal Justice System

The final disposition of cases brought against females was studied as they passed through the "channels of justice," with special attention given to the question of evenhandedness.

Final Disposition

In analyzing dispositions, the following categories were used: case still open, case not accepted at screening, case dropped after screening (including nolle prosequi, dismissal for want of prosecution, and grand jury ignoramus), not guilty, plea, guilty other than plea, and a residual category of other dispositions (mainly diversion programs).

Most cases, for both sexes, dropped out of the system either before or after screening rather than resulting in conviction. Offenses charged to women were accepted at screening relatively more often, but they also had a higher rate of being dropped at some point later.

There were some differences on racial lines (see Table 1.2). Females of both races had mostly similar dispositions, but white males seemed to fare better than their black counterparts: only 21 percent of the white males were found guilty, compared to 30 percent blacks; and 67 percent white males dropped out of the system before or after screening, compared with 56 percent blacks. But this difference might be explained by the different type and seriousness of the offenses committed by black and white males, and does not necessarily imply lack of evenhandedness.

TABLE 1.2

Percent Distribution of Offense by Type of Disposition
and Offender's Race and Sex

Disposition	Male			Female		
	White	Black	Total	White	Black	Total
Open	8.0	9.0	8.9	8.9	9.4	9.4
No paper	28.7	23.1	23.7	19.9	19.1	19.2
Dropped after papering	38.7	32.6	33.1	35.0	37.5	37.1
Not guilty	2.4	4.4	4.2	6.5	4.7	5.0
Guilty (plea or other)	21.0	30.1	29.3	28.3	28.9	28.8
Other	1.2	0.7	0.8	1.5	0.4	0.6
Total percent	100.0	100.0	100.0	100.0	100.0	100.0
Number of cases	1,195	11,406	12,601	403	2,011	2,414

Source: Compiled by the author.

When controlling for offense type, the findings show interesting differences in disposition: for "male-type" violent and property crimes, females had their cases dropped more frequently, and males were more often found guilty. For "female-type" victimless crimes, the picture was reversed, and males enjoyed more leniency (see Table 1.3). This supports the hypothesis that females are viewed as marginal to the male world and that when they commit male-type crimes, they are judged with patronizing leniency. But when they engage in female-type offenses, they violate the values society assigns to female morality; and since they pose a threat to the existing order, they are punished more severely. In light of the previous finding about the different offense patterns of white and black females, the question was raised as to the effect of race on disposition, controlling for offense type and sex.

TABLE 1.3

Percent Cases Dropped or Ending in Convictions
by Offense Type and Offender's Sex

Offense Type	Dropped before or after Papering		Guilty	
	Male	Female	Male	Female
Violent	58.4	66.0	26.0	21.3
Property	53.0	65.7	32.3	22.0
Victimless	60.0	46.0	29.4	36.4
Other	56.0	43.0	23.4	26.5

Source: Compiled by the author.

As an operational indicator of leniency (or the lack of it), rates of dropping out of the system as compared to rates of conviction were used. The following inferences could be drawn from this analysis (see Figure 1.4). White females fared better than white males in property crimes, worse in violent and victimless crimes. For blacks, females seemed to be dealt with more leniently than males in both violent and property crimes, more harshly in victimless crimes. Further, white females fared better than black females in the disposition of property and victimless crimes, but not in violent crimes. Finally, white males fared better than black males in all of the offense categories.

FIGURE 1.4

Percent Cases Found Guilty, by Offense Type and Offender's Race and Sex

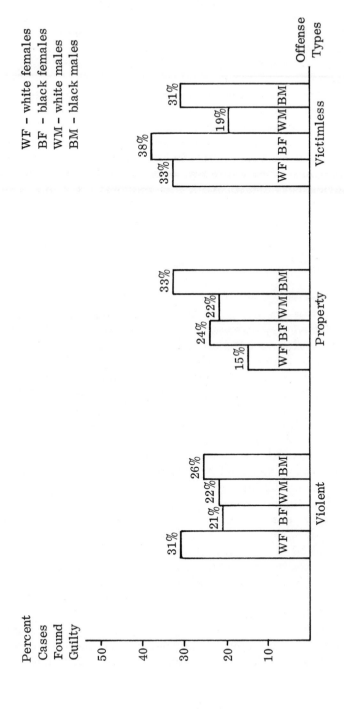

Source: Compiled by the author.

17

In view of these findings, the differential in disposition between males and females as hypothesized by Adler, and reported earlier in this study, seems to be accounted for mainly by the difference between black male and female offenders; that is, the hypothesis that females are treated more harshly in victimless crimes and more leniently in violent and property crimes seems to be supported when considering black male and black female offenders, but not whites. In interpreting these findings, one should be reminded of several other independent variables that might affect dispositions, such as seriousness of offense or offender's previous criminal history, which were not controlled for in the present analysis. Yet, at least in viewing victimless crimes that have equally low scores of seriousness and equal rates of recidivists for both sexes, a different criterion for disposition seems to be at work, that is, one based on the sex of the offender.

CONCLUSIONS

The data presented cover all known female offenses of one year in Washington, D.C. Although there are limitations to conclusions based only on known statistics from one city, the findings might suggest some insight into female crime.

In recent years, public opinion, shared by laymen and professionals alike, predicted an increase in the amount and seriousness of female crime. This prediction was not tested directly by these findings, but it is important to note that female crime is still only a fraction of all crime and includes mainly nonserious, victimless offenses. As this research continues into its second and third year, some further comparative analyses of female crime will be conducted to learn about trends and changes over time.

To sum up the major findings, the female offender in the District of Columbia tended to be young, black, and unemployed. Most frequently, she committed victimless crimes that had minimal ratings of seriousness. About one-fifth of the female crimes was violent, and its main targets were family and friends. Typically, younger women seemed to be involved in prostitution, middle-aged women in larceny, and older women in assault, which might suggest a relationship between women's offense patterns and their social roles at different points in their life cycles. Black female offenders were charged with a much larger proportion of violent and property crimes than their white counterparts, and this fact might be used as an indicator for the trend all female crime will follow in the future.

A relatively large proportion of the women had a previous arrest record, and about one in six female offenders had more than one arrest in the District of Columbia for 1973.

Generally, women seemed to fare better in the criminal justice system in terms of having their cases dropped and being convicted less. But this held true only for violent and property crimes: in the victimless crime category, the picture was reversed, and females were treated more harshly than males. A large proportion of these offenses are committed by recidivists, mainly prostitutes. These offenses place a serious burden on the law enforcement agencies, and the criminal justice system apparently has little effect on these crimes, with respect to deterrence or rehabilitation. It also appears that the ideal of evenhandedness is not completely fulfilled in regard to these female offenders.

This study clearly suggests that the legislator and the heavily overburdened criminal justice system should either legalize some offenses (namely the victimless ones) or stop prosecuting them. The first alternative is the more desirable because nonprosecution of legally forbidden behavior breeds contempt for the law, discrimination, and other possible undesirable practices.

If prostitution, gambling, and other "marginal" deviations were not considered illegal, the system could channel more of its time, manpower, and resources to deal with serious, violent crimes and guarantee a higher rate of arrest, prosecution, conviction, and more innovative and effective correctional programs for those offenders, male and female, who cause the most harm to society.

REFERENCES

Adler, F. S.
    1971   The Female Offender in Philadelphia. Ph.D. dissertation, The University of Pennsylvania.

Anderson, C. M.
    1967   The female criminal offender. American Journal of Correction 29(6): 7-9.

Bensing, R., and O. Schroeder
    1960   Homicide in an Urban Community. Springfield, Ill.: C. C. Thomas.

Bertrand, M. A.
    1969   Self-image and delinquency: a contribution to the study of female criminality and woman's image. Acta Criminologica 2: 71-144.

Bromberg, W.
　　1961　The Mold of Murder. Westport, Conn.: Greenwood Press.

Canadian Correctional Association
　　1968　Brief on the Woman Offender. Ottawa: The Association.

Chesney-Lind, M.
　　1973　Judicial enforcement of the female sex role. Issues in
　　　　　Criminology 8(2): 57-69.

Clinard, M. B.
　　1974　Sociology of Deviant Behavior. New York: Holt, Rinehart
　　　　　and Winston.

Cowie, J., V. Cowie, and E. Slater
　　1968　Delinquency in Girls. New York: Humanities Press.

deRham, E.
　　1969　How Could She Do That? A Study of the Female Criminal.
　　　　　New York: Clarson N. Potter.

Giallombardo, R.
　　1966　Society of Women. New York: John Wiley and Sons.

Hamilton, W. A., and C. R. Work
　　1973　The prosecutor's role in the urban court system: the
　　　　　case for management consciousness. Journal of Criminal
　　　　　Law and Criminology 64(2): 183-89.

Hannum, T.
　　1973　Differences in female prisoner characteristics, 1960-1970.
　　　　　Correctional and Social Psychiatry and Journal of Applied
　　　　　Behavior Therapy 19(3): 39-41.

Hoffman-Bustamante, D.
　　1973　The nature of female criminality. Issues in Criminology
　　　　　8(2): 117-36.

Klein, D.
　　1973　The etiology of female crime. Issues in Criminology
　　　　　8(2): 3-30.

Konopka, G.
　　1966　The Adolescent Girl in Conflict. Englewood Cliffs, N.J.:
　　　　　Prentice-Hall.

Landau, S., J. Drapkin, and S. Arad
   1974   Homicide victims and offenders. Journal of Criminal
          Law and Criminology 65(3): 390-96.

Landis, J., and F. Scarpitti
   1964   Delinquent and nondelinquent orientation and opportunity
          awareness. Interdisciplinary Problems in Criminology.
          Papers of the American Society of Criminology.

Landis, M. K.
   1970   Prostitution--delinquency's time bomb. Crime and
          Delinquency 16(2): 151-57.

McKissack, M.
   1973   Property offending and school-leaving age. International
          Journal of Criminology and Penology 1(4): 353-62.

Miller, E. E.
   1969   The woman participant in Washington's riots.   Federal
          Probation 33(2): 30-34.

Moses, E. R.
   1970   Negro and white crime rates. In M. Wolfgang, L. Savitz,
          and N. Johnston, eds., Sociology of Crime and Delin-
          quency. New York: John Wiley and Sons.

Payak, B. J.
   1963   Understanding the female offender. Federal Probation
          27(4): 7-12.

Pollak, O.
   1961   The Criminality of Women. New York: A. S. Barnes.

Radzinowicz, L.
   1937   Variability of the sex ratio of criminality. The Sociologi-
          cal Review 29: 76-102.

Reckless, W. C., and B. A. Kay
   1967   The female offender. Paper submitted to the President's
          Commission on Law Enforcement and the Administration
          of Justice, Washington, D.C.

Schenerman, K., and P. Kratowski
   1974   Incarcerated male and female offenders' perceptions of
          their experiences in the criminal justice system. Journal
          of Criminal Justice 2(1): 73-78.

Singer, L.
    1973   Women and the correctional process. American Criminal
            Law Review 11(2): 295-308.

Spencer, C., and J. Berecochea
    1972   Recidivism among Women Parolees. California Depart-
            ment of Correction.

The Statistical Abstract of the United States.
    1974

Sutherland, E. H., and D. R. Cressey
    1974   Criminology, 9th ed. New York: J. B. Lippincott.

Thomas, W. I.
    1907   Sex and Society. Chicago: University of Chicago Press.

Uniform Crime Report.
    1973

Velimesis, M. L.
    1969   Criminal justice for the female offender. Journal of the
            American Association of University Women (October):
            15-16.

Wolfgang, M. E.
    1961   Ceasare Lombroso, 1835-1909. Journal of Criminal Law,
            Criminology and Police Science 52(4): 361-73.

Wolfgang, M. E., and F. Ferracuti
    1967   The subculture of Violence. London: Tavistock.

2

AN ANALYSIS OF
MARITAL CHARACTERISTICS
OF PRISON INMATES

Ellen Handler and Lori Schuett

ARE PRISON INMATES REALLY "NAKED NOMADS?"

Some readers of George Gilder's book, <u>Naked Nomads: Unmarried Men in America</u>, may remember his catalog of miseries among unmarried males: a high incidence of suicide and illness, a high likelihood of being fleeced by massage parlors in Los Angeles, and a high crime and arrest rate. The last two could be of particular interest to criminologists, if these facts can withstand attempts to explain them away.

It is important to realize that all facts are not necessarily meaningful. In this particular case, it depends on whether the unmarried men studied by Gilder differ from the general run of men in other respects, such as age, health, and attractiveness, which could explain their special problems. The purpose of the present study was to determine whether in fact prison inmates actually have different marital patterns than the general population, and, if so, what implications these facts might have for correctional policies and practices. Therefore, our first and most important step is to determine whether our facts are meaningful.

Statistics collected by the U.S. Census Bureau tell us that prison inmates as a group are about (1) twice as likely to be never married; (2) three times as likely to be divorced, separated, or widowed; and (3) half as likely to be married and living with spouse as the general population. However, we also know that prison inmates are disproportionately young, 18-22 years of age, male, and nonwhite. Persons who are very young and, to a lesser extent, persons who are male and nonwhite, also show different marital patterns than the general population. Let us take an extreme example. About 90 percent of the total population 18-19 years of age has never been married. If we found that a very large fraction of prison inmates were 18-19 years old, we should not be surprised to find that a very large fraction had never been married. We would not attempt to draw up any special programs or policies on the assumption that prison inmates are a group with special needs, requiring special services. Instead, we would expect the anomalous marital characteristics of prison inmates to disappear through aging, much like acne does among adolescents. On the other hand, if we found that differences in marital status remained even when all other relevant factors such as age, race, and sex, were held constant, we should begin to think about special programming.

In order to test the validity of the summary census data, we carried out a research study in which we held constant the contaminating factors to see whether differences in marital status characteristics remained or disappeared. The study was carried out by means of a census of the population of the Illinois Adult Correctional Facilities on April 1, 1974, and comparisons were made with Illinois' general population characteristics, taken from the 1970 census tapes. Inmates admitted before 1968 or after 1972 were eliminated from the study to maintain comparability with the 1970 census data. Ages of inmates were calculated back to 1970. Illinois residents and prison inmates younger than 18 or older than 54 were eliminated from the analysis. Corrections inmates below age 18 fall outside the jurisdiction of the Adult Division of the Department of Corrections and corrections inmates above age 54 are too rare to warrant analysis.

Marital status was divided into three broad categories: (1) those who reported themselves as married (legally or common law) and living with spouse; (2) those who claimed to be single or never married; and (3) those described as separated, divorced, or widowed. Race was divided simply into black and white, the latter including the statistically small group of "other."

This report of the findings will begin with a comparison of the age composition of the Illinois prison inmates and general population. This will be followed by a discussion of differences in marriage patterns, holding age constant. Second, we will control for race as well as age. Third, sex will be added as a final controlling factor. In the fourth section we will examine differences in marital status within the prison population, comparing black and white inmates. Finally, we will spell out some of the implications of our findings for correctional practice.

THE AGE AND MARRIAGE PATTERNS OF PRISON INMATES AND THE ILLINOIS GENERAL POPULATION

Figure 2.1 gives a picture of the age composition of Illinois prison inmates and the general population. The bottom and longest block of the pyramid represents the 18- and 19-year-olds and the shortest block represents the 45-to-54-year-olds. The vertical line separates the two populations and the numbers on the horizontal line beneath the figure represent the proportion of each age group in each population. For example, you can see that 18- and 19-year-olds each constitute about 10 percent of the prison population but only 5 percent of the total Illinois population. In other words, this age group is disproportionately represented among prison inmates. The relative proportions are reversed in the upper age groups: 45-to-54-year-olds are a smaller proportion (6 percent of the prison population and a far larger fraction (24 percent of the general population).

FIGURE 2.1

Relative Age Composition of Illinois Prison Inmates
and Illinois General Population

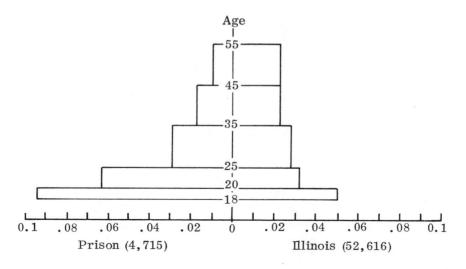

Age

Prison (4,715)   Illinois (52,616)

Source: Compiled by the author.

Notice that the age pyramid is very asymmetrical. The shape of the prison half of the pyramid is a deep curve with drastic reductions in size of proportions as age increases, whereas the general population is almost a straight line, except for the relatively large 18- and 19-year-old groups, who reflect the baby boom of the 1950s.

The marriage patterns are consistently different between the two populations within each age group. Except for the youngest age group, the prison inmates are less likely to be presently married, more likely to be single (never married), and more likely to be separated, divorced, or widowed. The last category particularly increases with age. Among the 18- and 19-year-olds, however, the pattern is reversed. Young prison inmates are more likely to be married than their age-mates in the general population. This finding is consistent with the lack of adult supervision and early assumption of adult roles by juvenile delinquents noted by many criminologists.

COMPARISON OF MARRIAGE PATTERNS WITHIN AGE AND RACIAL GROUPS

When we add race to the factors we are holding constant, some interesting similarities and differences emerge. Among both blacks and whites, differences in marriage patterns between prison inmates and the general population increase with age, but differences are much greater when white inmates are compared with white Illinois residents than when black inmates are compared with black Illinois residents. For instance, in the oldest age group, white prison inmates are about four times as likely to be separated, divorced, or widowed, three times as likely to be single, and about a third as likely to be married as whites of the same age in the general population. Black prison inmates above age 25 are only about twice as likely to be single as blacks in the general Illinois population and are about equally likely to be married or separated, divorced, or widowed. Maybe the differences among blacks are smaller because marriage patterns are related to income and the income differences between blacks who are inside and out of prison are less than income differences among whites.

COMPARISONS OF MARRIAGE PATTERNS WITHIN AGE, RACE, AND SEX GROUPS

In actual fact, this section will be limited to males because in the entire Illinois prison population at the time of the study, there were only 128 females, too small a number to permit further division or analysis. However, the differences within racial groups are accentuated when only males are included in the analysis. For instance, 18- and 19-year-old white male prison inmates are more than three times as likely to be married as white males of that age group in the general population. The reason that differences are greater when females are eliminated from the analysis is that females in general tend to marry at younger ages than males. When females are omitted from the comparison group, the number of young marrieds in the general Illinois population is greatly reduced. The difference in the proportion that are separated, divorced, or widowed are especially great among white males. Depending on their ages, prison inmates are anywhere from four to six times as likely to be separated, divorced, or widowed as Illinois white males generally. Differences of this order are far greater than national differences cited from the U.S. census data at the beginning of this chapter.

DIFFERENCES IN MARRIAGE PATTERNS BETWEEN
BLACK AND WHITE PRISON INMATES

In this section we will not compare prison inmates with the Illinois general population but will carry out an internal comparison of black and white prison inmates. Figure 2.2 shows the new age pyramid. In contrast to the asymmetrical Figure 1.1, which compared prison inmates with the Illinois general population, the present pyramid is virtually symmetrical. Differences in age distributions disappear within a prison population and so do differences in marital status. Virtually none of the differences in marital patterns between black and white prison inmates are as great as the national differences cited by the U.S. Census. In other words, the differences in marital patterns do not seem to be due primarily to age or race but are related to imprisonment itself.

WHAT DO THESE FINDINGS MEAN?

Before discussing the implications of these findings for correctional programs, it is legitimate to ask, are these figures reliable? The answer is maybe. The data on marital status are based on self reports at prison intake. No one knows how many married fathers may be describing themselves as bachelors to discard unwelcome wives and annoying child-support obligations. Also, we must remember that these figures offer a conservative description of the marital status of prison inmates. Virtually every state recognizes incarceration as legitimate grounds for divorce and "Dear John" letters are familiar occurrences for men inside. Therefore, the marital status at discharge would probably show even fewer married and more separated, divorced, and widowed inmates than data collected at intake.

FIGURE 2.2

Relative Age Composition of Black and White
Illinois Prison Inmates

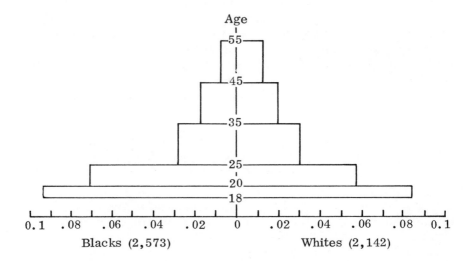

Source: Compiled by the author.

Do these findings mean that prison inmates are intrinsically less able or less willing to get or stay married than people in the general population? Only further research will tell. It is possible that prison inmates are less likely to be married because they have spent so much time in confinement that they have not had adequate opportunities for marriage. In order to answer this question, we would need to compare the marital status of men with different amounts of time at liberty. If some sort of intrinsic factors related criminality and marriageability, we would expect to find few differences between men with more and less time on the street.

Another confounding factor is the operation of the criminal justice decision process itself. Most serious offenders are subject to a presentence investigation. One of the objectives of this assessment is to estimate the risk of maintaining an offender under community supervision. One important component of risk assessment is stability of marriage ties. A man who is married and living with his spouse is considered a better risk (if all other factors are equal) and will be more likely to receive a recommendation for probation than one who is unmarried or whose marriage has been disrupted.   Therefore, a married man is less likely to become a prison inmate; we cannot conclude that our findings mean that a prison inmate is inherently less likely to assume the marriage role.

With all these qualifications in mind, do the data have any significance? The answer is yes. Studies comparing currently married and single prison inmates have found significantly more psychopathology among the latter (Payne, Howell, Roe 1971). Recidivism studies also show that currently married prison inmates are better parole risks than those without a stable marriage relationship (Taylor 1970).

Therefore, this study suggests two major conclusions. First, it seems clear that prison inmates are in fact less likely to be stably married and more likely to be never married or separated, divorced, or widowed than the general population, even when other demographic factors such as age, race, and sex have been controlled. The differences noted in the federal census data are indeed valid and should be incorporated into correctional program planning.

Second, we should modify our current programs to encourage the maintenance and establishment of marriage ties among prison inmates and provide family substitute arrangements for those who lack these stabilizing factors. As an example, let us consider our home and family furlough programs. Today, our furlough policies provide a reward for good behavior after most of a man's sentence has been served. Furloughs are not permitted sufficiently early in a man's sentence to help maintain existing family ties. Another example of needed program modifications is in services to prisoners' wives and families. Most states offer token services, if any, to the wives of inmates serving sentences, to help them cope with the stresses inherent in their situation and help them "hang on," to maintain contact during their husbands' confinement, and to anticipate and deal with the stresses of the early discharge period. Would such services reduce the number of "Dear John" letters ? It might be worthwhile to try.

Finally, we should devote far greater resources to postdischarge services for those lacking marital ties. Halfway houses today serve a minuscule fraction of the population in need and should be greatly expanded. Boarding houses, which served as homes to large numbers of unmarried men until the Great Depression, need to be reestablished. Drop-in centers of various sorts, where a man can find companionship and legitimate leisure time activites, are needed for lonely men who may be barred by conditions of parole from their habitual enjoyments of meeting friends in bars or driving out of the county (Handler 1974). The reentry problems of offenders have received scant attention from correctional policy

planners. Yet, in view of their meager family ties, postdischarge
services for offenders may spell the difference between success
and failure. Most people agree that factors other than institutional
rehabilitation programs are prime determinants of recidivism.
However, we have not translated this knowledge into policy and
practice. Maybe this study, showing clearly the characteristic lack
of social ties among the majority of prison inmates, will provide
greater support for programs that deal with this pervasive problem
of the correctional clientele.

REFERENCES

Gilder, G.
    1974   Naked Nomads: Unmarried Men in America. New York:
            Quadrangle.

Handler, E.
    1974   Family surrogates as correctional strategy. Social
            Service Review 48: 4.

Payne, I. R., R. J. Howell, and A. V. Roe
    1971   Marital status of prison inmates as a diagnostic index of
            personal characteristics and personality traits. Psy-
            chological Abstracts 28.

Taylor, C. U.
    1970   Who Are They? A Study of Illinois Parole Violators in
            Cook and Lake Counties. Illinois Department of Correc-
            tions, Division of Research and Long Range Planning.

U.S. Bureau of the Census
            Persons in Institutions and Other Group Quarters.
            Washington, D.C.: U.S. Government Printing Office.

3

DYSFUNCTIONAL IDEOLOGY:
THE BLACK REVOLUTIONARY
IN PRISON
Robert Johnson and Dennis D. Dorin

INTRODUCTION

The Sound before the Fury

The 1971 uprising at Attica had a dramatic impact upon the
American public for at least two reasons. First, the assault to re-
take the prison by state police and correctional officers resulted in
perhaps "the bloodiest one-day encounter between Americans since
the Civil War" (New York State Special Commission on Attica 1972:
xi). Second, the inmate leaders employed the mass media with an
unprecedented effectiveness to project an image of themselves as
revolutionaries.

The "whole world was watching" when inmate "security
guards" arrived at the DMZ* in their bizarre costumes of football
helmets, hoods, masks, and cloaks to escort state officials to
"negotiations" with their leadership. On-the-spot television focused

---

*The DMZ, so named by the inmate rebels, was a tunnel area
between Attica's A block, which was under the control of the authorities, and the door to A yard, which was inmate-controlled. As
such, it functioned as a no-man's-land or buffer zone between the
two contending forces.

The data for this chapter were collected under NIMH grant
5 RO1 MH-20696-02 ("Self-Destruction among Prison Inmates"),
directed by Hans Toch. We also are indebted to Dr. Toch for his
lucid discussion of militancy in Men in Crisis (1975). Finally, our
thanks to the editorial staff at Lexington Books for allowing us to re-
print materials published in slightly modified form by Robert
Johnson (1976).

upon the fiery inmate leader, L. D. Barkley, as he told the head of
New York's penal system that the insurrection was the result of
"unmitigated oppression wrought by the racist administrative network" of Attica, that all of its inmates had "set forth to change for-
ever the ruthless brutalization and disregard for the lives of prisoners [both within its walls] and throughout the United States," and that
the take-over was "but the sound before the fury of those who [were]
oppressed" (Wicker 1975: 34-35).

A nationwide audience observed the prisoners' defiant cheers
as Barkley read their unprecedented demands for complete amnesty,
the option of "speedy and safe transportation out of confinement to a
non-imperialistic country," direct federal jurisdiction over the
prison, and reconstruction of the institution by inmates and/or under
inmate supervision. *

Moreover, the media vividly projected the revolutionary atmosphere in which the uprising reached its tragic climax: the pas-
sionate speeches by black and white inmate leaders in which they
proclaimed their willingness to die, if necessary, for their cause;
poignant interviews with hostages who expressed their belief that
nothing but far-reaching concessions by the state could prevent
bloodshed; and the state's armed assault, complete with attack
helicopter and hostages displayed at knife-point by potential inmate
"executioners." [†]

It is thus no wonder that Attica raised profound questions for
students of corrections. It had served as a medium for a relatively
new image of the inmate leader--young, generally black, articulate,
disciplined, politically aware, indeed, a rebel prepared to take and
kill hostages and fight to the death in pursuit of nonnegotiable demands. Was this figure really the dedicated revolutionary he seemed?
And, if so, were he and Attica to be the models for "wars of liberation" within the prisons of the 1970s?

This chapter will critique the discipline of criminal justice's
attempts to answer these queries. Data obtained from in-depth interviews with a representative cross-section of post-Attica prisoners in New York's maximum security institutions subsequently will
be used to explore the viability of militant and revolutionary roles

---

*For a complete list of all of the inmates' demands, see
Wicker (1975: 401-04).

†See Wicker (1975: 341-80) and the New York State Special
Commission on Attica (1972: 366-403) for accounts of Attica's fatal
climax.

among black inmates. (For the purposes of this chapter, a militant posture is one that is actively aggressive, but not necessarily violent. A revolutionary role, however, is one that accepts, and attempts to employ, ideologically motivated violence.))

The Inmate Rebel: Establishment and Radical Perspectives

Surprisingly, correctional literature has produced only a handful of studies that attempt to gauge the prevalence of inmate revolutionaries or militants in the five years since Attica. Of these, an "establishment" interpretation proposed by Daniel Glaser and a "radical" one espoused by John Pallas and Bob Barber have received the most attention. (This work defines "establishment" perspective as the view commonly associated with the therapeutic or rehabilitative school of corrections. The "radical" approach refers to the positions generally expounded by the "radical criminologists".)

Within months of the insurrection, Glaser attempted to describe the "politicalization of prisoners" as a "new challenge to American penology." Prison rebels of the 1970s were presumed to differ from those of past decades:

> While inmate leaders of the 1950's sought mainly to
> publicize their complaints about correctional adminis-
> trators, many now address themselves primarily to
> the so-called "Third World" of oppressed peoples
> everywhere. They dream of joining forces in a
> global revolt against alleged "imperialist domina-
> tion." (Glaser 1971: 139)

This phenomenon was described as the result of the contemporary prisons' drawing their populations from groups that were the most excluded from participation in the policy-making processes of the country—ethnic minorities and youth (Glaser 1971: 140). A revolutionary movement might be particularly attractive to such prisoners because it permitted them to see themselves as patriots rather than pariahs (Glaser 1971: 143). The division of the prison community into a predominantly white Anglo-American prison staff and inmates drawn primarily from racial and cultural minorities provided an arena for new activist convict roles. (When a parole was denied and solitary confinement imposed for such conduct, a rebel's conclusion that he was being punished as a political prisoner, rather than as an ordinary criminal, would have strong appeal. The prospect of "guerrilla-type riots" loomed as a stable feature of modern prisons unless basic changes were made (Glaser 1971: 143).

Glaser's strategy for the reduction of prison militance was premised on the availability of "legitimate alternatives to rioting," which could "compete successfully with the appeal to rebelliousness" (Glaser 1971: 144). To this end, prisoners would be given an opportunity to effectively participate in prison management decisions, spend the last several months of their sentences in work release programs based in small community correctional centers, be supervised by a greater number of minority group guards, and be afforded a full and effective suffrage (Glaser 1971: 144-45).

Two years later, Pallas and Barber agreed with Glaser that a sharp distinction could be drawn between the "traditional prison riot(s)" of the 1950s and what they referred to as the "revolutionary upheavals of the late 1960s and early 1970s" (Pallas, Barber 1973: 341). The former, they contended, "were largely spontaneous uprisings against intolerable living conditions" (Pallas, Barber 1973: 342). They were unplanned and uncoordinated. The demands put forward by the inmates reflected their day-to-day needs. The unity of such movements, to the extent it existed, "concealed intense personal or racial hatreds, which the leaders, through force or personal persuasion, had to control in order to prevent the revolt from disintegrating" (Pallas, Barber 1973: 343).

More critically, the inmates in the riots of the 1950s did not question the legitimacy of the political system. They "challenged the abuse of power" rather than its source. Their trust in members of the prison staff, usually psychiatrists and counselors, reflected their belief in the idea of the "rehabilitated inmate." As minority groups outside the prison sought to become a part of the larger society through integration, many prisoners saw rehabilitation as their avenue to societal acceptance (Pallas, Barber 1973: 344). Their protests accordingly were modified by their perceived investments in the conventional social order.

Attica and similar prison disturbances, by contrast, suggested a "radically new dimension in the prison struggle" (Pallas, Barber 1973: 341). American society in the late 1960s and early 1970s, unable to respond to rising pressures for reform, had turned increasingly to repressing such challengers of its institutions as proponents of the black power and antiwar movements. At the same time, U.S. interventions in Vietnam and the Dominican Republic revealed that the roots of our foreign policy were in imperialism and its concomitant, racism (Pallas, Barber 1973: 348). Continued opposition to the state thus grew more radical and militant and was met with increased repression. Participants in ghetto riots, campus revolts, Black Panther party activities, Third World Liberation groups in local communities, and revolutionary movements in Latin America and Asia

articulated an understanding of the inter-relationships
of domestic and foreign repression, of the role of
racism as an ideology used to divide people of different races in the interest of economic exploitation,
and of the necessity for international solidarity among
the victims of imperialism. They proceeded to act
upon these analyses, thus providing models of both
revolutionary theory and practice, a general atmosphere of confrontation for prisoners. (Pallas,
Barber 1973: 348)

The impact of these developments upon the American prison
population could not be overestimated. Black and Chicano prisoners, in particular, were quick to make the connection between the
struggles of Third World peoples around the world and their own.
At the same time, black, Puerto Rican, and other Third World
people active in radical groups and white participants in the antiwar
movement constituted a new influx of inmates into American prisons
who brought with them not only their revolutionary perspectives on
politics but also their considerable organizing skills (Pallas, Barber
1973: 348).

Advocates of the radical perspective thus viewed Attica as a
dramatic example of the new prison revolution these forces had
spawned. In the rebels' demands for the resignation of the warden
and amnesty, they were attempting to establish the precedents that
they had a right to participate in (if not control) the process of
choosing who ruled them, as well as to revolt without fear of punishment. The demand for amnesty, in particular, unlike those for
no reprisals in the 1950s, denoted a relationship between political
actors--an attempt to legitimize the take-over as a proper inmate
tool (Pallas, Barber 1973: 352).

The prisoners at Attica were unlike their counterparts in the
1950s because they had no trust in the prison officials with whom
they were dealing. Indeed, they challenged the ideology and structure of both the penal system and the larger society. From their
radical perspective, American prisons were not only institutions
for the suppression of society's lower classes but also part of a
global pattern of class oppression called "imperialism" (Pallas,
Barber 1973: 354).

The Attica rebels and their successors also were presumed
able to overcome racial mistrust and hatred. Leadership was based
on mutual consent and represented an apportionment of responsibilities among the various inmate groups. The movement was the result of an organizing campaign within the prison based on remedial
education of inmates and systematic exposure to the tracts of various

past and present revolutionaries. Operating in conjunction with
many sympathetic groups outside the prison, it had been in the van-
guard of revolutionary change in America (Pallas, Barber 1973: 353).

Was it to thus be "the sound before the fury" that Barkley had
predicted? Would the 1970s see a series of similar insurrections?
Pallas and Barber maintained that an escalating cycle of dissent and
repression would set the stage for radical prisoner activity, ultimately feeding the fire of rebellion:

> Traditional techniques were still used to prevent rebel-
> lions: attempts to turn inmates against each other
> along racial lines; promises of early parole and good
> treatment for docility; and threats, segregation, tor-
> ture, and assassination for alleged "troublemakers."
> [But] the growth of the prisoners' movement with wide-
> spread outside support [limited] the effectiveness of
> these tactics. (Pallas, Barber 1973: 354)

The diffusion of political consciousness among inmates was making
it more difficult for officials to promote internecine racial violence
or to induce convicts to behave passively through bribes and threats.
In addition, the increased public concern for the fate of prisoners,
particularly after the slaughter of inmates at Attica, was making it
more difficult for the authorities to hide or defend the practice of
"mass murder and torture" behind the walls (Pallas, Barber 1973:
355).

The prison system, according to Pallas and Barber, was thus
forced to look for new techniques to suppress prison disturbances.
Authorities would increasingly resort to electronic surveillance,
mind-altering or pain-inducing drugs, brain surgery, and electric
shocks to induce conformity (Pallas, Barber 1973: 355).

Moreover, a new breed of penologist would come to the fore.
Liberal, academically trained, and sophisticated enough to understand the revolutionary movement and its appeal to prisoners, he
would attempt to undercut dissent with far-reaching reforms. He
would be sympathetic to the drives of Third World inmates for cultural and racial identity, and would talk about opening lines of com-
munication and sharing power with responsible inmates. However,
such reformers would be ready and willing to use whatever force
was necessary to deal with prisoners who did not cooperate with the
system (Pallas, Barber 1973: 355).

The pervasiveness of this "liberal totalitarianism" in the
prison system was alleged to have implications for the society as a
whole. Many of the techniques for suppression of inmates would be
applied to other nonconformists in the population at large. More

and more people outside the walls would discover that they were not free, but merely held prisoner in "minimum," rather than "maximum," security prisons. Prison revolutionaries such as George Jackson, who had illuminated the true nature of American society, would serve as "models of leadership for the movement as a whole" (Pallas, Barber 1973: 341). Thus, the fate of the prison revolution would continue to be inseparable from that of the revolutionary forces outside the walls (Pallas, Barber 1973: 355).

Foundations of Sand: The Rebel Inmate in Correctional Literature

Despite what are sometimes radically different ideological perspectives, the implications of Attica developed in correctional literature are comparatively uniform.) Both the Glaser and Pallas-Barbar studies, for example, relied upon sociohistorical approaches to explain and predict the occurrence of such phenomena, and both works were influenced heavily by the political currents of their time. Thus, each placed substantial emphasis upon the Third World appeals of inmate rebels to conclude that the "guerrilla-type riots" or "revolutions" of the 1970s were distinct from the "riots" of the 1950s, and each predicted that such revolutionary insurrections would recur unless marked sociopolitical changes were made.

Yet, even given these significant areas of agreement, research on the radical or militant prisoner seems far from conclusive. While hindsight comes easy, the fact remains that the "politicalization" described by Glaser as permeating the society appears to be very much on the wane. And the militant groups and rampant dissent that Pallas and Barber saw stoking the fires of revolution in prison have largely disappeared from the scene.* (The U.S. withdrawal from Vietnam has, of course, sounded the death knell for the anti-war movement. The campus unrest of the late 1960s and early 1970s appears to have been replaced by political apathy and a

---

*The suicidal quality of groups like the SLA was characterized recently by a black felon who, although an escapee from a California maximum security institution, allegedly refused, despite physical threats from Donald DeFreeze, to become one of its members: "They were living out of books, man. . . . They weren't living everyday experience. You can't readily equate what you read in books with reality. . . . To the people out there, trying to survive takes priority over dreams" (Blauner 1975: 12A).

concern with career preparation among students. The Black Panthers
seem to have vanished as a force in American politics. Eldridge
Cleaver's repatriation and recent political statements suggest that
the Panther's revolutionary zeal has dissipated.)

There is thus the distinct possibility that researchers put too
much stress on the revolutionary rhetoric of the Attica and other
inmate leaders in their attempts to describe the new militant. For
example, Pallas and Barber emphasized that the rebels at Attica demanded amnesty, rather than the promise of no reprisals sought by
their counterparts two decades previously. Yet the leaders at Attica
defined "amnesty" in their list of demands as "freedom from any
physical, mental and legal reprisals" (Wicker 1975: 402). If the
distinction between these two terms was as crucial as Pallas and
Barber asserted, it apparently escaped the rebels themselves. *
The demand that the warden be fired was similarly not unique to the
1970s, but had been an important feature of earlier riots (Sykes 1966:
114). And the suggestion that the disturbance was planned and exe-
cuted by a unified inmate constituency finds no support in detailed
accounts of the uprising provided by the Attica Commission and Tom
Wicker, a journalist involved in the negotiations.†

If correctional research on the new inmate has produced ques-
tionable distinctions between current and past prison disturbances,
its prognosis for prisons of the future seems even more suspect.
None of the system changes advocated to prevent Attica-type insurrections have been implemented. Penitentiary inmates remain essentially powerless to influence management decisions. The prison
staff is still predominantly nonminority (and nonurban), and prisoners remain disenfranchised.‡ Work release, an alleged panacea,
has been found to have variable impact, in some instances producing
stress and alienation among participants (Waldo et al. 1973). Other

---

*It should be recalled that a correctional officer had been
beaten to death by inmates during the early stages of the take-over
and that the prisoners who so avidly sought amnesty were acutely
conscious that they faced possible indictments for a capital crime.
See also the enormous number of crimes with which the leaders of
the Attica insurrection were charged in Wicker (1975: 392).

†See, for example, the New York State Special Commission
on Attica (1972: 104-13) and Wicker (1975: 18-22).

‡For an account of minor reforms implemented at Attica in
wake of the insurrection, see New York State Special Commission
on Attica (1972: 466-70).

prescriptions for administrators have been ignored or only partially observed, yet guerrilla uprisings have failed to materialize. (Few inmate systems, for example, have followed a Glaser suggestion to systematically disperse violent militants. Some, like New York's, appear to be consolidating radicals in one prison, and recurrently express interest in developing maxi-maxi units to further this end.)

Nor did the apocalyptic view of some analysts produce a reliable charting of inmate rebellion. The mayhem caused by the indiscriminate firing of shotguns, .270s, and pistols and the vicious beatings by the state police and correctional officers who crushed the Attica revolt suggested strongly that the state's functionaries would stop at nothing in their efforts to suppress such uprisings. Nevertheless, the inclination toward revolution on the part of inmates has apparently not become so powerful that the state has resorted to the full panoply of "1984" techniques that had been envisaged.

The most serious deficiency in scholarly descriptions of the new radical inmate, however, relates to the absence of attempts to measure the extent to which inmates subscribe to militant or revolutionary ideologies and actually put their tenets into practice. We see a series of conclusions based largely on inmate rhetoric. While questionnaire or interview surveys can document the extent to which such modes of expression exist (see, for example, Faine, Bohlander 1975), the Attica rebels themselves seem skeptical about rhetorical pronouncements, noting that talk in prison comes exceedingly cheap. Violent action against guards and other system officials, they note, costs dearly, sometimes pricing self-proclaimed militants out of the market. *

To produce full-bodied portraits of today's prison inmate, we have therefore drawn upon data that may allow us to look more closely at human responses to the penitentiary. We aim to provide baseline estimates of militancy and to explore its variations and consequences in the prison context.

METHODOLOGY

The Data

The data for this chapter originate from an interview survey of inmates confined to each maximum security penal institution in

---

*For a revealing discussion of prisoner rhetoric between Roger Champen, one of the most important inmate leaders of Attica, and Tom Wicker, see Wicker (1975: 312).

New York State and two major New York City jails between 1971 and 1973. * The project was designed to explore the nature of psychological survival and breakdown in confinement (Toch 1975). The information of primary relevance to this study stems from a stratified random sample of 146 prisoners drawn from the various penal institutions that was used to delineate the pressures of confinement for the "typical" or "average" inmate. This sample was comprised of 67 black, 31 white, and 48 Latin interviewees; these inmates were comparable on all major demographic and criminal career variables to noninterviewed prisoners from each ethnic or racial group.

The interviews conducted with this representative sample were open-ended. Each man was asked to describe in his own words and in chosen sequence the pressures created by confinement and the personal modes of adjustment used to combat stress. These interviews were therefore not designed explicitly to measure militancy. But they do provide baseline information about the nature of prison coping and stress, and on whether (and in what fashion) militant ideologies influence prison adjustment. Each respondent's description of his prison experience is also tied to concrete incidents, and thus may afford a comparatively realistic view of his ideology. An opportunity sample of crisis-prone inmates (the focus of the original survey) may on some occasions also shed light on the role of militancy in prison adaptation.

Interviews were in all cases tape-recorded with the consent of the interviewee. Time and financial constraints, however, made it possible to transcribe less than a quarter (30) of them. The procedure for nontranscribed interviews entailed the interviewer and two independent observers to listen to the interview and to arrive at a group summary of the problem sequences and coping strategies described by the respondent.[†] These summaries were subsequently transcribed. All transcribed interviews and interview synopses

---

*The prisons surveyed include: Attica, Auburn, Clinton, Elmira, Green Haven, Great Meadow, and Sing Sing (Ossining). The New York City jails sampled were the Manhattan House of Detention for Men (subsequently closed by court order) and the Adolescent Remand Shelter on Riker's Island.

[†]The prison interviews were conducted by Robert Johnson and James G. Fox and the jail interviews were conducted by John J. Gibbs, graduate students in the School of Criminal Justice at the State University of New York at Albany during the survey. The project was directed and monitored by Hans Toch, a professor of Criminal Justice at SUNYA. All three men also served as interview coders.

were classified according to a content analytic scheme evolved by
Toch to describe salient concerns voiced by interviewees. *

Two prominent themes emerged in the prison interviews that
may relate to militancy: the inmate's perception of himself as a
victim of arbitrary abuse by the criminal justice system or its
agents (victimization) and difficulties in managing feelings of anger
and resentment produced by prison pressures (aggression control).
These themes may tap perspectives that have been linked to prisoner
militancy: the issues of systemic inequity, class oppression, and
violence as a strategy for political change (Faine, Bohlander 1975).
Detailed accounts of reactions to prison contained in transcribed interviews and interview summaries allow us to explore the shape of
political militance among men who are prone to feelings of victimization and explosiveness while confined.

Findings

Analysis of interview content shows that black convicts are
more likely than their white or Latin counterparts to view themselves as victims and to harbor feelings of resentment and violence.
As can be seen in Table 3.1, over 40 percent of the black interviewees describe themselves as targets of arbitrary treatment at the
hands of the criminal justice system (victimization), while only approximately half as many white and Latin inmates experience similar feelings in confinement. Table 3.2 depicts a comparable (though
less statistically reliable) pattern with respect to aggression control problems. While one of every three black prisoners reports
pronounced anger and resentment as a salient feature of his prison
existence, such responses occur less frequently among other inmates.

These findings suggest that a comparatively high proportion of
confined blacks confront adjustment pressures that are in some respects analogous to those described for radical or militant prisoners.
But full-blown political ideologies comparable to positions espoused
by George Jackson or Eldridge Cleaver are virtually absent in this
survey. In fact, only a handful of convicts (at most, three) described
themselves in terms that even approximated the role of the revolutionary. And in each instance the personal consequences of a militant stance were destructive.

---

*More detailed accounts of sampling procedure, interview
format, and content analysis are available in Toch (1975) or Johnson (1976).

TABLE 3.1

Relative Prevalence of the Victimization Theme
among Representative Samples of Black, White,
and Latin Inmates, in Percent

| | Ethnic Group | | |
Victimization Theme	Black	White	Latin
Present	41.8	22.6	20.5
Absent	58.2	77.4	79.5
Total percent	100.0	100.0	100.0
Total number	67	31	48

Note: $Chi^2 = 6.99$; probability $= .05$.
Source: Compiled by the authors.

TABLE 3.2

Relative Prevalence of the Aggression Control Theme
among Representative Samples of Black, White,
and Latin Inmates, in Percent

| | Ethnic Group | | |
Aggression Control Theme	Black	White	Latin
Present	32.8	19.4	18.8
Absent	67.2	80.6	81.2
Total percent	100.0	100.0	100.0
Total number	67	31	48

Note: $Chi^2 = .3.66$; probability $= .16$.
Source: Compiled by the authors.

DISCUSSION

Militant Scenarios: Violent Challenge and Defeat

To the alienated, prisons pose threats that seem designed to
promote a radical response. One prisoner, for example, claimed
prisons exercise illegitimate power. They seek through brute force

to debase and dehumanize their captives, to render helpless already
defenseless men. The critical issue posed by confinement, as this
man saw it, was whether it would be possible to physically survive
in prison while remaining psychologically and spiritually intact:

> It's when you're totally stripped of any option, then you
> have a decision to make, whether you become a tool,
> whether you will conform and suppress your own ideals,
> principles, orientations, and conform at least overtly
> with theirs . . . knowing it's only a matter of time be-
> fore that overt conformity will definitely influence your
> principles. (Interview A)

This prisoner embarked on a series of campaigns that were
calculated to assert his personal dignity and worth. He flouted orders, cursed guards, threatened violence and retribution. Such responses were ineffective, however, because prison proved obdurate
and inflexible. Bids for autonomy and recognition, occasional frontal
assaults on the legitimacy of the system, resulted primarily in repeated and extended periods in segregation. It was here, in this
prison-within-prison, that our man confronted the stark power of
the penal system. "To be in the maximum security unit," this respondent observed, "was like the end of the line in terms of you being able to control the situation to any degree." He set fire to his
cell in a suicide attempt, which documented the extent of his impotence and despair.

Rebellious postures, when they emerge, may be destructive
for reasons other than the apparent futility of protest. There are
various conditions presented by prison in which indignities and inequities are evident, and in such situations bitterness and resentment are likely to run high. In segregation units, for example,
there is often a palpable degree of tension in the air, and rhetoric
of violence (and even insurrection) is not uncommon. However, the
man who puts such words into practice, who bridges the gap between
talk and action, may not be a leader or an impressive inmate figure.
He may even be a stooge, an individual whose antics produce added
personal difficulties and provide a perverse form of entertainment
for his more restrained peers.

> Like I might be with six Panthers, and me. And I get
> so involved up in doing it, and because this is--like
> they give me three months, six months in the box, and
> this is my life for six months. Now sometimes like
> they try to draw attention on the conditions that we're
> in. We have to do something, man, we got to do

something, because this ain't going to get it, right?
So like to draw their attention they say you have to do
certain things, and like most of the time, the certain
things that be done by them it's just talking, but by me
I really do it. I go through and do it. Like they say
"no pig will walk down this gallery." And nine times
out of ten times I'm in the first fucking cell. And like
I'm not going to back down. . . . Like say for instance I was over here in the blocks. I was in the
first cell. I had made up my mind not to get involved
no more, just to get out of here. So when I was in
the first cell, they had a beef about the windows, and
they passed the word all the way down to me. They
said, "Tell that pig down here to close these windows."
So I say, "Officer, they want the windows closed." So
he came down to my cell and he said, "Listen, something wrong with you?" "No, nothing wrong with me."
"What you hollering for me for?" I said, "The inmates want the windows down." "Wait a minute, what
are you hollering for? Is that bothering you?" I said,
"No, it's not bothering me, I'm just --." "Listen,
mind your own business, before I come in there and
mind it for you." I said, "You motherfucker," and I
had a bowl or something and "spquuuuuue." And then
they go and get the vice squad, boom, boom, boom,
and I wind up in the box, you know? (Interview B)

A more tragic sequence is involved when a facade of militance masks terror in prison. Out of fear, some men may loudly
announce their independence from prison rules and defy their keep-
ers. They may advocate rebellion, claim comrades-in-arms, or
produce minor skirmishes with prison personnel. Such sequences
may involve unflattering characterizations of staff--who may be
variously referred to as "white pig motherfuckers," "devils," or
related appellations; obstinate refusals to comply with routine orders; and invitations to violence from guards. But while such
claims of power and autonomy may have a Promethean ring, they
are more likely to be exposed as merely a bluff by those who may
fear prison the most. On the one occasion this syndrome was observed, the interviewee ultimately backed himself into segregation,
closed off all retreat options, and panicked. He took his life to
avoid what he perceived to be a more painful fate at the hands of
his omnipotent captors (Toch 1975: chap. 10).

A stance of violent militance, then, may be both comparatively
rare in prison and counterproductive when it occurs. The reasons

for this may not be hard to discern. The radicalized prisoner,
after all, stipulates the existence of a monolithic power structure
that is purposely arranged to wreak damage upon him as a helpless
member of the underclass. There is, as we have mentioned earlier,
the concession of personal impotence in the face of such threats and
the view that the only way out is through a violent mass insurrection.
While there is, in theory, an army of similarly alienated persons
ripe for conscription, most of these potential recruits have suffered
at the hands of their fellow convicts and have come to view them
with suspicion. To engage in revolutionary action, the prospective
militant must develop faith in an unimpressive group of peers, and
must then gird himself for what may easily degenerate into a Pyrrhic
victory--short-term ascendance following a bloody prison riot. And
if our rebel is prisonwise, he may well fear the reign of inmates and
the backlash from guards more than the disturbance itself.

Yet there are forces that can make men desperate in prison,
and desperate men are apt to defy the odds. The ghetto man, as we
have seen, may be particularly susceptible to radicalization. In
prison, where factors that spawn bitterness and resentment in the
ghetto are magnified, the black convict group might plausibly contain a sizable number of men who are ready to court danger to right
longstanding wrongs and assert their autonomy. But comparatively
few such individuals populate prisons because the very factors that
might predispose ghetto men to violent protest create a more conservative perspective--a focus on survival in an unpredictable and
often arbitrary world.

Ghetto and Prison: Settings for Survival

Ghetto socialization encourages the development of skills and
perspectives that promote survival in inhospitable settings* (Phillips
1960). Primarily, the ghetto man must learn to cope with power-
lessness and vulnerability. He must be equipped to play the role of
victim. The ability to assume such a pose has proven relevant to
survival in a variety of stress situations with which lower-class
blacks have been forced to contend. Lee Rainwater, an astute ob-
server of slum life and a gifted sociohistorian, suggests that

---

*See pages 164-65 of "Another Man's Poison," a chapter con-
tributed by Robert Johnson to Men in Crisis (Toch 1975), for a more
detailed description of ghetto socialization.

The cultural mechanisms which Negroes have developed for living the life of victim continued to be ser-
viceable as the victimization process was maintained
(after emancipation) first under the myths of white
supremacy and black inferiority, later by the doc-
trines of gradualism which covered the fact of no im-
provement in position, and finally by the modern
Northern system of ghettoization and indifference.
(Rainwater 1966: 174)

The view that prisons, like ghettos, are geared to abuse and
harass their inhabitants is one shared by many black convicts (see
Table 3.1), a fact that is not surprising given the close interplay
between these settings. Black prisoners are able to point to a
variety of prison conditions that they feel are calculated to deal
them injustice. The victim perspective can encompass wrongs that
relate to substantial inequities (such as being railroaded), or to the
cumulation of petty confrontations and incursions by officials that
are designed to emasculate and abuse. The perceptions of two interviewees who harbored such feelings have been summarized as
follows:

This man feels that he has been an innocent victim of
repeated abuses, not only on this bust, but including
virtually all the treatment he's received in the past
at the hands of the criminal justice system, both inside and outside prison. . . .) For example, he describes himself as being repeatedly harassed,
arrested without evidence and by the same precinct
on many occasions. (Interview C)

This is an inmate who feels he's been singled out by
some corrections officers for harassment. It's a
continuing problem of sensitive skin and it's painful
for him to shave and these officers are constantly
creating problems by insisting that he shave or locking him in because he hasn't shaved. . . . He points
out that he has been the object of a lot of abuse, most
of which is racial . . . and he definitely conceptualized his degenerating encounters with guards in ethnic terms. For instance, beyond the premise of
this sensitive face, he talks about the endemic problems of blacks with sensitive faces being harassed
by white guards as policy. (Interview D)

But a sense of victimization, as we have observed, only rarely blossoms into a violent militant pose. Some prisoners, by contrast, seem unmoved by their victim status. While the majority feel bitter and resentful over abuses they feel are perpetrated against them, few see themselves as helpless targets of harassment, or as devoid of resources or options. The primary response called forth by the experience of victimization involves striking back (physically or verbally) at the source of discomfort. But this response, Toch has observed, is self-defeating. While some men may give vent to their feelings (when they are young or novice prisoners), Toch argues that the legitimate target of an inmate's anger is either out of his reach (such as courts or parole boards) or is in a position of power (for example, guards). In either case, the offending party is capable of taking revenge. Expressing aggression against the "system" or its representatives thus offers the prospect of enhancing one's status as a victim (Toch 1975: 295). (Attacks on staff have always represented a small proportion of violent incidents in prison. In California, where the specter of inmate militancy seems most on the minds of correctional administrators and staff, inmate-staff attacks represented only 11 percent of violent acts committed in that system during 1975. While this represents an increase over figures available for a decade earlier, the proportion of such acts that were ideological in character remains unknown. See Toch [1974].)

The sequence in which injustice spawns rage, which in turn must be suppressed or ventilated in indirect (safe) ways, is a theme that is related to the "cool role" of black ghettos. The man who must live in a world comprised of arbitrary and often powerful others must cultivate a pose of detachment--whenever possible he must avoid trouble and refrain from actions that are likely to invite unmanageable confrontations (Hannerz 1969; Sutter 1972). An extreme concern for suppression of feelings and the appearance of self-control is shown by some convicts. They feel that in order to survive in a world that poses threats a person must equip himself with a "shell" that provides protection from noxious stimuli and from personal reactions to insults. Such persons feel they can become solitary men, callous and impervious to hurt. For example, one such respondent was summarized as follows:

> Our man tells us that he's built an emotional wall
> around himself and he defines problems as nonprob-
> lems and he lets them roll off his back. . . . He
> says he can't be hurt, by anyone or by the criminal
> justice system. He also withdraws from most human
> contact and he's an insular man. He talks a lot about
> constructing this nonemotional shell around himself.

> And remaining by himself most of the time. And he
> considers this the only way he can cope both with the
> prison world and the outside world. . . . He de-
> scribes the shell as a product of repeated injustices
> and unfair treatment that he has received in his life.
> He says in effect that he needs this shell to resist the
> impact that things might have on him otherwise. . . .
> It's a kind of philosophy of life as he sees it, and it's
> a very workable philosophy of life; and it's evolved in
> order to cope with a world that requires that sort of
> philosophy. In fact, he makes it quite clear that even
> when he walks out of prison he's going to be facing a
> world that is treacherous and where there is a lot of
> unpredictable crime going on, so he isn't going to be
> able to relinquish this stance. (Interview E)

The most common (and effective) response to feelings of victimization in prison involves more balanced efforts to keep one's
cool and maintain a low profile. The inmate strives to reduce the
chance of abrasive, self-defeating contacts with authority figures.
Most black prisoners, in other words, come to terms with their impotence and strike a pragmatic compromise. Survival for them is
not an all-or-nothing issue, in which one turns off the world and
kills feelings in order to maintain personal equilibrium. Nor do
such men advocate blind militancy, in which one challenges--and
inevitably falls prey to--omnivorous captors. Rather, these men
take a middle ground; they recognize that they have limited power,
and they realistically assess the boundaries within which they can
operate. The element of risk, the harm that may result from refusals to comply with prison routine, lingers as a theme that rein-
forces a posture of conformity. To maintain poise, many black convicts deploy a battery of resources, ranging from physical activity
or work (which can distract and ameliorate tension) to peers who
provide meaningful activities and supports, offer feedback on the
appropriateness of personal reactions, or simply lend an ear to
grievances. Attempts to negotiate difficulties with staff may be
used to break the victimization cycle or to air complaints. Primarily, however, a man must rely on his own capacity to appraise
situations and exert self-control.

The perspective of an interviewee in his early twenties who
illustrates these observations was summarized as follows:

> This inmate paints a picture of prison as a tension-
> provoking and humiliating environment. He sees him-
> self as a survivor and his survival strategy is one of

of compromise. He tells us that although prison routine is degrading, you have to comply with it to some extent because prison is a violent environment and if you don't comply there's a high probability that you'll be beaten. . . . On the other hand, he doesn't advocate suppressing a sense of injustice or passively taking what is dished out to him. He sees himself in a sense walking a tightrope and the tightrope has to do with issues of equity, power, and manhood. He is, objectively speaking, powerless, though he has some play: at junctures where people transcend even the limits of decency, he might surface the issue and try to get his resentment on the table; and, in some instances, he shares it with his peers who help him gain a sense of proportion. But by and large, he feels that his perceptiveness, his ability to control his own actions, keep him in a position of militant passiveness and survival. (Interview D)

Experiences of victimization and resentment in prison thus typically spawn a pragmatic and cynical "militancy," not the uncompromising stance of the ideologue. The summary of our more sophisticated inmate proceeds as follows:

He describes some of the "younger" inmates getting extremely resentful about things, and he says this is sometimes seductive, but rather unhealthy. He would describe himself as being "aware" just as the younger militant who feels all this resentment is aware, but yet in the sense of being more aware in other respects, because he's not only aware of the grounds for resentment; he's also aware of his own need to keep his cool so that he doesn't win battles and find himself losing the war of survival as a consequence. (Interview D)

The realization that a person must cope with limited resources in contests that are often no win/multiple lose affairs is a lesson many black prisoners feel they have learned in the ghetto. In prison, where this lesson may be most applicable, the typical response to inequity and abuse is likely to involve an element of qualified but informed consent.

CONCLUSIONS

This chapter provides a view of prison from the standpoint of black prisoners. Salient modes of adjustment are described. The findings indicate that adaptations that approximate that of the revolutionary or violent militant are both atypical and dysfunctional in confinement. By contrast, a more mature, pragmatic, and non-ideological stance may be a more representative and viable response to prison pressure.

The radical or revolutionary prisoner thus may represent a less common and effective mode of prison adjustment than has been assumed elsewhere. To be sure, such men exist in penal institutions and on occasion play catalytic and highly visible roles in prison violence and insurrection. And prisons, as we have observed, increasingly house the young, the alienated, and the violence-prone, populations that are bound to produce some tension and unrest. But there appear to be substantial forces that operate to undermine or defuse a radical prisoner movement. For ghetto blacks, men to whom penal settings may be most plausible, who evoke a revolutionary response, the conservative road to survival may be preferred to more hazardous (and unrewarding) prison confrontations.

REFERENCES

Blauner, R.
     1975   Convict explains why SLA fizzled. Charlotte Observer
             (November 23): 12A.

     1970   Black culture: lower class result or ethic creation. In
             Soul, ed. L. Rainwater. N.J.: Transaction.

Faine, J. R., and E. Bohlander
     1975   Prisoner radicalization: an investigation of the solidifi-
             cation of radical attitudes. Paper delivered at the Annual
             Meeting of the American Society of Criminology, Toronto,
             Canada.

Glaser, D.
     1971   Politicalization of prisoners: a new challenge to Ameri-
             can penology. In Corrections--Problems and Prospects,
             ed. D. Peterson and C. Thomas. Englewood Cliffs,
             N.J.: Prentice-Hall.

Hannerz, U.
    1969   Soulside. New York: Columbia University Press.

Horton, J.
    1967   Time and cool people. Transaction 4 (April): 5-12.

Jackson, G.
    1970   Soledad Brother. New York: Coward-McCann.

Johnson, R.
    1976   Culture and Crisis in Confinement. Lexington, Mass.:
            Lexington Books, D. C. Heath.

New York State Special Commission on Attica
    1972   Attica--The Official Report of the New York State Special
            Commission on Attica. New York: Bantam Books.

Pallas, J., and B. Barber
    1973   From riot to revolution. In Criminal Justice in America,
            ed. R. Quinney. Boston: Little, Brown.

Phillips, W.
    1960   Survival techniques of black Americans. In Black Life
            and Culture, ed. R. Goldstein. New York: Coswell.

Rainwater, L.
    1970   Behind Ghetto Walls. Chicago: Aldine.

    1966   Crucible of identity: the Negro lower class family.
            Daedalus 95: 172-216.

Sutter, A.
    1972   Playing a cold game: phases of a ghetto career. Urban
            Life and Culture (April): 77-91.

Sykes, G.
    1966   The Society of Captives: A Study of a Maximum Security
            Prison. New York: Atheneum.

Toch, H.
    1975   Men in Crisis: Chicago: Aldine.

    1974   The shape of prison violence. Manuscript.

Wallo, G. , et al.
   1973   Community contact and inmate attitudes: an experimental
          assessment of work release. Criminology 2 (December):
          345-81.

Wicker, T.
   1975   A Time to Die. New York: Ballantine Books.

4

STYLES OF DOING TIME IN A CO-ED PRISON: MASCULINE AND FEMININE ALTERNATIVES
Nanci Koser Wilson

INTRODUCTION

The burgeoning literature on female emancipation and on sex role differences has given impetus to the study of differences in male and female criminality (a body of literature that is still quite small, but is beginning to grow). At the same time the recent phenomenon of cocorrections (housing male and female offenders together in prisons where they often interact with each other) gives us a unique opportunity to study differences in masculine and feminine reactions to imprisonment. Previous studies of this topic have been limited to comparisons of data from studies of all-male and all-female prisons. Because the two types of facilities differ so radically (in population count, programming, degree of security, and the like), the comparisons made between Fronters or Alderson and male prisons are difficult to evaluate. This chapter presents preliminary findings from the study of a minimum security correctional center, which in the last year has moved from an all-male facility to cocorrectional status. It is one of only a handful of prisons in the country to make this change.

RELATED LITERATURE

Data on the feminine response to imprisonment has come from three important studies of female prisons--David Ward and Gene Kassebaum's study of Frontera (Ward, Kassebaum 1965), Rose Giallombardo's study of Alderson* (Giallombardo 1966a), and

------

*Giallombardo (1974) has also researched juvenile facilities for females, but as this chapter focuses on adults we will not consider these findings.

Esther Heffernan's work on Occoquan (Heffernan 1972). The authors
compare their findings with the previous findings from studies of
male prisons. In addition Charles Tittle has compared male and
female responses to incarceration in a federal drug treatment hospital. These studies have emphasized basic differences between
masculine and feminine reaction to incarceration in terms of two
important variables--solidarity and homosexuality.

As to homosexuality, the authors seem to be in general agreement (with the exception of Tittle) that the rate of female homosexuality during confinement is greater than the male rate. Table 4.1
depicts these reported differences.

TABLE 4.1

Reported Differences in Male and Female Homosexuality

Researcher	Type of Institution	Percent of Inmate Population		Basis of Estimate
		Male	Female	
Clemmer	Maximum security male prison	40	--	Overt homo-sexuality
Giallombardo	Maximum security female prison	--	85	Participation in pseudo-families
Heffernan	Maximum security female prison	--	48 cool* 58 life 31 square	"Playing"
Sykes	Maximum security male prison	35	--	Overt homo-sexuality
Tittle	Co-ed drug hospital	23	24	Self-reports and patient estimates of homosexual activity
Ward and Kassebaum	Maximum security female prison	--	50	Overt homo-sexuality

*Hefferan provides different estimates for each type of inmate.
Source: Compiled by the author.

The more important sex-linked difference in homosexuality reported, however, lies in the meaning of homosexuality. Most authors think that for males there exists a need to validate their masculinity. The corollary is not true, however. Giallombardo, for instance, indicates that the need to assert or defend one's feminity in the same way that the male inmate must prove his masculinity "clearly does not arise for the female offender" (Giallombardo 1966b: 447). John Gagnon and William Simon's (1968) and Ward and Kassebaum's (1965) works both maintain that a woman has fewer problems managing sexual deprivation, and that her greatest deprivation is that of emotionally satisfying relationships. They see female prison homosexuality as fulfilling primarily physical needs.

A second theme in the literature asserts that inmate solidarity is lower in the female inmate community than in the male. Table 4.2 presents these reported data.

Giallombardo accounts for the differences as attributable to general features of the American culture (which socializes women to be less aggressive and more emotionally dependent, and depicts women as competitors rather than friends). But Gagnon and Simon and Ward and Kassebaum point to differences in offense history and suggest that women prisoners are less likely to have extensive criminal histories or long histories of penal confinement, both of which are "relevant to the development of criminal maturity and a con-wise prison orientation" (Ward, Kassebaum 1965: 67).

The two themes of homosexuality and solidarity are not unrelated. Many authors think of the "play families" that women create in prisons as a functional alternative to the solidary inmate culture created and maintained by adherence to an inmate code. Tittle aptly summarizes this position, for which he found some support in his study of a co-ed drug hospital. He maintains that the previous evidence suggests that male inmates "tend to organize into an overall symbiotic structure characterized by a shared normative system epitomized in a prison code, but that within that community considerable individualism and personal isolation prevail." In contradistinction, "female inmates are characterized neither by overall cohesion nor by individual isolation. Instead they tend to organize into relatively enduring primary relationships often involving dyadic homosexual attachments and extensive 'family' relationships" (Tittle 1969: 492).

In summary, then, the existing literature seems to suggest that clear masculine and feminine alternatives for "doing time" exist. While men cope with the pains of imprisonment by forming a solidary inmate culture supported by adherence to the inmate code, women form play families to provide emotional support. This basic difference is reflected in the lower rates of solidarity and the

TABLE 4.2

Reported Differences in Male and Female
Inmate Solidarity

| Researcher | Type of Institution | Percent of Female Population | | Basis of Estimate |
		Male	Female	
Giallombardo	Maximum security female prison	--	Almost all	Snitching
Heffernan	Maximum security male prison	--	50	Of inmates stated there was "no inmate loyalty"
			22 Cool* 61 Life 9 Squares	Received tickets for fighting
			69 Cool 60 Life 5 Squares	Adherence to inmate code
Sykes	Maximum security male prison	41	--	Were informers
Tittle	Co-ed drug hospital	40	21	Attitude scale of cohesion (high score)
		34	36	Sharing
		42	34	Awareness of normative system
		55	48	Believed snitching would entail risk
Ward and Kassebaum	Maximum security female prison	--	50 90	Snitching

*Heffernan provides different estimates for each type of inmate.
Source: Compiled by the author.

higher rates of homosexuality in the female versus the male prison
environment. It also reflects the important differences between
men and women as their roles are defined in the outside world.

RESEARCH SITE

The cocorrectional prison gives us a unique opportunity to
address the issues of sex-role differences in confinement. It allows
us to measure, with the same instruments, differences between
men and women exposed to roughly the same prison environment,
rather than forcing us to compare work done on men by one set of
authors with research on women done by another set of authors.

The findings presented here represent preliminary and tentative
conclusions from the study of a minimum-security facility. The
findings are applicable only to the rather unique type of correctional
facility studied and should not be generalized to larger, more
secure, one-sex prisons.

Correctional Center is a minimum security facility that is part
of one of the largest state correctional systems in America. Within
the system are several large maximum-security adult male prisons,
a medium-security farm for males, a maximum-security female
facility, numerous work-release centers, and various juvenile reformatories and camps. Rarely is an individual sent directly from
the reception and diagnostic center to the minimum-security Correctional Center. Rather, most inmates serve from two to ten
years in one or more of the maximum-security facilities prior to
transfer to the Correctional Center. This transfer is based partially on their behavior in the larger prison and partially on their
proximity to a "board date" (the first time at which the inmate's
case is heard by the parole board, for possible parole-release).

Correctional Center is a modern, treatment-oriented prison.
Terminology changes include the use of the term "correctional
center" rather than prison, while guards are "correctional officers,"
inmates are "residents," and the yard is called "town square."

But the differences between Correctional Center and other
prisons within the same state go deeper than mere label changes.
Physically, the Correctional Center has no wall or fence of any
kind. Its facilities consist of numerous small buildings, including
dormitories, a dining hall, chapel, and a gym. The effect is that
of a small college campus. Each resident has his or her own room
and wears his or her own clothes. Although the men and women
eat and are housed in separate buildings, they interact frequently
on their work assignments, in classes (a complex college and vocational program is maintained), and in certain recreational areas.

Residents have a great deal of freedom in moving from one area of the institution to another, in control over their own rooms (from decorating them to possessing their own keys to them), and in many other areas of institutional life.

As a consequence of all this, the resident at Correctional Center has fewer "pains of imprisonment" with which to cope. The relative freedom of movement, the private rooms with keys, the access to personal clothing, and the like all significantly reduce feelings of loss of autonomy, liberty, and goods and services, which may be felt in the other prisons in the system. Because almost all of the residents have a very short "time to the board" (the first time a resident's case is heard by the parole board), there is also much more of a "street orientation" among the residents. Also, as a concomitant of the free availability of goods and services, there are few if any jobs in the prison that may be thought of as "power jobs" (such as kitchen worker, clerk, and the like). In fact, "power plays" in the form of fighting, gang "warfare," and generally disruptive behavior are practically nonexistent for the simple reason that the threat of transfer back to one of the more maximum security prisons is a potent social control mechanism.*

It is within this setting, then, that this study attempts to compare the way that men and women "do time." So far, because the study is still in progress, only impressionistic data on the issues of homosexuality and solidarity (which the earlier comparisons focused on) are available. The majority of the data relied upon for this chapter focuses on program agreements made by the residents and on disciplinary ticket information. However, even in the absence of hard data, a few comments on solidarity and homosexuality may be in order.

SOME OBSERVATIONS ON SOLIDARITY
AND HOMOSEXUALITY

From observation and from scattered interviews with residents it is my impression that the level of solidarity is not less for women than for men within this cocorrectional setting.

In general, solidarity appears to be directly related to (1) the size of a prison, (2) the security level of the prison, (3) the amount of time the average inmate has to do (and concomitantly the turnover rate), and (4) the presence or absence of a "treatment" orientation.

---

*See Wilson (1975) for a further discussion.

Because Correctional Center is a minimum-security facility, has a relatively small population (some 400-50 residents), has a definite treatment orientation, and because the residents generally have a short time left to serve on their sentences (which results in a high turnover of residents), we may expect that the traditional phenomenon of a solidary inmate culture will not obtain.

While we have no information on the differential degree of solidarity that may exist between the maximum-security female prison and the maximum-security male prisons within this same system, this much seems clear--as expressed in interviews, both men and women experience a lower amount of solidarity when they arrive at Correctional Center.

In commenting on the lower degree of inmate solidarity at Correctional Center, one resident noted that there are "so many snitches here that you can't estimate the number." Female residents also report less solidarity at Correctional Center than at the female maximum-security prison in the system. Male and female residents alike noted that "you can't take care of a snitch" at Correctional Center, attributing this to fear of being transferred back to a maximum-security prison.

We have no hard data yet on the types of sexual involvements of the residents. There is some reason to believe that the play families that women are reported to create in all-female prisons still exist, and so does homosexual involvement. The extent of both homosexuality and of play families is unknown, but there is some reason to believe that the rate of homosexuality for both men and women is lower at Correctional Center.

A male resident who asked whether he felt the rate of male homosexuality was different at Correctional Center commented: "At [a maximum-security prison in the system] all the young guys are girls--now they're coming out of their man bag. . . . They're playing big man with the women."

On the differences between male and female homosexual involvement while in prison, a resident drew the following distinction. While both men and women seek advice and emotional fulfillment from such a relationship, the methods by which the more aggressive partner introduces a "square" to homosexuality vary. "A bull-dagger's main desire is to mentally destroy a girl [by telling her] she is ugly, piggy, etc." She convinces herself that she cannot get any other friends. The bulldagger is then able to dominate her by taking care of her. "You can cop a boy more easily," he continued, "because of his relationship to fear, cowardice, and laziness. You can cop a girl through openness, tenderness, and a strong relationship." The young girl is looking for "an all and all mighty adviser --a mother," while the young boy "finds a father." From this inmate's perspective, at least, the meaning of male and female prison homosexuality is not very different.

Although we have only impressionistic data on homosexuality from this study at the present time, we do know that it is still a pattern. The administration has rather strictly controlled hetero-sexual involvement, with a definite and stringently enforced rule against physical contact of any sort between the male and female residents. (For discipline purposes, physical contact tickets have been written for such minor amounts of contact as holding hands.) Homosexual contact is much more difficult to control, although tickets are still written for a resident "being in bed" with another resident during the night. Because the homosexual activity is so much more difficult to control, some residents have concluded that the administration does not discourage it. "Down here they would rather see a woman with a woman and a man with a man," one resident commented. Other residents feel that the presence of the opposite sex actually stimulates homosexuality. "They sit down with a man and get horny--they sit with a man all day and go take care of their needs [with a woman] at night."

Heterosexual involvement in the cocorrectional prison is, of course, the topic that most catches the imagination of the general public and therefore is the issue that makes the cocorrectional prison administrator walk on eggs most of the time. To the re-searcher, however, the meaning of heterosexual involvement is much more important than the extent of the physical relationship.

Residents indicate that heterosexual involvement within the prison, is "a way to do time." One couple, who had had a stable romantic relationship for a number of months was asked whether they thought most residents wanted to get involved or to stay away from it. The female half of the couple responded:

> I think most of it's just like for conversation you know.
> Maybe to help 'em--for each other to do time. Now you
> can get involved, you know, within time, like we did. I
> don't think anyone comes here with the idea "I'm gonna
> fall in love" and you know, "I'm gonna do all this."
> They just come here and find someone they can relate
> to, someone of the opposite sex and they just sit and
> talk or whatever, you know, they relate to them.

The man noted that the male residents

> don't come here lookin' for no love affair--nothin'
> like that. . . . If a man finds a woman . . . they're
> doing their time, maybe they're sharing things

together--to them if you will look at it it's therapeutic,
you know, because like they're sharin' things back and
forth and that helps do time.

A larger percent of the females get involved in heterosexual
relationships simply because of the imbalanced sex ratio. (The sex
ratio at Correctional Center is almost 1 to 8, or approximately 50
women and 400 men). There are some women who do remain
heterosexual isolates, however, and some men who appear to choose
to remain uninvolved. It is hoped that the research project will
eventually be able to identify what type of resident is most likely to
seek a heterosexual relationship as a method for doing time.

STYLES OF DOING TIME

Data that are available at the present time that would give us
some clues as to how men and women differentially respond to the
prison environment are of two kinds. We have data on the number
and kinds of disciplinary tickets received by women and men. We
also have the program agreements that are made by the men and
women.
Formal record is made of disciplinary procedures, which
include the offense for which the individual is cited and the disposition of the "ticket." Program agreements are made by each new
resident with his counselor, upon entrance to the prison. Each
resident is asked to specify his goals while in Correctional Center.
The counselor then makes note of the method for achieving these
goals, and the resident is finally asked to specify his long-range
goals.
We have these data on all women who have been incarcerated
at the center. The large number of men makes it impossible to
collect data on the entire population. For this reason, two units,
which usually hold about the same amount of men as the female
unit, were selected at random for the male sample. This sample
was chosen rather than a random sample of all male residents to
facilitate sociometric data gathering. It does mean that certain
types of comparisons between men and women are difficult to make,
however, as we shall see.

SEX DIFFERENCES

The first thing we discover is that the women seem to get
more disciplinary tickets than do men in our sample (disciplinary

ticket data are available for 44 men and 52 women and computations are based on these totals). The men had an average of 2.846 tickets. This average is misleading, however, since the men in our sample tended to have served more time than the women (10.3 months for the men, 6.4 months for the women). Controlling for this by computing the average number of tickets per month served gives us the following figures: .143 tickets per month served for the men and .446 per month served for the women.

The program agreements specify what kinds of institutional programs the men and women intend to get involved in. Some residents, however, fail to enroll in or complete programs that they request. Hence, we cannot infer that all requested programs are actually fulfilled. With this caution in mind, we can look at the prison programs that men and women request. Table 4.3 presents these differences.

TABLE 4.3

Prison Programs Requested by Men and Women

Type of Program	Male Residents (N = 52)		Female Residents (N = 78)	
	Percent	Number	Percent	Number
Academic (total)	57.7	30	67.7	52
GED	11.5	6	48.7	38
A.A. or A.S.	21.2	11	1.3	1
College courses	17.3	9	16.7	13
Learning lab	7.7	4	6.4	5
Vocational	73.1	38	74.4	58
Counseling	9.6	5	35.9	28

Note: Figures indicate percentages of the male–female residents who requested this program. Percentages do not total to 100 as residents may request more than one program.
Source: Compiled by the author.

More women (66.7 percent) than men (57.7 percent) appear to be involved in academic programs. Of the various types of academic programs, we find a much larger percentage of the women in the General Education Degree (GED) program (48.7 percent women, 11.5 percent men). Approximately the same percentage of men and women are involved in learning lab, and in taking college courses. However, a larger percent of the men (21.2 percent men, 1.3 percent women) set a goal of gaining an Associate of Arts or Associate of Science degree in the college program.

Although the data indicate that a much higher percent of women desire to engage in counseling while in prison, these data are not interpretable as representative of overall male-female differences at Correctional Center. When the male units were selected to form the sample, all units that would contain an extremely atypical sample of the male inmate population were deliberately excluded from choice. These units were: a unit composed of older men, a unit devoted to those men with drug problems, and a special unit devoted to transactional analysis (TA). Because of this composition, it is highly likely that men who wish to engage in counseling will take advantage of the therapeutic community offered in either the drug or the TA unit. These two units comprise about 12 percent of the male population. With this in mind, we can see that male-female differences in desire for counseling probably are not great.

The institution has an extensive vocational education program and many residents take advantage of it. The percentages of men (73.1) and women (74.4) requesting vocational education are nearly equal. In terms of type of vocational education, we do see some sex differences. Most of the vocational programs are oriented toward traditionally male vocations, since the institution only recently became cocorrectional. Hence, there is not a wide variety of choice in terms of sex-linked occupational training. However, the sex differences that do appear are predictable from a knowledge of the general cultural attitudes toward "masculine" and "feminine" jobs. No women requested training in meatcutting, air conditioning repair, or water-waste management; and few women were interested in welding or office machine repair. Concomitantly, no men requested the sewing program although one enrolled in the upholstery course. More women (16.7 percent) requested cosmetology training than men (7.8 percent). The most popular program at the institution is training as an emergency medical technician (EMT). It appears to be equally appealing to men and women, with 17 of the 66 female requests and 22 of the 51 male requests being for the EMT program.

It is in the prisoners' long-range goals that we see the greatest sex differences. When asked to specify a long-range goal, 34.3 percent of the women and 42 percent of the men were unable to do so (see Table 4.4). Only two men mentioned their personal life (for example, marriage, children, home ownership, and the like) as part of their long-range goal, but 12.9 percent of the

women did so. Of the men responding, 11 percent confidently predicted that they would own their own business, while only 5.7 percent of the women set such a goal for themselves. Some inmates
were able to think only in terms of the prison life itself. When
asked to specify a long-range goal, they mentioned further programs
they would like to engage in. This was true for 15.7 percent of the
women, but only 4 percent of the men. Approximately the same
percentages of men (38.8) and women (38.6) were job-oriented;
that is, they mentioned a specific job they intended to have as a
long-range goal.

TABLE 4.4

Long-Range Goals of Men and Women

Type of Goal	Men (N = 45)		Women (N = 70)	
	Percent	Number	Percent	Number
No long-range goal specified	42.2	19	34.3	24
Personal life was mentioned	4.4	2	12.9	9
Owning business	11.1	5	5.7	4
Prison-oriented	4.4	2	15.7	11
Job-oriented	38.8	17	38.6	27

Note: Percentages do not total to 100 because a resident
could appear in more than one category.
Source: Compiled by the author.

We find, then, that in terms of coping with imprisonment, the
women are more apt to "get in trouble," as evidenced by their higher
number of disciplinary tickets. This may, however, be a function
of their higher visibility within the institution, rather than their
actual behavior. In terms of how residents "fill their time" during
institutionalization, these data do not show many sex differences.
We estimate that about the same amount of men and women engage
in counseling and in vocational programming. Only a slightly higher
percentage of women than men engage in academic programming.

When we move from a consideration of how men and women "do their time" to a consideration of their plans for the future, however, we begin to see traditional sex differences emerge. Women are much more likely to think of the future in terms of marriage and babies, and, when it comes to work, men are more likely to think of themselves as business owners and women as workers.

DIFFERENCES IN "FELONIOUS IDENTITY"

It was felt that the technique of looking only at the gross differences between the two categories male and female was likely to be misleading, however. Those who have studied the female prison have noted that the female prison population is much different than the male counterpart in many important respects other than sex (see, for example, Ward, Kassebaum [1965: 67]).

Further, the work of John Irwin (1970), Irwin and Donald Cressey (1962), and Heffernan (1972) strongly suggests that there are differences in the reaction to imprisonment based on the type of identity the convict brings with him to prison. Heffernan in particular found strong differences between her three categories of prisoners--the square, the cool, and the life. Therefore, it was felt that the differences between the sexes might be more accurately assessed by making comparisons within various categories of prisoners--the categories to be based on preprison identities.

Irwin (1970) has developed a method for classifying inmates' preprison identities (or felonious identities as he calls them) by taking into account such factors as offense, offense history, race, occupation, age, previous prison experience, drug use, and a number of other indicators. He devised eight different categories. In applying this typology to the residents at Correctional Center, we found that although Irwin devised the scheme for use with men, it "worked" equally well with women. That is, a high percentage of residents clearly fell into one of the Irwin categories, using his scoring technique.

As we would expect from previous studies of the female inmate population, it differs rather markedly from the male prison population, as depicted in Table 4.5. The literature suggests that women are less likely to be professional criminals, and this is evidenced by the much larger percentage of male (28.4 percent) than female (8.8 percent) thieves. A larger percentage of women than men shows up in the hustler category, although the numbers are extremely small. The same is true of the "head" category. A major difference appears in the percentage of women (17.6 percent) who are "disorganized criminals" compared with men (4.5 percent).

TABLE 4.5

Felonious Identities of Men and Women

Felonious Identity	Men		Women	
	Percent	Number	Percent	Number
Thieves	28.4	19	8.8	6
Squares	22.4	15	16.2	11
Drug addicts	14.9	10	17.6	12
Lower-class persons	20.9	14	19.1	13
Hustlers	1.5	1	5.9	4
State-raised	6.0	4	5.9	4
Disorganized criminals	4.5	3	17.6	12
Heads	1.5	1	8.8	6

Source: Compiled by the author.

        In comparing men with women within each of these categories,
we are limited to comparisons between men and women thieves,
squares, drug addicts, and lower-class persons. (The numbers in
the other categories are too small to allow for comparison of data.)
In the following analysis, however, the reader will note that the
differences between the four types of felonious identities appear to
be much more striking than the overall differences between men
and women (see Tables 4.6 and 4.7).
        Thieves within our sample were very unlikely to experience
trouble with the administration. They received, on the average
.115 tickets per month. The literature suggests that this is a category of felon who "pulls time" easily. The finding of a low number
of tickets is thus explainable within this framework. Of both men
and women thieves, 18 percent expressed desire for counseling in
their program agreements. This is consistent with the notion that
thieves may be prisonwise enough to engage in counseling to please
the parole board, but are not generally oriented to counseling.
About two-thirds (59 percent) of the thieves expressed no long-range
goal, and 29 percent of them expressed long-range goals that were
job oriented.
        A clear contrast to the thieves is found in the category of
squares. These individuals also received a low average amount of
tickets (.172 per month), consistent with the theory that squares
attempt to please the administration, although they are perhaps not

TABLE 4.6

Differences in Program Agreements and Disciplinary
Tickets among Felonious Identity Types,

	Thieves	Squares	Drug Addicts	Lower-Class Persons
Average number of tickets per month	.115	.172	.511	.252
Percent desiring counseling	18.0%	25.0%	39.0%	9.0%
Long-range goal				
None	59.0	31.0	38.0	32.0
Job-oriented	29.0	63.0	56.0	36.0
Prison-oriented	5.9	6.3	6.3	27.0

Source: Compiled by the author.

TABLE 4.7

Differences in Program Agreements and Disciplinary
Tickets among Felonious Identity Types,
by Sex

	Average Number of Tickets Per Month	Percent Desiring Counseling
Thieves		
Males	.063	12.5
Female	.316	33.3
Squares		
Male	.151	9.1
Female	.212	44.4
Drug addicts		
Male	.595	14.3
Female	.456	54.5
Lower-class persons		
Male	.127	0.0
Female	.450	16.7

Source: Compiled by the author.

as adept at avoiding trouble as are the prisonwise thieves. A larger percent (25) of the squares desire counseling, and their long-range goals are much different than the thieves. Only 31 percent of the squares failed to specify a long-range goal, whereas 63 percent of them expressed long-range goals oriented toward jobs or education.

Drug addicts are most likely to do time poorly, at least as far as avoiding trouble with the administration is concerned. They received an average of .511 tickets per month. But 39 percent of them expressed an intention to engage in counseling, which is the highest percent of any of the four categories. Two possible interpretations are: (1) drug addicts know they have to engage in some form of therapy related to their drug problem, if they have any hope of favorably impressing the parole board, and/or (2) they recognized their own need for counseling to deal with this problem. Approximately 38 percent of the drug addicts failed to specify a long-range goal, and 56 percent of them expressed a goal oriented toward getting a job.

Lower-class persons received a fairly high amount of tickets (.252 per month served), indicating that they neither attempted to please the administration as squares do, nor to stay out of trouble as a general policy for doing time well, as we would expect of the thieves. Consistent with findings from the "outside world" as well as within the prison, we find that lower-class persons do not find themselves comfortable with counseling. Only 9 percent of them expressed an intention to receive counseling as part of their program; 32 percent had no long-range goal; and 27 percent had long-range goals that were oriented to prison life. Only 36 percent had job-oriented goals, which is slightly higher than the percentage of thieves who had these goals, and much lower than the percentages for drug addicts and squares.

Comparisons between men and women within the four categories show us some interesting differences, as depicted in Table 4.7. The overall patterning in regard to counseling is repeated for both men and women, with the exception that male thieves are more likely to engage in counseling than are the "square Johns." The finding that more women than men engage in counseling in this sample is repeated within each felonious identity type. (However, the reader is again cautioned that these probably do not represent true differences because of the way in which the male sample was selected.)

The patterning of "trouble with the administration" as evidenced by average number of tickets is somewhat different for men than for women. For both sexes, it is the drug addicts who are most likely to receive tickets. But lower-class women rank second in average number of tickets while lower-class men rank third.

Male thieves are the least likely of all males to receive tickets, while female thieves rank third in number of tickets. "Square Janes" are the least likely to receive tickets, while square Johns rank second in this regard. It will be noted that not only is the patterning of tickets different for men and women but also that, in every category except drug addict, the women receive more tickets than the men, reflecting that general finding for all men as compared with all women. However, the differences between the men and women within each category are smaller than is the overall difference.

Comparisons of the long-range goals of men and women within each category would not be meaningful as the numbers are too small.

CONCLUSIONS

These data are limited, being based on a relatively small sample of men and women. Further, they speak to only a small portion of the question: Are there differences in the ways that men and women do time? However, one thing does seem clear. While we find some differences in reaction to incarceration when we compare men with women, we see more striking differences when we compare different types of felons with each other. It is a general finding that women are more likely to attract the attention of the administration through disciplinary tickets, but drug addicts, be they male or female, are the most likely of any of the four categories of felons to receive tickets. Drug addicts, be they male or female, are the most likely types to engage in counseling and lower-class men and women are the least likely. The differences between felon types is also clearly evident in their long-range goals. While we see very little if any difference between men and women in terms of their being "job oriented," we see strong differences between the various types of felons in this regard. For example, while 63 percent of square Johns and Janes are job oriented, only 29 percent of thieves are so oriented.

This chapter, then, presents support for the theory that the way in which felons "do time" is a function of their preprison identities. Further, a felon's sexual identity appears to be less important than his "felonious identity." Square Janes are more similar to square Johns than they are to drug addicts or thieves. Lower-class women are more similar to lower-class men than they are to other women, and so forth.

The differences in male and female inmate culture reported in the literature may hold true for one-sex prisons. And this research project may yet discover striking differences between men and women at Correctional Center. But the evidence that is thus far available suggests that when men and women do time in a similar environment, the differences in their styles of doing time are not great. Instead, the types of preprison identities that they bring to the incarceration experience dictate the ways in which they will do their time. In short, masculine and feminine styles of doing time may exist, but the clearest differences in styles of doing time are between thieves and squares (or drug addicts and lower-class persons) rather than between men and women.

REFERENCES

Clemmer, D.
    1940   The Prison Community. New York: Holt, Rinehart and Winston.

Gagnon, J., and W. Simon
    1968   The social meaning of prison homosexuality. Federal Probation 32, 1 (March): 3-29. Reprinted in Knudten, Crime, Criminology and Contemporary Society: 367-78.

Giallombardo, R.
    1974   The Social World of Imprisoned Girls: A Comparative Study of Institutions for Juvenile Delinquents. New York: John Wiley and Sons.

    1966a   Society of Women: A Study of a Woman's Prison. New York: John Wiley and Sons.

    1966b   Social roles in a prison for women. Social Problems 13 (Winter): 268-88. Reprinted as The female inmate social system. In Guenther, Criminal Behavior and Social Systems. Chicago: Rand McNally.

Heffernan, E.
    1972   Making It in Prison: The Square, the Cool and the Life. New York: Wiley Interscience.

Irwin, J.
    1970   The Felon. Englewood Cliffs, N.J.: Prentice-Hall.

Irwin, J., and D. Cressey
    1962   Thieves, convicts and the inmate culture. Social Problems (Fall): 142-55.

Sykes, G. M.
    1958   The Society of Captives.   Princeton, N.J.: Princeton
            University Press.

Tittle, C.
    1969   Inmate organization: sex differentiate and the influence
            of criminal subcultures.   American Sociological Review
            34, 4 (August).

Ward, D. A., and G. Kassebaum
    1965   Women's Prison: Sex and Social Structure.   Chicago:
            Aldine.

Wilson, N.
    1975   Speak softly and carry a big stick.   Paper presented at
            the meetings of the Southern Sociological Society,
            Washington, D. C.

5

CRIMINAL MATURITY, PRISON ROLES, AND NORMATIVE ALIENATION

Werner Gruninger, Norman S. Hayner,
and Ronald L. Akers

Research on the prisoner community suggests two sets of variables that account for the emergence of the inmate contraculture found in prison: the social and criminal background an offender brings with him to prison and the situation of prison life to which an inmate must adapt upon admission. The inmate contraculture may be defined in terms of association patterns among inmates, their professed values and attitudes, the collective resistance shown to staff-imposed treatment and training programs, and the corruption of authority and control instituted by custodians. The principal consequence of membership in the contraculture is prisonization, that is, an increasing hostility toward the goals of the institution, a crystallization of criminal values and self-identification, and alienation from the values of law-abiding society.

The situation-response model of prisonization, developed by Clemmer (1959), Sykes (1948), Adamek (1968), Schrag (1949), Giallombardo (1966), and Ward and Kassebaum (1965), among others, asserts that the inmate group serves as a buffer against the pains of imprisonment, such as material impoverishment, stigmatization, involuntary celibacy, loss of personal autonomy, and other deprivations of prison life. It also appeared, in the work of Street, Vinter, and Perron (1966) that variations in prison situations generated variations in inmate orientations to staff goals and patterns of association.

In contrast to the functional model of prisonization, a number of researchers, among them Garabedian, Garrity, Wheeler, Cline, and Irwin, found that the life history of the offender and his personal characteristics were the more crucial determinants of inmate orientations. The import model is based on the major premise that the organizational patterns and the content of the prisoner subculture are a continuation of values and attitudes learned prior to incarceration, becoming somewhat more pronounced under conditions of confinement with other offenders of similar social and criminal experience.

Attempts to determine the relative magnitude of effects of either of the two sets of variables generally failed, since most studies were based on the analysis of a single prison, making statistical controls for levels of deprivation difficult. It was suspected that offender characteristics and situationally determined variables were confounded with each other. More sophisticated offenders may have been sent to harsher, more depriving institutions, while leniently run correctional facilities may have contained a larger proportion of naive or first offenders, especially in those jurisdictions where a variety of different prisons are available for prisoner rehabilitation. The two studies in which a variety of prisons were simultaneously analyzed, with adequate controls for levels of deprivation, came to opposite conclusions. Wheeler (1961), in his research in 15 Scandinavian prisons, found that inmate responses were a function of the social relationships that prisoners retained with members of the outside community, and that the pains of imprisonment had only a transitory effect, varying, however, with levels of deprivation. Street, Vinter, and Perrow (1966), in their research on four juvenile institutions, showed that levels of deprivation accounted for inmate responses; but the relationships between inmate cohesion and antisocial responses were quite different from those found in adult prisons. One possible explanation is that juveniles have, as yet, not developed self-images as criminal offenders and lack the crystallized antisocial attitudes of more sophisticated adult lawbreakers.

Schrag (1949), in a study of argot role types, found that inmate role adaptations were based both on the social and criminal history of the offender and on the expectations that other inmates had of him, based also on the offenders' prior characteristics. Prisoners, therefore, had a license to engage in certain patterns of action, and differences in orientation and attachment were expected. Inmate attitudes were shown to vary both with the individual's social background and degrees of deprivation, as measured by security sections.

The present study was designed to shed light on the relative importance of the import model as against the situation-response model of prisonization. Twenty-five prisons were selected in the United States, Mexico, Spain, Germany, and Great Britain, representing a wide range of custody and treatment prisons with varying levels of deprivation, measured by architecture, administrative goals, classification and diagnostic procedures, inmate employment, education and training programs, security and custody practices, personnel qualifications, and degrees of contact with outsiders

permitted to inmates.* Questionnaire data were obtained from
1,310 male prisoners, representing a prison population of 17,114
offenders. The findings presented here are part of a larger research
project still in progress.

THE HYPOTHETICAL MODEL

The recent literature on prisonization, taken as a whole, appears to support the import model of prisonization, even though the
pains of imprisonment may aggravate the antisocial orientations of
inmates. A causal model was developed with the assumption that
causal linkages between criminal background and prisoner role adaptations can be established, as Schrag (1949), Irwin (1970), and
others had previously demonstrated. In addition, the role adaptations a prisoner makes upon admission are hypothesized to determine his professed attitudes, the imputation of attitudes to other inmates and the prison climate he observes, the ways in which the individual is structured into the inmate group, and the participation in
staff-initiated programs. The hypothetical model, therefore, rests
on the assumption of a developmental sequence. An individual is
conditioned in his life experiences to assume a given role and self-
conception, and the acting out of that role sets the pattern for prison
adaptation. One should therefore expect linkages between background and roles, and between roles and behavior. Various measures of deprivation were expected to modify the relationships, such
that the normative alienation of the prisoner becomes more severe
under harsh conditions of confinement. If the assertion that the
prisoner utilizes the group as a buffer against deprivation is valid,
one should find a more cohesive group structure and more resistance to prison programs in custodial prisons. Time factors may
also affect the relationships. The multiple indicator model shown
in Figure 5.1 contains the hypothesized relationships among concepts, indicators, and control variables.

CRIMINAL MATURITY AND INMATE
ROLE ADAPTATIONS

The independent conceptual variable, criminal maturity, was
measured in terms of the age at first arrest, the number of juvenile

---

*See Akers, Hayner, and Gruninger (1974). Details of mea-
surement are contained in that article.

FIGURE 5.1

Causal Model of Hypothesized Relationships

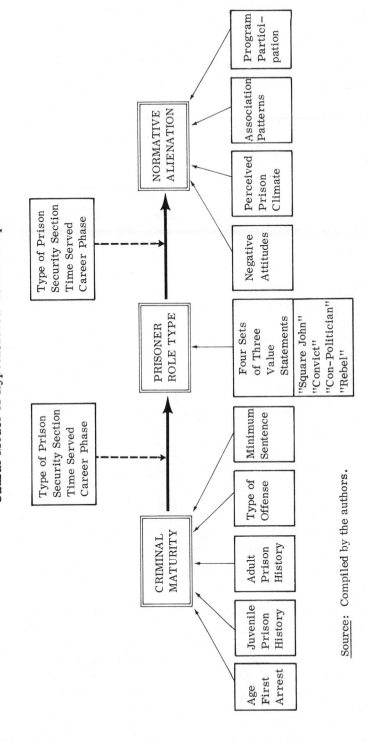

Source: Compiled by the authors.

75

sentences served, the number of adult sentences served, the type of offense, and the minimum sentence handed down by the court. As can be expected, these variables are correlated. The gamma values are shown in Table 5.1.

TABLE 5.1

Gamma Values for Associations among
Indicators of Criminal Maturity

	Number of Juvenile Prison Sentences	Number of Adult Prison Sentences	Type of Offense	Minimum Sentence
Age at first arrest	.83*	.46*	-.44*	.28*
Number of juvenile prison sentences		.61*	-.38*	.12
Number of adult prison sentences			-.32*	.10
Type of offense				.65*

Source: Compiled by the authors.

Individuals who had been arrested early in life, before reaching age 18, have an excellent chance of being incarcerated numerous times thereafter, in both juvenile and adult prisons, because their exposure to the risk of incarceration is longer, and because some genuine criminalization seems to occur as a result of association with others in prison that has consequences for postrelease adjustment; the released offender, of course, also becomes a member of a police suspect pool. There are two offense patterns apparent from our original tabulations on which the gamma values were based. The probability that the instant offense is committed against a person or is a sex offense increases with an increased age at first arrest, and varies negatively with the number of prior juvenile and adult prison commitments. The reverse is true for property offenders. Career criminals are chiefly engaged in the illegal redistribution of wealth. They are typically arrested for the first time before reaching age 18, three-fourths of them admit to having been in juvenile prisons two or more times, and an equally high proportion state that they have served three or more adult prison terms.

Schrag (1949), Garabedian (1959), Garrity (1956), and Irwin (1970) made very similar observations.

Age at first arrest, the number of juvenile sentences served, and the number of adult sentences served--being the most efficient indicators with respect to the dependent variables measuring prison- ization responses--were selected to form an index of criminal matur- ity. The scores give equal weight to each of the three variables, and the summed scores were categorized into four criminal matur- ity types: professional, habitual, occasional, and novice or first offender. At one extreme, a professional offender can be described as an individual whose criminal career began at an early age, and who served a number of adult and juvenile sentences in the past. At the other extreme, there is the offender who had no previous contact with law enforcement agencies, and his first arrest came relatively late in life. Two intermediate categories were also formed. Of the 1,310 prisoners, 6 percent were defined as profes- sionals, 17 percent were habitual offenders, 31 percent were de- fined as occasional criminals, and 46 percent were, by their own admission, naive first offenders.

The utility of prisoner role types for the study of prison ad- justment, parole prediction, and recidivism had been shown in previous research. Here, inmate argot roles were again used as a major variable. With minor modification, the measurement of role types is the same as that used by Garabedian (1959) in his study of Western Penitentiary. The method of assigning an inmate to a role category, however, is markedly different, yielding a greater pro- portion of inmates who could be typed. Inmates were asked to re- spond to a set of Lickert-type value statements, each set of three questions measuring a different Schrag role type. The set of ques- tions for which an individual received the highest summed Lickert score determined the inmate role to which the prisoner was as- signed. In the case of ties, the inmate was defined as prosocial when at least one of the sets referred to prosocial, or "square John," orientations; when both tied sets were in the antisocial direction, the prisoner was defined as antisocial in the tabulations involving only two categories: the social and the antisocial offenders. No social role identifications were available for Mexico. The rela- tionship between criminal maturity and social role types is shown in Table 5.2.

The relationship between criminal maturity and social roles is only significant when the three antisocial role types are collapsed into one category, in part because there is no inherent order in the Schrag role types. When the collapsed categories are analyzed, there is a moderate relationship between criminal maturity and antisocial role playing. When the type of prison, custody and treatment, is held constant, the relationship between criminal maturity and social roles becomes somewhat stronger in tough custody prisons and weakens in treatment prisons; the gamma values are -.40* and -.17, respectively. The less sophisticated offender is more likely to play the prosocial "square John" role under conditions of strict confinement, perhaps separating himself from the more hardened inmates. In the treatment prison, criminal maturity has little effect on role identifications. Table 5.3 demonstrates the relationships.

TABLE 5.2

Criminal Maturity and Prisoner Role Adaptations, in Percent

| | Criminal Maturity | | | | |
	Professional	Habitual	Occasional	Novice	Total
Four Schrag role types (gamma = -.07)					
Number of cases	61	108	240	233	642
Social	5	7	8	17	11
Convict	23	31	28	22	26
Politician	15	11	8	7	9
Rebel	56	51	56	54	54
Two role types, including ties (gamma = -.34*)					
Number of cases	78	143	336	316	873
Social	6	8	14	21	15
Antisocial	94	92	86	79	85

Source: Compiled by the authors.

The suspected interaction between criminal maturity and the possibility of confinement in differing prison types on that basis is not apparent in our data. Custody and treatment prisons do not differ significantly in the type of inmates they receive; when security sections are held constant, it is found that various criminal maturity groups are not segregated from each other within the prison either. Prison administrators apparently fail to segregate sophisticated from naive offenders, thereby making criminal contamination possible.

TABLE 5.3

Criminal Maturity and Role Adaptations,
with Type of Prison Held Constant

| Criminal Maturity | Percent of Inmates Who Play Antisocial Roles in Prison | | | | | |
| | Treatment Prisons | | Custody Prisons | | All Prisons | |
	Number	Percent	Number	Percent	Number	Percent
Professional	23	91	55	95	78	94
Habitual	47	94	96	92	143	92
Occasional	93	86	243	86	336	86
Novice	96	87	220	76	316	79
Total	259	88	614	84	873	85
Gamma		-.17		-.40*		-.34*

Source: Compiled by the authors.

When the amount of time served and the amount of time left to be served are held constant, the relationships between criminal maturity and social role adaptations are not significantly changed. Inmates play the same social role at various time periods of their sentence, lending support to the hypothesis that the social role adopted has its origins in conditions present prior to confinement. Since the data are cross-sectional and not repeated measures on the same inmate over time, this hypothesis warrants further study in a longitudinal design.

INMATE ROLES AND NORMATIVE ALIENATION

The dependent conceptual variable, normative alienation, was measured in terms of an attitude index, where prisoners were asked to state their solutions to various hypothetical prison situations, and in terms of a climate index that measured the inmates' assessment of the solutions they felt other prisoners would have offered to the same situations (Gruninger 1974*). In addition, the extent of inmate-inmate contact and inmate-staff contact, the manner of leisure time

---

*This document contains a detailed description of the measurement procedures used.

association, leadership patterns, and participation in staff-initiated activities, were used as indicators of normative alienation from prison goals. Associations among indicators are shown in Table 5.4.

TABLE 5.4

Gamma Values for Linkages between Indicators
of Normative Alienation

	Climate Index	Inmate-Guard Contact	Treatment Staff Contact	Inmate-Inmate-Contact	Leisure Time with Inmate Group
Attitude index	.58*	-.11	-.10	.04	-.04
Climate index		-.06	-.18	.24*	-.08
Inmate-guard contact			.39*	.58*	-.28
Treatment contact				.13	-.08
Inmate-inmate contact					-.33*

Source: Compiled by the authors.

The tabulations indicate that some 40 percent of the prisoners would have solved the hypothetical prison situations contained in the attitude index in an antistaff, prisonized manner. At the same time, three-quarters of the inmates held that their fellow inmates would be antistaff in their orientations, as measured by the climate index. This finding validates Garabedian's assertion that collective ignorance attributes more antistaff climate to the prison than actually exists (Garabedian 1959). While the inmate's own attitudes are independent of the amount of contact he has with other inmates and with staff personnel, his perception of the prison climate is significantly related to the frequency of contact maintained with fellow prisoners. The questions designed to measure the extent of contact with various groups of the prison community generally show two patterns of inmate association. The majority of prisoners have high contacts with inmate, treatment, and custody personnel, while other prisoners shun all association and remain social isolates. Tabulations of association patterns against the measures of normative alienation showed only small relationships, but in the expected direction. Prisoners who have high contact with other inmates are slightly more antisocial in orientation, while those having high contact with either guards or treatment workers are slightly more prosocial in orientation. These findings are consistent with Wheeler's conclusion that the prisoner community and the amount of interaction between inmates determine the individual's nonconformity (Wheeler 1961).

When inmate role adaptations were tabulated against the indicators of normative alienation, none of the relationships was statistically significant when the four Schrag role types were used. Collapsed categories of social and antisocial role types yielded one statistically significant association: those inmates who play antisocial roles in prison are more likely to solve given hypothetical situations in the prisonized manner. Levels of deprivation do not affect the relationships appreciably (see Table 5.5).

TABLE 5.5

Social Role Types and Antistaff Orientations

Social Role Type	Inmates Who Are Antistaff on the Attitude Index		Inmates Who Perceive Others as Antistaff on Climate Index	
	Number	Percent	Number	Percent
Four Schrag types				
Social	24	33	56	78
Convict	97	59	135	82
Politician	34	60	51	90
Rebel	159	46	279	80
Total	314	49	521	81
Gamma	.04		.00	
Two collapsed types				
Social	45	35	106	82
Antisocial	388	52	603	82
Total	433	50	709	82
Gamma	-.29*		.02	

Source: Compiled by the authors.

Since the attitude index and the climate index are positively related, the presence of an association between social role types and the attitude index (gamma = .29*) and, at the same time, the lack of statistical association between social role types and the climate index (gamma = .02), suggested that the nonassociation might be spurious. A very similar inconsistency was found in tabulations involving the relationships between criminal maturity and

the attitude and climate indexes. It was expected that greater criminal maturity should mean more prisonized attitudes on the part of
the inmate and also a perception of greater prisonization on the part
of fellow inmates.

When the present age of the respondent was held constant,
however, the relationships between criminal maturity and the attitude index, and the relationship between criminal maturity and the
climate index, are consistent and in the expected direction; the initially spurious association emerges as a positive statistical association. The relationships are weaker for young offenders. Attitude
differences are greater and more consistent than are the differences
among criminal maturity categories in their assessment of the
prison climate, as Table 5.6 shows.

THE EFFECTS OF DEPRIVATION

When the type of prison, measured by a custody-treatment
continuum, was related to inmate role adaptations, it was found that
custody and treatment prisons do not differ significantly in the distribution of social role types found in each, nor do they differ in the
criminal maturity levels of their clientele. One may conclude,
therefore, that the impact of levels of deprivation is not confounded
with the impact of the criminal history of the offender. However,
the finding that more than one-half of the respondents had previously
spent time in an adult prison and that one-third had served sentences
in juvenile institutions still raises the possibility that the previous
institutional experience contributes to the role identification and to
the attitudes of the prisoner. Recidivist offenders more often play
an antisocial role and more often hold antistaff attitudes. A joint
consideration of type of prison and criminal background demonstrates that the effects of levels of deprivation are nonsignificant
within categories of criminal maturity.

A tabulation of type of prison against the attitude index and
the climate index shows that neither index is related to levels of
deprivation. When criminal maturity is held constant, the relationship between deprivation levels and the attitude index remains constant in the partial tables; the relation between deprivation and the
climate index, on the other hand, shifts somewhat. Career offenders housed in maximum-security prisons perceive less antistaff
climate than do career offenders in treatment prisons. Unsophisti-
cated offenders perceive much less antistaff climate in either type
of prison. Tables 5.7 and 5.8 show that larger percentage differences occur as a result of criminal background than occur as a result of degrees of deprivation. Other tabulations of deprivation

TABLE 5.6

Criminal Maturity and Attitudes, with Age Held Constant

Criminal Maturity Index	Less than 25 Years of Age		Age 25 and Over		Total, All Age Groups	
	Number	Percent	Number	Percent	Number	Percent
Percent of prisoners holding antistaff attitudes						
Professional	22	59	58	64	81	63
Habitual	72	51	34	49	166	50
Occasional	193	53	215	47	655	29
Novice	170	29	485	29	655	29
Total	457	44	853	38	310	40
Gamma		.29*		.37*		.34*
Percent of prisoners who perceive antistaff climate						
Professional	22	86	59	85	81	85
Habitual	72	76	94	75	166	75
Occasional	193	82	215	80	408	81
Novice	170	69	485	64	655	65
Total	457	76	853	71	1,310	73
Gamma		.22		.31*		.29*

Source: Compiled by the authors.

83

TABLE 5.7

Type of Prison and Attitude Index, with Criminal Maturity Held Constant

| | Percent of Prisoners Holding Antistaff Attitudes: Criminal Maturity Index | | | | | |
| | Professional and Habitual Offenders | | Occasional and Novice Offenders | | Total, All Criminal Maturity Groups | |
Type of Prison	Number	Percent	Number	Percent	Number	Percent
Treatment prisons	70	51	274	37	344	40
Custody prisons	170	55	789	37	966	40
Total	247	54	1,063	37	1,310	40
Gamma		-.10		-.03		-.03

Source: Compiled by the authors.

TABLE 5.8

Type of Prison and Climate Index, with Criminal Maturity Held Constant

| | Percent of Prisoners Who Perceive Antistaff Climate: Criminal Maturity Index | | | | | |
| | Professional and Habitual Offenders | | Occasional and Novice Offenders | | Total, All Criminal Maturity Groups | |
Type of Prison	Number	Percent	Number	Percent	Number	Percent
Treatment prisons	70	89	274	69	344	73
Custody prisons	177	75	789	72	366	73
Total	247	79	1,063	71	1,310	73
Gamma		.47*		-.04		.04

Source: Compiled by the authors.

levels against the attitude and climate indexes, with social role type held constant, show that the small and nonsignificant differences that do occur are also attributable to role identifications rather than to levels of deprivation.

While levels of deprivation, when used as an independent variable, are not significantly related to any of the measures of normative alienation, it is nevertheless the case that the type of prison in which an inmate is housed produces a number of interaction effects. Deprivation levels, when held constant, create conditional relationships, and joint effects are apparent. In the more repressive custody prison, criminally mature offenders are more likely to make an antisocial role identification; in contrast, the treatment prison reduces the impact of criminal maturity on role identifications. But, at the same time, the least sophisticated offender remains more prosocial in orientations when housed under harsh conditions. This phenomenon had once been described by Bettelheim (1943) in his discussion of concentration camps. The pains of imprisonment, therefore, have varied impact on different offender categories.

In addition to a measure of deprivation based on a custody-treatment continuum, information was available on the security section in which an inmate was housed within the prison. Maximum-security prisons may contain medium-and minimum–security facilities, sometimes outside the wall, while treatment prisons may contain tight security tiers and wings. The question arose, therefore, as to whether or not the type of prison, in a universe of prisons, would have the same subjective meaning to an inmate as does the relative deprivation he may perceive when he compares his custodial status within a given prison. When security section is used as an index of relative deprivation, the effects of the pains of imprisonment become apparent, as Tables 5.9 and 5.10 show.

The greatest degree of antistaff orientation is observed for mature criminals held under repressive custodial care, while the least antistaff orientations are observed for first offenders who also are held in the maximum–security section of a prison. This finding conflicts with that of Garabedian (1959), who found that inmates in custodial wings of the prison are more antistaff in their orientations. When one examines the tables, it is evident that lenient situations of incarceration create slightly more normative alienation than do repressive situations. It is still the case, as in previous tabulations, that the percentage differences among criminal maturity categories are larger than the differences among deprivation levels.

Somewhat different effects are shown for the climate index. When type of prison is controlled, the relationship between criminal maturity and the climate index becomes stronger in lenient prisons.

TABLE 5.9

Criminal Maturity and Attitude, with Levels of Deprivation Held Constant

Percent of Prisoners Who Hold Antistaff Attitudes

Criminal Maturity Index	Treatment Prisons		Custody Prisons		All Prisons		Minimum Security Section		Maximum Security Section		All Security Sections	
	Number	Percent	Number	Percent	Number	Percent	Number	Percent	Number	Percent	Number	Percent
Professional	23	74	58	59	81	63	39	62	42	64	81	63
Habitual	47	40	119	54	166	50	92	45	74	57	166	50
Occasional	102	47	306	51	408	50	209	52	199	48	408	51
Novice	172	31	483	28	655	29	333	35	322	22	655	29
Total	344		966		1,310		673		637		1,310	
Gamma		.34*		.35*		.34*		.20*		.48*		.34*

Source: Compiled by the authors.

TABLE 5.10

Criminal Maturity and Perceived Climate, with Levels of Deprivation Held Constant

Percent of Prisoners Who Perceive Antistaff Climate

Criminal Maturity Index	Treatment Prisons		Custody Prisons		All Prisons		Minimum Security Section		Maximum Security Section		All Security Sections	
	Number	Percent	Number	Percent	Number	Percent	Number	Percent	Number	Percent	Number	Percent
Professional	23	91	58	83	81	85	39	85	42	86	81	85
Habitual	47	87	119	71	166	75	92	74	74	77	166	75
Occasional	102	84	306	80	408	81	209	79	199	83	408	81
Novice	172	60	483	67	655	65	333	69	322	62	655	65
Total	344	73	966	73	1,310	73	673	74	637	72	1,310	73
Gamma		.57*		.20*		.29*		.21*		.37*		.29*

Source: Compiled by the authors.

When the relative deprivation measure is held constant, the relationship between criminal background and perceived climate becomes weaker in lenient situations. Theoretically, it should become weaker in the lenient condition of deprivation, since the attitude index and the climate index are positively related (gamma = . 58*); hence, the changes in relationship introduced by an additional variable should be similar in direction. Both Tables 5. 9 and 5. 10 show that the effect of relative deprivation is to create a polarization of sophisticated and naive offenders under conditions of intense pains of imprisonment. The polarization is less severe in lenient prison situations. This finding is consistent with other information that suggests that the pains of imprisonment create changes in role identification on the part of naive offenders, who are more often "convicts" in the treatment prison and more integrated members of the contra-culture, while they would have played the "square John" role more often in the tough prison situation.

CONCLUSION

The conclusion from these findings is that the pains of imprisonment are chiefly felt by naive offenders, who may lack the defense mechanisms of the recidivist offender for whom prison adjustment seems to be less problematic. It should be noted, however, that inmate adjustment for naive offenders is in the opposite direction as that predicted in the situation-response model of prisonization, while the model holds for mature offenders. In both cases, the prior life experiences of the prisoner are more important determinants of role adaptation and normative alienation than are the levels of deprivation. At the same time, the measure of criminal maturity used here, based in large part on previous institutional experience, may be a measure of the delayed effects of the pains of imprisonment that includes earlier socialization toward criminal behavior, further criminalization in juvenile and adult prisons, readjustment difficulties following previous releases, and further alienation as a result of new apprehension and conviction. There is a selective factor that returns offenders to prison as recidivist. Among first offenders, 29 percent are antistaff in attitudes. This percentage increases to 50 percent when they return for the second and third times to prison, and increases further to 63 percent for offenders who have served five or more prison terms. When time served or time left to serve is held constant, the relationships remain stable, indicating that the present incarceration experience has no immediate effect on alienation. A similar trend can be observed for the prison climate that an inmate perceives. For each increment in repeated commitment to prison, there are increments in the percentage of inmates who become antisocial and who attribute antisocial attitudes to others. But the process of alienation takes place outside the prison, and the prisonization hypothesis as commonly understood oversimplifies the relationships and fails to take into account the feedback effects that the present data suggest.

The pains of imprisonment have varied effects on inmate groups. Normative alienation increases with increased deprivation for mature offenders, but decreases for naive offenders. For the inmate group studied as a whole, importation factors appear to be the more crucial element in creating role identifications and normative alienation than do deprivation levels. However, there are important national differences that arise from the various control patterns observed in different countries, related to Auburn and Pennsylvania prison regimes. These national differences are the subject of Chapter 6 of this book. In addition, there are a number of structural effects that appear in the relationships between criminal sophistication and some forms of deviant inmate behavior in prison (Akers, Hayner, Gruninger 1974). For these reasons, the relative impact of the two competing models of prisonization remains, at present, unclear.

REFERENCES

Adamek, R. J., and E. Z. Dager
  1968   Social structure, identification, and change in a treatment-oriented institution. American Sociological Review (ASR) 33: 931-44.

Akers, R. L., N. S. Hayner, and W. Gruninger
  1974   Homosexual and drug behavior in prison: a test of the functional and importation models of the inmate system. Social Problems 21: 410-22.

Bettelheim, B.
  1943   Individual and mass behavior in extreme situations. Journal of Abnormal and Social Psychology 38: 417-52.

Clemmer, D.
  1959   The Prison Community. New York: Holt, Rinehart and Winston.

Garabedian, P. G.
  1959   Western Penitentiary: A Study in Social Organization. Ph.D. dissertation, University of Washington.

Garrity, D. L.
1956   The Effects of Length of Stay upon Parole Adjustment.
        Ph.D. dissertation, University of Washington.

Giallombardo, R.
1966   Society of Women. New York: John Wiley & Sons.

Gruninger, W.
1974   Criminalization, Prison Roles, and Normative Alienation:
        A Cross-Cultural Study. Ph.D. dissertation, University
        of Washington.

Irwin, J.
1970   The Felon. Englewood Cliffs, N.J.: Prentice-Hall.

Schrag, C.
1949   Social Types in the Prison Community. M.A. thesis,
        University of Washington.

Street, D., M. Vinter, and C. Perrow
1966   Organization for Treatment. New York: Free Press.

Sykes, G.
1948   The Society of Captives. Princeton, N.J.: Princeton
        University Press.

Ward, D. A., and G. G. Kassebaum
1965   Women's Prison: Sex and Social Structure. Chicago:
        Aldine.

Wheeler, S.
1961   Socialization in correctional communities. ASR 26:
        697-712.

6

PRISONIZATION IN FIVE COUNTRIES: TYPE OF PRISON AND INMATE CHARACTERISTICS

Ronald L. Akers, Norman S. Hayner,
and Werner Gruninger

THE CONCEPT OF PRISONIZATION

With the adoption of the Auburn system of congregate labor
and housing of more than one person per cell (later in cottages and
dormitories) and relaxing of the silence rule for most American
prisons (Rothman 1971), the structural conditions for the emergence
and maintenance of a cultural and social system among inmates
were set (Cloward 1960). Sociological study of this system began
in earnest in the 1930s. The staff-inmate conflict within the prison
was studied, distinctions between the prison community and the
prisoner community were made, the existence of a separate inmate
culture with an anticonventional code of conduct was noted, and
interactional patterns were studied (Hayner, Ash 1939, 1940;
Clemmer 1938; Hayner 1943; Haynes 1948). Clemmer (1938: 299)
coined the term "prisonization" to refer to the inmate's initiation
into and adoption of this prisoner society, the "taking on in greater
or less degree of the folkways, customs, and general culture of the
penitentiary." He likened prisonization to a process of assimila-
tion. His concept is fairly broad as it includes taking on a subordi-
nate status, learning prison argot, adapting to prison-style eating
habits, "wising up," picking up the best way of doing time, engaging
in various forms of deviant behavior such as gambling and "abnormal
sex behavior," developing hostile attitudes toward guards, and becoming acquainted with the inmate "dogmas and mores" (Clemmer
1938: 299-300). While researchers still see prisonization as a
process, it has become conceptualized as one of adult "socialization" (as contrasted with the institution's attempt at "resocialization") of the offender. The content of this socialization process has
tended to be narrowed to the adoption of the normative content of
the inmate code, although any of the features outlined by Clemmer
may be included. Prisonization also is used to refer to the extent
to which inmates have adopted the inmate code at a given time,

without reference to process (McCorkle, Korn 1954; Wheeler 1961a;
Garabedian 1963; Wellford 1967; Thomas 1973; Thomas, Foster
1972).

The code is described as expressive of inmate solidarity
against the prison staff and administration (thus allowing rejection
of the rejectors, to use McCorkle and Korn's terms) and is
hence characterized as containing tenets that are opposed to the
expectations of prison rules and conventional norms combined with
loyalty to other inmates (Sykes, Messinger 1960). While there may
be aspects of the code that make no reference to official norms of
the prison, it is most often presented in the literature as a form of
contraculture in which what is wrong from the prison staff's point
of view is right from the perspective of the inmate culture. Therefore, "adherence to the inmate code means rejection of the administrative code of conduct" (Wellford 1967: 198).

It is by this logic that Wheeler (1961a, 1961b) measured degree of adherence to the inmate code (prisonization) by the extent
to which inmates were in low conformity to staff norms. Garabedian
(1963) notes that Wheeler's measure of prisonization was of a movement away from staff norms and that Clemmer's notion was one of
moving toward adoption of norms of the inmate culture. Concep-
tually, "adoption of the prison culture may or may not involve
movement away from staff norms" (Garabedian 1963: 140). Nonetheless, Garabedian also measured prisonization as a degree of conformity or nonconformity to staff norms, and others have used
similar measures (Glaser 1964; Wellford 1967, 1973; Schwartz
1971, 1973). Other researchers have developed prisonization
scales that involve the inmate's endorsement of, or positive adherence to, items stating normative prescriptions and proscriptions
of the inmate culture rather than measuring his nonadherence to the
administrative code (Tittle 1969, 1972; Thomas 1973; Thomas,
Foster 1973; Ward and Kassebaum [1965] use both). But whether
alienation from staff norms or conformity to inmate norms is the
conception that is used, all of these studies view the inmate culture
as oppositional, anticonventional, and hostile to the institutional
norms.

Others have countered this "solidary opposition" concept with
a "solidary cooperation" concept, so in some correctional institutions the inmate culture is compatible with staff expectations and is
imbued with prosocial norms and positive attitudes toward the staff
and institution (Schwartz 1973). Research by Grusky (1959) and
Berk (1966) in adult institutions and research by Street, Vinter, and
Perrow (1966) in juvenile institutions indicate that in more treatment-
oriented institutions, because of the freer interaction allowed among
inmates, a cohesive inmate system develops but the inmate culture

is not hostile or oppositional. Ward and Kassebaum (1965) and Giallombardo (1966) found little solidarity in adherence to an inmate code among female prisoners and believe that the solidarity of the inmate group in male prisons has been overstated (see also Heffernan 1972).

Inmate solidarity and the existence of an inmate subculture does not, of course, require that all inmates become highly prisonized. Clemmer and most others since recognize that prisonization is a matter of degree; many, if not most, inmates do not become fully socialized into the inmate normative system and remain in varying degrees of isolation from its influence (see McCorkle, Korn 1954; Wheeler 1961a; Sykes, Messinger 1960). Besides the normative element the inmate system also includes patterns of social interaction and behavior, and prisonization has sometimes been used to label the extent to which inmates become incorporated into inmate groups, interact with other inmates, and take on certain roles within the inmate social structure. The assertion that there is an identifiable inmate social system within the larger prison system does not mean that all or even most of the prisoners are caught up in its central structure; as with any system there are core participants, leaders, followers, and isolates.

There is no assumption that the system is invariably oppositional or that it is always cohesive or involves a majority of inmates. The typical inmate may be one who remains relatively insulated from the culture and unaffiliated with the social system. The only assumption is that the inmate normative system is pervasive enough to be recognized and that enough inmates participate in the social system so that we may speak of a system that sets the tone and style for the entire inmate group.

THEORETICAL PERSPECTIVES

The efforts to account for variations in prisonization can be fitted into two principal theoretical models: a functional, situation-response model and an importation, prior socialization model. The thrust of Clemmer's analysis, especially in his concern with prisonization as a function of time served, with the role of inmate primary groups in the prisonization process and "universal factors" of the prison in prisonization is essentially functional, although he did list background factors as influencing the extent to which inmates are prisonized. Other early studies, such as Hayner and Ash (1939), likewise assumed that the prisoner society (with its "conniving" code of behavior) was a response of solidary opposition to the environment provided by the official system of the prisons.

Similarly, later analyses pointed to the functions for the inmate and the prison administration served by the inmate culture (McCorkle, Korn 1954; Cloward 1960; McLeery 1961).

The classic statement of the functional model is that by Sykes (1954; Sykes, Messinger 1960). Syke's explanation of the inmate code is that it is a collective adaptation to the "pains of imprisonment," the deprivation and degradation of incarceration. The deprivation of liberty, goods, services, heterosexual relationships, autonomy, and security all present problems to inmates to which they must adapt. The more inclusive the system in its solidary opposition to the official system the less painful imprisonment is.

The classical statement of the importation model is that of Irwin and Cressey (1962), which called attention to the fact that the inmate code bears great resemblance to criminal norms on the outside. Participation in lower-class and deviant subcultures on the outside provide the behavior patterns, maxims, and proscriptions that are brought into the prison by offenders, and which then become part of the inmate culture into which inmates are socialized. The later statements of the importation model carried on this line of thought and hypothesized that the antisocial content of the inmate culture is a consequence of traits and social histories that are external to the situation found in the prison. Such characteristics exist prior to and after incarceration and are brought into the institution when the inmate arrives (Irwin 1970; Thomas 1975; Thomas, Foster 1972).

Research has been reported that supports the importation model (Thomas 1973; Thomas, Foster 1972; Schwartz 1973; Ward, Kassebaum 1965; Giallombardo 1966, 1974; Heffernan 1972). At the same time, research has been reported that is more supportive of the functional model of the inmate culture (Wheeler 1961a; Garabedian 1973; Berk 1966; Street, Vinter, Perrow 1966; Tittle 1961, 1972) and some has been reported that finds support for certain aspects of both (Wellford 1967; Cline, Wheeler 1968; Schwartz 1973). Evidence can be found, then, in support of both perspectives, and the issue of which better accounts for which features of the inmate system has yet to be settled empirically.

The research reported here is an attempt to move closer to taking an approach that differs from previous research. Most of the research mentioned above has been done in single institutions. In a study of one prison the impact of the institutional environment can be observed in the processual sense that length of time served and sentence stage measure differential exposure to the prison environment. Another approach is to measure variations in individual inmate's subjective perceptions of the pains of imprisonment. There have been very few studies that take a more structural

approach, as we do here, by comparing different types of institutions
to observe systematic differences in the objective organization environment (Berk 1966; Street, Vinter, Perrow 1966; Cline, Wheeler
1968; Giallombardo 1974). By using the same measures of variables
in the several prisons, this approach overcomes the difficulties of
comparability of measurements encountered in trying to make comparisons from one case study to another. We extend this approach
here by conducting the organizational comparisons in five different
countries--the United States, Mexico, England, West Germany, and
Spain--using the same measure of variables. Thus, we are able to
study the inmate system not only cross-organizationally but also
cross-culturally. To our knowledge no prior research has done this.

Our cross-cultural analysis is largely descriptive, since we
do not have independent measures of characteristics of the national
cultures by which we may account for observed cross-cultural differences in prison organization and inmate response. Given the
embryonic stage of cross-cultural research on correctional organizations, however, even descriptive and illustrative findings
are important enough to report as guides to future research. In
addition, there is some apparent analytic significance that can be
attributed to the findings in the various countries. If the very fact
of being incarcerated has an impact on inmate response to the
prison as a total institution, then that impact should be similar across
the societies from which the inmates are drawn. If variations in
the harshness of that incarceration beyond the irreducible amount
found in any prison (as captured by placement on the custody-
treatment continuum) make for variations in degree of prisonization, they should do so in a similar way from one society to the
next. Further, if the larger culture from which the inmates come
influences their response to prison, there should be significant
differences in the levels of prisonization found among the inmates
in the different countries. Finally, if criminal values and anti-
administration attitudes are imported into the prison, then they
should be most strongly adhered to by the most criminalistic offenders, regardless of the larger cultural context.

SAMPLE AND DATA COLLECTION

Data were collected from seven prisons for men in the United
States, eight prisons in Mexico, three in West Germany, two in
England, and two in Spain.* The prisons were selected on a

---

*In addition, some data were collected from one British, one
Spanish, and one Mexican prison for women and the female section

judgment basis to provide as wide a variety as possible of different institutions for adult felons and as much assurance as possible of research access. Interviews with top administrators of the various institutions were tape-recorded, as were observations made by the investigator at each institution. The interviews lasted from two to three hours and the total time spent at each institution averaged two to three days. The interviews and observations were designed to elicit answers to a set of predetermined questions that would yield information about architecture, the administrative goals, classification, inmate employment, education and training, treatment program, security practices, personnel, and policy on visitation and outside contact of each institution.

At each institution a sample of inmates was drawn and a questionnaire administered designed to elicit information on the inmate's characteristics and the inmate system. The design called for a 10 percent random sample of inmates from each prison. But the peculiarities of the various institutions made random selection difficult. As a consequence of the deviations from the sampling plan under actual field conditions and the nonrandom way in which the institutions were selected, the samples of inmates and institutions obtained cannot be considered truly representative of those found elsewhere in the respective countries. Some questions were excluded in the Mexican questionnaire and some items were included in the American phase of the study that were not included elsewhere. On the whole, however, the items were kept as closely comparable as possible in the five sets of questionnaires for the five countries. Within each country, the same questionnaire was administered to all prisons; thus, the items are exactly comparable among prisons in the same country.*

Independent Variables: Type of Prison and Inmate Characteristics

The tape-recorded interviews and observations were transcribed into descriptive statements on each of the nine dimensions mentioned above. On the basis of agreed-upon, written specifications, each judge rated each prison on each dimension on a seven-point scale from the most custodial to the most treatment-oriented.

---

in six of the Mexican institutions for men. Only data from the male prisons are included here.

*The total number of respondents completing questionnaires was 1,310: 547 in the United States, 391 in Mexico, 102 in England, 193 in Germany, and 77 in Spain.

The ratings were summed and averaged and a total score was assigned to each prison, which was then used to classify that institution as custodial, intermediate, or treatment (which is what is
meant here by "type of prison"--the functional variable).

The scores for the nine items for each prison were summed
and averaged for the three raters with a minimum of 63 indicating
the most treatment-oriented. The scores were trichotomized as:
custody type--score of 29 or less; intermediate type--score of
30 to 44; and treatment type--score of 45 or more. The actual
averaged scores within each country came out separated by sufficient numbers to allow fairly easy and clear-cut division into three
types. The scores and typing of the prisons for each country are
shown in Table 6.1.

TABLE 6.1

Type of Prison, as Scored on Scale Ranging from
Most Custodial- to Most Treatment-Oriented

Country	Treatment	Intermediate	Custodial	Total
United States				
Number	3	1	3	7
Score	50-57	30	16-21	16-57
Mexico				
Number	1	3	4	8
Score	46	all 38	24-29	24-46
England				
Number	1	1	--	2
Score	55	35	--	35-55
Germany				
Number	--	1	2	3
Score	--	32	17-24	17-32
Spain				
Number	1	1	--	2
Score	51	30	--	30-51
Total				
Number	6	7	9	22
Score	46-57	30-38	16-29	16-57

Source: Compiled by the authors.

The conception is that the ratings reflect significant, objectively observable differences in the overall prison environment or overall organizational atmosphere confronting the inmates. At one extreme the type of prison facing the inmate is "custodial," degrading, and punitive. At the other "treatment" end, this milieu is nonpunitive, imbued with humanitarian concern for the welfare of the prisoners, and not unduly deprivational beyond the basic and undeniable deprivation of freedom in which the effort is to induce positive changes in inmate behavior and attitudes. It should be emphasized, however, that there is no assumption that institutions that we have specified as lying toward the high end of the scale are in fact effective "treatment" institutions. It may be that none of the dimensions has anything at all to do with rehabilitation, and we have no follow-up data by which to assess the issue. The only assumption is that an institution coming closer to the ideal typical treatment institution presents a more open and less harsh environment for the inmate than does the one coming closer to the custodial model.

Questions on age, education, marital status, and rural-urban residence were included on the questionnaires in each prison, and these are treated in a straightforward way as imported social characteristics.* Offense, length of sentence, age at the time of first arrest, prior juvenile commitments, and prior adult commitments were solicited on the questionnaire as imported criminal characteristics. The latter three were combined into another variable, which we label "Criminality Index" and use as a general measure of

---

Race was not asked of the individual inmate in any institution. The percentage nonwhite (mainly black) inmates was obtained for each institution in the United States. This aggregate level piece of information, of course, cannot be related to individual questionnaire responses and therefore is not used in this analysis. To the extent that the proportion of inmates perceiving a high level of nonconformity can be taken as an aggregate measure of the inmate normative climate, then its relationship to the racial composition can be legitimately measured. There is a relationship (gamma = -.38) for the seven American prisons, but it is not clear that it is what would be expected from importation theory--that is, the prisons with a relatively high proportion of black inmates are less likely than those with a low proportion of blacks to have an antistaff climate. Other than educational level, no measures of socioeconomic status or social class were obtained anywhere.

extensiveness of criminal background. The possible range of scores on this index (3 to 19) were divided into four categories: "novices," who were arrested at a later age and were first offenders; "occasional" offenders, who were not first offenders but were only slightly more involved in crime prior to the current incarceration; "habitual" offenders; and "professional" offenders, scored as having the most criminal background (although there is no pretense that they are, in fact, professional thieves).

The Inmate Culture: Inmate Attitudes and the
Normative Culture

The degree of prisonization is first measured here by the technique developed by Wheeler (1961a, 1961b). Three hypothetical vignettes taken from Wheeler (who used five) were presented to the inmate respondents. In the first vignette, a prisoner is described as defending the behavior of a guard in writing up a violation report on another inmate. In the second situation, an inmate hides money (this was changed to marijuana in Mexican prisons where money is not contraband) for a fellow prisoner who has smuggled it into the institution. In the third situation, one inmate is forced by two others to steal a crowbar for an escape attempt, which the two plan to make, but he is caught with the crowbar and unless he clears himself by squealing on the escape plan he may lose a year of good time.

Both the inmate's own attitude toward the behavior or the action taken and his perception of how other inmates would respond under the conditions described were elicited for each situation. From the report of his own feelings for all three situations we constructed an "Attitude Index." From his report of how other inmates would respond we constructed a "Climate Index." The Attitude Index is viewed as a measure of degree of individual prisonization and the Climate Index as a measure of the normative orientation existing among the general inmate population.

The indexes were constructed as follows:

Attitude Index. According to Wheeler, disapproval of the inmate's defense of the guard in the first situation is a response not in conformity with staff expectations, and scores of 1 to 4 were assigned to a response range from strong approval to strong disapproval by the respondent. Approval of hiding the money in the second situation is a prisonized response and scores of 4 to 1 were assigned to the response range for this hypothetical situation. On the third situation a score of 4 was assigned to the response that the

inmate should keep quiet and take his punishment as a response coun-
ter to staff expectations and in conformity to the inmate code. A
score of 1 was assigned to the response that the inmate should tell
and clear himself. A score of 3 or 4 on each item is a prisonized
response, and a score of 1 or 2 on each is in conformity with staff
norms. The index was constructed by summing each respondent's
scores across the three items. The summed scores were then
trichotomized: 6 or less = high conformity to staff norms; 7-8 =
ambivalent attitudes or medium conformity to staff norms; 9-12 =
antistaff attitudes, low conformity to staff expectations, and highly
prisonized.

Climate Index. On the first two hypothetical situations, the
respondent was asked how many other inmates would approve of the
actions described; in the third situation, how many others would
feel that the one caught with the crowbar should tell and clear himself. The response categories were all, three-fourths, half, one-
fourth, and none. For the first and third items these responses
were scored 1 through 5, and for the second item (since it goes in
the other direction) they were scored 5 through 1. These scores
were summed across the three items, a higher score indicating a
perception of a strong antistaff normative climate and a lower score
indicating a climate of conformity to staff norms. The summed
scores were trichotomized: 6 or less = perception of a conformist,
prosocial climate; 7-8 = ambivalent appraisal or perception of a
moderate level of conformity to staff norms; 9-15 = perception of
nonconformist, antistaff climate or a highly prisonized normative
climate among inmates. Thus, the perception of an antistaff climate means that on the average half or more of the other inmates
are seen as being antistaff, at least regarding their expected actions
in the described situations.

Table 6.2 presents the percentage distribution of the inmates'
own prosocial or antisocial attitudes and their perception of a normative climate of conformity or nonconformity to staff expectations.
The data shown in this table make it clear that, at least as reported
by inmates themselves (on the Wheeler items), there is a definite
inmate culture defined by a climate of hostility toward conventional
standards of the prison administration. In all but two prisons, a
majority of inmates (in most cases a large majority) perceived an
antisocial normative climate. When all prisoner responses within
a given country are combined we see that a majority of inmates in
each country report a prisonized culture among inmates. The data
leave little doubt that the notion of an antisocial inmate culture,
first formulated and applied to prisons in the United States, is applicable to prisons in some other societies. In every prison we

TABLE 6.2

Attitudes and Climate of Conformity to Staff Norms,
by Prison and Country

Prison Number	Number	Attitude Index[a]--Percent Whose Own Attitudes Are:		Climate Index[b]--Percent Perceiving Climate in Which Most Other Inmates Hold Attitudes of:	
		Nonconformity	Conformity	Nonconformity	Conformity
United States					
1	129	66.7	15.5	86.0	6.2
2	69	37.7	37.7	69.6	10.1
3	41	63.4	19.5	68.3	17.1
4	70	52.9	34.3	74.3	8.6
5	94	73.4	17.0	81.9	9.6
6	54	44.4	37.0	83.3	1.9
7	90	62.2	17.8	91.1	1.1
All U.S. prisons	544	59.0	23.9	81.0	7.1
Mexico					
1	96	9.4	61.5	52.1	31.3
2	17	17.4	52.9	52.9	5.9
3	37	32.4	40.5	62.2	16.2
4	45	24.4	66.7	42.2	40.0
5	64	23.4	46.9	64.1	25.0
6	22	31.8	63.6	50.1	27.3
7	38	13.2	57.9	55.3	26.3
8	72	12.5	77.8	38.9	27.8
All Mexican prisons	384	18.2	60.4	51.8	27.8
England					
1	34	41.2	38.2	91.2	0.0
2	68	38.2	36.8	92.6	2.9
All English prisons	102	39.2	37.3	92.2	2.0
West Germany					
1	106	32.1	38.7	79.2	7.5
2	67	32.8	34.3	91.0	3.0
3	20	20.0	75.0	80.0	20.0
All German prisons	193	31.1	40.9	83.4	7.3
Spain					
1	52	44.2	26.9	63.5	7.7
2	25	32.0	40.0	68.0	16.0
All Spanish prisons	77	40.3	31.2	64.9	10.4

[a]Percent holding ambivalent attitudes (medium conformity) omitted.
[b]Percent reporting ambivalent perceptions of climate omitted.

Source: Compiled by the authors.

studied, regardless of the country in which it is located, there is an awareness of a prevailing inmate contraculture.

While these findings lend strong credence to the concept of an inmate culture standing in "solidary opposition" to the conventional culture of the staff, those on the inmate's own attitudes present a more ambiguous picture. That most inmates recognize the pervasive influence of the inmate culture does not mean that they all hold private allegiance to it (see the discussion of pluralistic ignorance below). The data presented in Table 6.2 show that, based on prisoners' own attitudes, the solidary opposition concept holds primarily for American prisoners and that the development of an inmate culture standing in "solidary cooperation" with the institutional staff holds primarily in the Mexican prisons. In all but two of the American prisons the majority makes oppositional responses, and even in those two about two out of five inmates gave prisonized responses. In all but two of the Mexican institutions, on the other hand, the majority of inmates stands in conformity with the prosocial staff norms. The inmates in the other countries report attitudes somewhere in between these two, and are fairly evenly split between conformity and nonconformity to staff norms.

Pluralistic Ignorance

In each prison the proportion of inmates reporting their own attitudes as hostile toward staff norms is much less than the proportion reporting that other inmates hold antistaff attitudes. Thus, we have encountered in a large number of prisons from several different countries exactly the same "pluralistic ignorance" that Wheeler (1961b: 249), and Cloward before him, found in studies of single American institutions.

The question is whether the overestimation of others' adherence to a prisonized code is characteristic of all inmates regardless of their own attitudes or only of the more conventionally oriented ones. Is it true that the more conventional one's attitudes are the more likely one is to believe that others are antisocial ("everybody else in here is a crook"), and that the more antistaff one's position is the more likely one is to believe that others are proadministration ("I'm the only real convict in here")" The answer from our data is that most inmates overestimate the antistaff hostility of others and that the more the inmate believes other prisoners are antistaff the more likely he is to report highly prisonized attitudes of his own. There is a consistently strong positive association between the perception of the normative climate prevailing among inmates and inmates' own attitudes. (In the United States, the gamma = .41**; in Mexico, .59*; in England, .52; in Germany, .48*; in Spain, .69; and in all prisons, .58**.) The strength of the relationship varies by type of institution (stronger in custodial prisons where gamma = .51** and weaker in intermediate and treatment institutions, gamma = .32* and .33*, respectively), but it remains in all types. Thus, the pluralistic ignorance is all in one direction; very few see other prisoners as being less prisonized than themselves, and the more antisocial the normative climate the more antisocial the individual inmate's attitudes.

Type of Prison, Inmate Background, and Prisonization

Inmate Attitudes and the Normative Climate

The majority perception of a hostile inmate culture in nearly every prison and the sizable portion of inmates (especially in American prisons) that seems to adhere to its code (except in Mexican prisons) provide general support for the functional view by suggesting that the inmate culture represents a generalized adaptation to the irreducible deprivational conditions of imprisonment in whatever society that imprisonment takes place. Also, the variations from one prison to another shown in Table 6.2 support the functionalist portion in that the inmate culture varies by whatever differences in organizational environment there are from one institution to the next. However, it is apparent from Table 6.3 that those differences in organizational environment are only partly reflective of differences in architecture, administrative goals, programs, and the other features of the organization we have used to measure type of prison. The perception of a hostile inmate culture is found to very much the same extent in all types of prisons, from the most custodially oriented to the most treatment-oriented institutions. Positive associations are found in Mexico and Germany but none in England and Spain, and in the American prisons the finding is opposite from expectations. However, the relationships between the inmates' own attitudes and type of prison are in the expected direction in four of the five countries. Therefore, the hypothesis that the type of prison would affect prisonization as measured by the Wheeler method is only partially supported by the data.

The importation model does little better, however, in accounting for the differences found. None of the social characteristics is related to prisonization. Moreover, as can be seen from Table 6.4 the inmate's criminal background is weakly predictive in the expected direction but only of his own degree of prisonization (and not of his perception of prisonization among others), and then only in one instance is the relationship statistically significant. Nonetheless, the strength of the association between the Criminality Index

TABLE 6.3

Type of Prison and Attitude and Climate of Nonconformity to Staff Norms, by Country

	Country											
	United States		Mexico		England		Germany		Spain		All Countries	
Type of Prison	Percent	Number	Percent	Number	Percent	Number	Percent	Number	Percent	Number	Percent	Number
Antistaff attitudes[a]												
Treatment	49.8	213	12.5	72	41.2	34	--	--	32.0	35	39.8	344
Intermediate	66.7	129	17.1	205	38.2	68	20.0	20	44.2	52	36.7	492
Custodial	64.4	205	23.7	114	--	--	32.4	113	--	--	43.7	492
Gamma =	.18		.25*		.01		.52*		.24		.07	
Antistaff climate[b]												
Treatment	82.2	213	38.9	72	91.2	34	--	--	68.0	25	73.0	344
Intermediate	86.0	129	53.7	205	92.6	68	80.0	20	63.5	52	70.3	474
Custodial	76.6	205	57.9	114	--	--	83.8	113	--	--	74.8	492
Gamma =	-.14		.16		.08		.19		-.02		.03	

[a]Percent inmates holding nonconforming, antistaff attitudes.
[b]Percent inmates perceiving an antistaff climate in which most other inmates hold nonconforming attitudes.
Note: * = significant at .05.
Source: Compiled by the authors.

and the Attitude Index is comparable to that of the association between type of prison and the Attitude Index in the United States.
Prisonization is more strongly related to criminality in Mexico and
England but more strongly related to prison type in Germany and
Spain. The general tendency across societies is for both type of
prison and inmate criminal background (but not social background)
to be related to prisonized attitudes but for neither to be related very
much to the perception of a prisonized normative climate. Therefore, both the functional and the importation model apply to some ex-
tent--the most prisonized responses are apt to be made by the habitual offender in a custodial institution. The magnitude of the associations suggest relatively low levels of explained variance by either
model, however, and we must conclude that more powerful explanations lie in sets or combinations of variables other than we have here.

TABLE 6.4

Associations between Criminal Background and Attitude and
Climate of Conformity to Staff Norms, by Country
(gamma)

	United States	Mexico	England	Germany	Spain
Age at first arrest					
Attitude Index	.15	.10	.27	.17	-.04
Climate Index	.08	.08	.16	.07	.01
Prior juvenile incarcerations					
Attitude Index	.13	.21	.27	.12	.45
Climate Index	.12	.01	.20	.16	.27
Prior adult incar- cerations					
Attitude Index	.11	.24	.07	.13	.06
Climate Index	.01	.04	-.08	-.19	.03
Criminality Index					
Attitude Index	.17	.33*	.21	.20	.15
Climate Index	.13	.14	-.09	-.14	-.02

Note: * = significant at .05. Positive gamma indicates expected direction--the younger the age at first arrest the greater number of prior juvenile or adult incarcerations, and the higher the
criminality score the greater the antistaff attitudes or perception
of antistaff climate.
Source: Compiled by the authors.

General Orientation to the Institution

The Wheeler approach measures situation-specific responses
that are in conformity or nonconformity with the prosocial response
that would be ideally expected from the inmate in that situation by the
prison staff. Another indication of the inmate's degree of prisonization used here is his general positive or negative orientation to the
prison and its administration. This general orientation should be
reflected in the prisoner's perception of the prison administration
as primarily interested in punishing him and other inmates; his
willingness to take part in treatment, training, and recreational
programs offered by the institution; his feeling that the institutional
programs are beneficial or harmful to him both at the time and for
his postrelease success; and his judgment as to whether or not he
has been handled fairly or harshly by the staff and administration.

The questionnaire contained a series of items on the kinds of
programs in which inmates had participated (from which a Participation Index was constructed) and in what ways they had benefited
(if at all) from their stay in the institution (from which a Benefit
Index was constructed). Obviously, the inmate's response to these
items is not totally a function of his hostile or positive attitudes
toward the institution. Participation especially is also apt to reflect the objective opportunities and release requirements for getting
involved in various programs. The inmate's feeling that he has
benefited from the programs is conditioned also by how many possibly beneficial programs are available. Nonetheless, the existence
of a highly antiadministration inmate culture and his socialization
into it should reduce participation and perception of benefit from
whatever is available.

In addition to the Benefit and Participation Indexes there are
four single items that are indicators of the inmate's orientation
toward the institution. One asks the inmate about his postprison
expectations of the effect (helpful or harmful) of the present incarceration, and the other asks whether or not he feels he has received
"just" or fair treatment in the institution. The third item asks
whether the inmate feels that the main purpose of the prison in
which he is confined is to punish or help him. The fourth asks
whether he views the guards (and the administration) or the treatment personnel as more important in what happens in the daily lives
of the inmates.

The functional model would hypothesize that the responses to
each of these varies by type of prison. The more custodial the institution the more likely inmates are to refrain when possible from
prison programs and the less likely they are to feel they have been
helped by them; the more inmates will view themselves as having

been dealt with unjustly and the more pessimistic they will be about
the beneficial effects of having been imprisoned; and the more likely
they will be to see punishment as the major institutional goal and
the custodial personnel as having the greater influence in prison.
In general, the functional expectations are met. The Participation
Index is related to type of prison in the combined sample (gamma
= .23*) and in each country; the Benefit Index also is related to type
of prison in the expected direction--although the associations tend
to be weak and approach   zero in Spain (see Table 6.5).

TABLE 6.5

Associations between Type of Prison and Measures
of Positive or Negative Orientation to
the Institution, by Country
(gamma)

Type of Prison	United States	Mexico	England	Germany	Spain
Participation Index	.24*	.25*	1.0**[a]	1.0*[a]	.53
Benefit Index	.19	.14	.23	.13	.03
Effect of incarceration	.23*	-.23*	.77*	.04	.50
Treated justly in prison	.29*	.28*	.32	.14	1.0**[a]
Perception of prison goals	.43**	.29*	.42	.42	.46
Which staff has most daily influence	-.24*	.00	-.17	.05	.00

[a]Very small numbers; 9 and 13.
Note: * = significant at .05; ** = significant at .01. Positive
gammas indicate that relationship is in expected direction.
Source: Compiled by the authors.

There are higher levels of negative feelings about present
treatment and postprison expectations among inmates in the more
custodial institutions (except those in Mexico), and they are less
likely than those in the treatment institutions to feel that their imprisonment will have a negative effect on their chances of success
on the outside. Similarly, those in custodial institutions are more
likely than those in intermediate or treatment institutions to believe
that punishment is the major purpose of the prison. The exception

to this general support for the functional view is with regard to the inmates' perception of which set of personnel wields most influence in the prison (see Table 6.5). Thus, the data on the extent to which inmates are "prisonized" toward a negative orientation to the institution are supportive of the functional model with only some cross-cultural variation.

Of all the possible relationships between the various social characteristics and the several items used to measure orientation to the institution, only two show any strength much above zero. The inmate's age is significantly related to his feeling that he has been treated justly in the United States (gamma = .26*) and in Mexico (gamma = .31*). It is unclear whether or not even these two relationships are in line with the importation model, however, because there is no theoretical indication as to whether the younger or the older offenders would feel more hostile toward the institution. The importation model would lead to arguing that the greater the inmate's prior criminal socialization the more developed his hostility toward prison authority and the more likely he is to have an anti-administration orientation. The data in Table 6.6, however, demonstrate that this argument does not hold. The positive or negative orientation toward the institution, as measured by the items in the table, are largely unrelated to criminal background, and in those instances where there does appear to be some association it is opposite from expectation.

Orientation toward and Interaction
with Staff and Inmates

The degree of prisonization also refers to the extent to which the inmate is positively oriented toward and interacts with other inmates, on the one hand, and with staff, on the other. The functional model and prior research (Street, Vinter, Perrow 1966; Berk 1966; Grusky 1959; Stephenson, Scarpitti, 1969) predict that the atmosphere engendered in treatment-oriented institutions produces a more positive disposition not only toward other inmates but also toward staff and a freer interaction with both. Table 6.7 presents the values for the gamma measures of associations between type of prison and four items on positive or negative attitudes toward, and interaction with, other inmates; Table 6.8 does the same for attitudes toward, and interaction with, staff.

The data presented in these tables show support for the functional hypothesis, but that support is made somewhat equivocal by cross-cultural variations. In the U.S. treatment institutions, inmates definitely have a more positive orientation toward other inmates but they are only slightly more likely to interact with, or spend time with, them than do prisoners in intermediate and

TABLE 6.6

Associations between Criminality Index and Measures of Inmate's
Positive or Negative Orientation toward the
Institution, by Country
(gamma)

Criminality Index	United States	Mexico	England	Germany	Spain
Participation Index	-.04	.01	-.81[a]	-1.0[a]	-.42
Benefit Index	.07	.27	-.24	-.23	.04
Effect of incarceration	-.03	.04	-.24	-.09	-.13
Treated justly in prison	-.07	-.31	-.09	-.23	-.02
Perception of prison goals	-.02	.00	-.17	-.17	-.03
Which staff has most daily influence	-.08	-.27	-.08	-.19	.44

[a]Very small numbers; 9 and 13.
Note: Positive gammas indicate relationship is in the expected direction.
Source: Compiled by the authors.

TABLE 6.7

Associations between Type of Prison and Orientation toward and
Interaction with Other Inmates, by Country
(gamma)

Prison Type	United States	Mexico	England	Germany	Spain
Like inmates[a]	.23	--	.18	-.19	.33
Interaction with inmates[b]	.03	.16	.43	-.30	-.22
Spend free time with other inmates[c]	.10	.14	.29	-.18	-.23
Prefer to have more time with other inmates[d]	.26*	.14	.07	.06	-.37

[a]A positive gamma indicates that inmates in treatment institutions are more likely than inmates in custodial institutions to like other inmates.

[b]A positive gamma indicates that inmates in treatment institutions are more likely than inmates in custodial institutions to interact with other inmates.

[c]A positive gamma indicates that inmates in treatment institutions are more likely than inmates in custodial institutions to spend their free time with a buddy or in a group of inmates.

[d]A positive gamma indicates that inmates in treatment institutions are more likely than inmates in custodial institutions to say that it is all right now or that they prefer to have the chance to have more time with other inmates. Custodial inmates want more time alone.

Note: * = significant at .05.
Source: Compiled by the authors.

custodial prisons. In England, inmates confined in the treatment institution interact with each other more and are somewhat more favorably disposed toward one another than those in the intermediate institution. In Mexico the relationships are in the expected direction but are weak. In Germany and Spain the type of prison does have an effect on inmates' attitudes toward each other and their interaction, but not in the way expected (Table 6.7). While there is only a slight tendency for inmates in the more treatment-oriented institutions to have more positive attitudes toward staff, the relationships between type of prison and informal interaction with both guards and treatment staff are stronger (for the combined sample, gamma = .26** and .27**). The differences by type of prison are repeated in each country although there is some variation. In the U.S. prisons the significant relationship is that between type of prison and inmates' interaction with treatment staff, while in the other countries the differences occur in contact with guards (Table 6.8).

TABLE 6.8

Associations between Type of Prison and Orientation and
Interaction with Staff, by Country
(gamma)

Prison Type	United States	Mexico	England	Germany	Spain
Like guards[a]	.10	--	.11	.59	-.20
Interaction with guards[b]	.03	.53**	.60**	.40	.66*
Interaction with treatment staff[b]	.21*	.13	.17	.07	.27

[a]Positive gammas indicate that inmates in custodial institutions are more negative toward guards than inmates in treatment institutions.

[b]Positive gamma indicates that inmates in treatment institutions are more likely than inmates in custodial institutions to interact with guards and treatment staff.

Note: * = significant at .05; ** = significant at .01.

Source: Compiled by the authors.

    The importation model does not fare as well as the functional
model because orientation toward, and interaction with, inmates and
staff tend not to be affected by the extent of prior criminality or by
the social characteristics of the inmates. In those instances where
some association is found the cross-cultural variations point to opposite conclusions. In the two English prisons the less extensive
the inmate's previous criminal involvement the less likely he is to
have positive attitudes toward other prisoners (gamma = .33) and
to spend his time with them (gamma = .19). However, in the Mexican and German institutions the association between criminality and
spending time with other inmates is in the opposite direction (gamma
= -.23 and -.19).

    While there are differences by country that qualify the support
for the functional model provided by these data, that support is
greater than it is for the importation view. The custodial environment tends to produce negative inmate attitudes and greater social
distance among inmates and between inmates and staff in each of
the societies in which the prisons are located.

                              CONCLUSIONS

    We conclude from the data reported that, while there are
some notable cross-cultural differences, most of the research
findings related to prisonization in the United States are clearly
generalizable to other societies. Although U.S. prisoners are
more prisonized than those in other countries, prisonization does
occur to a significant degree in institutions located in other countries (the notable exception being Mexico), and a recognizable nonconformist inmate culture is found everywhere. Pluralistic ignorance wherein inmates overestimate the degree to which other
inmates adhere to this inmate culture is found everywhere. The
strong relationship between the perception of an oppositional code
and one's own prisonized attitudes persists cross-culturally. In
each country, individual prisonization is related more to type of
prison and inmate criminality than is the perception of a prisonized
normative climate.

    Cross-cultural comparisons are important in themselves.
However, the central issue examined here was not the general
similarities and differences across societies. Rather, it was testing the functional and importation models of the inmate system.
The functionalist position that emphasizes in-prison variables
recognizes that inmate characteristics intervene in the adoption
of the inmate code, and those adhering to an importation perspective, who stress preprison and extraprison variables, recognize

that organizational variables affect the inmate culture. Thus, although the differences have been great enough to continue to discuss them as two different and competing theories, there has been recognition of the interaction of functional and importation variables and the need for integration of the two models. The obvious argument is that both sets of variables are involved in the formation and nature of the inmate system. The problem is to specify to what extent or in what way each is involved. The data here have allowed us to move closer to specifying which aspects of the inmate systems are better accounted for by the functional theory, which by the importation theory, and which by neither.

The data on the normative orientation of inmates, as measured by their judgment of the climate of opinion prevailing in the prison population and their own orientation, give some small comfort to both models. However, the other findings come out fairly clearly in favor of the functional theory that prisonization (as measured by positive or negative orientation toward the institution and its programs and the social distance inmates keep between themselves and other inmates and the staff) is greater in the more custodial prisons. Other data, reported elsewhere, also favor a functionalist explanation with regard to patterns of deviant behavior found in prison. To this point, our analysis has revealed only one aspect of the inmate system: namely, the inmate social roles adopted, which appears based more on preprison, rather than in-prison, variables.

We must move further, however, to assess the potency of some integrative models. For instance, one model suggests that the existence of collective solutions in the inmate culture and social structure is based on the common problems of adjustment to the institutions while the content of those solutions and the tendency to become prisonized or not reflects the criminal and other values and behavior patterns imported from the larger society (Thomas 1970; Peterson, Thomas 1973). One clear instance of this appears in the explanation of drug use in prison. Our findings indicate that the general level of drug behavior among inmates is clearly a function of the more or less severe adjustment problems presented by the type of prison environment. Thomas and Cage (1975) find, on the other hand, that almost all of those using drugs in one prison had preprison drug experience and that very few first took up drugs during their current incarceration. This suggests that both functional and importation processes are operative in that the type of prison determines the general level of drug activity that can be expected, but which inmates will engage in drug use rather than some other adaptation and hence contribute to this level of drug activity is determined by whether or not they have had prior experience with drugs.

It remains to examine in detail the combined and interactive
effects of type of prison and inmate characteristics on several
aspects of the inmate system. This is an enterprise that we contend can best be done by future research projects that use comparative organizational analysis.

REFERENCES

Berk, B.
    1966   Organization goals and inmate organization. American
            Journal of Sociology 71 (March): 522-34.

Carter, R., D. Glaser, and L. Wilkins, eds.
    1972   Correctional Institutions. Philadelphia: J. B. Lippincott.

Clemmer, D.
    1958   The Prison Community. New York: Holt, Rinehart and
            Winston. (Paperback edition, 1958.)

Cline, H. F., and S. Wheeler
    1968   The determinants of normative patterns of correctional
            institutions. In Scandinavian Studies in Criminology,
            ed. N. Christie, vol. 2: 173-84. London: Tavistock.

Cloward, R.
    1960   Social control in the prison. In Theoretical Studies in
            Social Organization of the Prison, ed. R. Cloward et al.,
            pp. 20-28. New York: Social Science Research Council.

Garabedian, P. G.
    1963   Social roles and processes of socialization in the prison
            community. Social Problems 11 (Fall): 139-52.

Giallombardo, R.
    1974   The Social World of Imprisoned Girls. New York: Wiley
            Interscience.

    1966   Society of Women. New York: John Wiley & Sons.

Glaser, D.
    1964   The Effectiveness of a Prison and Parole System.
            Indianapolis: Bobbs-Merrill.

Grusky, O.
   1959   Organization goals and the behavior of informal leaders.
           American Journal of Sociology 65 (July): 59-67.

Hayner, N.
   1943   Washington state correctional institutions as communi-
           ties. Social Forces 21 (March): 316-22.

Hayner, N., and E. Ash
   1940   The prison as a community. ASR 5 (August): 577-83.

   1939   The prisoner community as a social group. American
           Sociological Review 4 (June): 362-69.

Haynes, F. E.
   1948   The sociological study of the prison community. Journal
           of Criminal Law, Criminology and Police Science 39
           (November-December): 432-40.

Heffernan, E.
   1972   Making it in Prison: The Square, the Cool, and the Life.
           New York: Wiley-Interscience.

Irwin, J.
   1970   The Felon. Englewood Cliffs, N.J.: Prentice-Hall.

Irwin, J., and D. R. Cressey
   1962   Thieves, convicts, and inmate culture. Social Problems
           10 (Fall): 142-55.

McCleery, R. H.
   1961   The governmental process and informal social control.
           In The Prison, ed. D. R. Cressey, pp. 149-88. New
           York: Holt, Rinehart and Winston.

McCorkle, L., and R. Korn
   1954   Resocialization within walls. Annal 293 (May): 88-98.

Rothman, D.
   1971   The Discovery of the Asylum. Boston: Little, Brown.

Schwartz, B.
   1973   Peer versus authority effects in a correctional commu-
           nity. Criminology 11 (August): 233-57.

   1971   Pre-institutional vs. situational influence in a correc-
          tional community. Journal of Criminal Law, Criminol-
          ogy, and Police Science 62 (September): 532-42.

Stephenson, R. M., and F. Scarpitti
   1968   Argot in a therapeutic milieu. Social Problems 15
          (Winter): 384-95.

Street, D., R. D. Vinter, and C. Perrow
   1966   Organization for Treatment. New York: Free Press.

Sykes, G. M.
   1960   The inmate social system. In Theoretical Studies in
          Social Organization of the Prison, ed. R. Cloward et al.,
          pp. 5-19. New York: SSRC.

   1956   The Society of Captives. Princeton, N.J.: Princeton
          University Press.

Thomas, C. W.
   1973   Prisonization or resocialization? External factors asso-
          ciated with the impact of imprisonment. Journal of
          Research in Crime and Delinquency 10 (January): 13-21.

   1970   Toward a more inclusive model of the inmate contracul-
          ture. Criminology 8 (November): 251-62.

Thomas, C. W., and S. Foster
   1972   Prisonization in the inmate contraculture. Social Prob-
          lems 20 (Fall): 229-39.

Tittle, C. R.
   1972   Society of Subordinates. Bloomington: Indiana University
          Press.

   1969   Inmate organization: sex differentiation and the influence
          of criminal subcultures. American Sociological Review
          34 (August): 492-505.

Ward, D. A., and G. G. Kassebaum
   1965   Women's Prison: Sex and Social Structure. Chicago:
          Aldine.

Wellford, C.
    1973   Contact and commitment in a correctional community.
           The British Journal of Criminology (April): 108-20.

    1967   Factors associated with adoption of the inmate code: a
           study of normative socialization. Journal of Research in
           Crime and Delinquency 58 (June 2): 197-203.

Wheeler, S.
    1961a   Socialization in correctional communities. American
            Sociological Review 26 (October): 699-712

    1961b   Role conflict in correctional communities. In The Prison,
            ed. D. R. Cressey. New York: Holt, Rinehart and
            Winston.

7

THE PROFIT MAKERS BEHIND THE WALLS: PHARMACEUTICAL MANUFACTURERS' EXPERIMENTS ON PRISONERS

Peter B. Meyer

Profits are now being made, and enhanced, by private firms operating behind prison walls. The practice of pharmaceutical product testing on humans in the nation's prisons and jails provides, on the basis of conservative estimates, some $200 million annually in reduced operating costs for drug firms (Meyer 1976: chap. 7).

Bernard L. Diamond, of the University of California at Berkeley, has characterized such experimentation succinctly:

> In the prisons where inmates serve as guinea pigs for
> the testing of new drugs, the research may have little,
> if any, scientific or medical value. Such research is
> frankly commercial, and is solely for the purpose of
> allowing pharmaceutical companies to meet Govern-
> ment requirements for the introduction of new drugs.
> (Diamond 1973: 878)

We can examine the profits made possible in this example in terms of the shares accruing to the companies involved, the correctional institutions, and the inmates themselves. This case is more simple than most since participation in medical experiments is a type of work for which little competition from workers on the "outside" may be expected (Martin et al. 1968). This form of prison employment, therefore, is not subject to the pressures from the free labor market that could arise with free workers unemployed and inmates guaranteed work.

THE CURRENT PRACTICE: DRUG TESTS

Pharmaceutical tests are required by the Federal Food and Drug Administration prior to the marketing of new drugs, and experiments are thus one part of a manufacturing and marketing

116

process. Prisoners are the major source of subjects for the most dangerous tests, at Phase I, in which toxicity is examined. Cost savings are realized through provision of free institutional services to experimenters, and through personnel wage costs that lie below outside rates. The former component derives from the complementarities of incarceration and experimentation, while the latter is a reflection of routine prison wages for nonexperimental work. We can look at these elements in turn.

Institutional Services

The critical problem confronting experimenters has been described by one leading clinician in the question:

> Where do you find a bundle of people on whom you can collect their blood day and night, on whom you can collect their urine day and night quantitatively, and follow their blood pressure and temperature and pulse and liver function and kidney function for days and weeks? (McMahon 1973: 17)

The answer is, clearly, some institutional setting. Thus, in order to conduct Phase I tests on nonincarcerated subjects, pharmaceutical companies would have to recruit volunteers and induce them to move into special residential facilities and subject themselves to extensive medical monitoring. Prisons and jails that maintain their physical plant and provide institutional services to their residents for correctional purposes should, therefore, be able to charge experimenters for access to their services and facilities.

In practice, correctional institutions do not charge experimenters for services rendered, with the result that the companies save the full costs of housing and food services for active subjects as well as for a modicum of institutional social control and for physical facilities in which to conduct medical monitoring tests. These savings amounted to some $7.75 per active experiment subject-day in 1975, based on the costs of dormitory facilities and related provisions (Meyer 1976: chap. 7). The correctional system, therefore, could easily have charged experimenters $7.00 per subject-day for services rendered and still saved the companies money, but no institution did so.

Personal and Subject Services

Daily inmate wages in the United States in 1972 were solidly under $1.00 for the less than 80 percent of the prison and jail

residents with employment (Lenihan 1974: 17). We can assume
such wages now average $1.50. The experimenters have contributed
to higher average wages for inmates by paying $2 to $5 per day.
These are premium rates in the institution context, but still wages
far below the economically feasible payments. Health Sciences
Association, a private firm conducting Phase I drug tests for pharmaceutical manufacturers, routinely pays $50 to $100 a day, plus
compensation for loss of job pay and travel costs to noninmate subjects (Dickinson 1975: 2). Based on these fees, the inmate–subjects
could easily be paid $45 per day by experimenters with the latter
still enjoying cost savings from utilization of correctional institutions as experiment sites.

     The presence of experiments in prisons and jails provides
nonsubject inmates with some employment as experiment staff.
Thus experimenters gain from reductions in the wage bills they pay
for lower echelon project staff. Based on typical staff/subject
ratios, wage scales for nonunionized hospital workers, and inmate
staff wages of $1.50 per day, the cost saving to experimenters
amounts to some $2.25 per subject–day (Meyer 1976: chap. 7). A
$2.00-per-subject-day charge would leave the companies better off
than they would be using outside staff.

Direct Cost Savings

     The pharmaceutical industry, which experiments in order to
legally market its products, thus is currently not being billed for
some $54 per active subject-day for institutional, subject, and staff
services they receive. These funds could be demanded by host institutions and the companies would still prefer prisons to free con-
texts as localities for experimentation, since they would still save
money. The fact that these funds are not pursued presents a problem for proponents of profit-making industry behind prison walls.

     Experience with medical and pharmaceutical experimentation
on inmates suggests that the benefits from profit makers' access to
inmate labor will accrue exclusively to the companies in question
due to correctional system malleability. The potential for positive
impact is present, but its realization is problematic at best: the
current implicit subsidies to experimenters in the prisons, with an
annual level of some $200 million, could be diverted to provide
about $1,000 in gate money to every discharged inmate (Meyer 1976:
Postscript). Instead of contributing to easier reintegration of ex-
convicts into the social system from which they have been removed,
however, these funds are now used to increase the profits of drug
manufacturers.

GENERALIZING PROFIT MAKING IN PRISONS

Based on the pharmaceuticals testing experience, we can derive a series of questions requiring resolution before pursuit of profit is introduced wholesale into the correctional setting. We need to consider the obligations of institutions to inmates as well as to the invited in-house industries, the relationship of the private to the public sector generally, and the role and objectives of the "corrections process" and how it acts on institution inmates. Correctional functions and objectives served or undermined by an industry presence may be spelled out under different possible conditions of operations imposed on such private enterprises.

THE ECONOMIC FUNCTIONS OF
CORRECTIONAL FACILITIES

Consider the criminal justice system as having the dominant function of providing protection services to the community or nation that it serves; following Kenneth Avio, we can then characterize correctional facilities as: "Non-profit firms which produce two services intermediate to protection services: (1) incarceration services, and (2) training services" (Avio 1973). Incarceration services may be further described as affecting protection through both "removal" and "deterrence" effects. Training, on the other hand, may include outputs serving to increase the potential legitimate incomes of exprisoners upon their release, but it also could include apprenticeships in the skills of criminality--"positive" or "negative" training (Avio 1973). Utilizing these three outputs, we can characterize certain aspects of the relative efficiency in the production of each associated with different types of facilities, and the impact of the introduction of a contribution to private profit into the mix of correctional system outputs. A number of basic productivity interlocks should first be noted, however.

Incarceration and Training

High incarceration levels require a large institutional setting, which is typically a context in which extensive negative training occurs and little positive training is possible. Community correction centers, by contrast, exist to provide minimal incarceration and to make possible extensive positive training for inmates. Thus, incarceration and training outputs, while possibly complements in the justice system's production of protection, are in part mutually exclusive correctional system outputs.

Incarceration and Profit

Profits for private industry are more easily enhanced by institutional than community corrections settings. The opportunities for alternative employments and earnings are lower for institutional residents than for the denizens of halfway houses and other community-based facilities. To the extent that wage rates may reflect these opportunity costs, pay scales will be lower in closed institutions. Incarceration and profit opportunities thus appear to be complementary outputs.

Training and Profits

Insofar as a profit-making enterprise requires labor with specific skills, the pursuit of profits behind the walls will promote positive training outputs. However, since there is a cost incurred in the provision of training, the profitable enterprise will want to train those inmates who will remain in the institutions for the longest possible time periods. Maximization of either positive training or profits will engender the sacrifice of one system objective to another. Other things being equal, training recipients will tend to be persons facing long minimum incarceration periods.

INTRODUCING PROFIT-MAKING FIRMS:
SOME QUESTIONS

Five major issues present themselves to any correctional system contemplating pursuit of profits behind the walls. Each issue has been made evident by our experience with drug company tests on inmates. Moreover, the pharmaceutical test experiences serve to indicate the direction of the resolution of policy questions that will probably emerge in other grants to profit makers who have access to correctional institution settings.

Job Security and Competition

If profit-making industries produce with prison labor, will noninmates lose jobs? In an economy with surplus labor and high unemployment, could not guaranteed prison jobs at competitive wages increase crime as people attempt to access scarce jobs? To avoid such a trend, should correctional facilities make sure that inmates are paid less than free labor would earn? If this is done,

would not the benefits to prisoners of profitable industries' presence
in prisons be reduced? On average, inmates serving as drug experiment subjects "work" for one-tenth the wage that would be required to attract free-living subjects. Moreover, noninmates without jobs are willing to serve as human guinea pigs, so the citizen
response to provision of jobs in industry to inmates at the expense
of the unincarcerated unemployed will probably render such a policy
politically untenable.

Selection of the Industries and Jobs

Any scheme devised for the recruitment or selection of employers, industries, and jobs available in prisons may produce new
negative training and high deterrence (due to mandatory work on
dangerous or unpleasant jobs, perhaps), as well as company profits.
The technology used in production will affect the value of positive
training provided, as will job assignments offered prisoners. It is
thus critical that noncoercive, constructive means of job rationing
across inmates be developed. Pharmaceutical experimentation
selects subjects on the basis of relevant medical and physical criteria as well as prisoners' disciplinary records, so access to higher
pay is unequal; this access then becomes a new tool for coercion of
inmates.

Profit-Related and Other Prison Jobs

If new profit-producing jobs are introduced into the prison
setting, will these jobs be remunerated at the existing wage rates
for inmates or at higher levels? If current inmate rates are paid,
industry wage cost savings are astronomical, and competitive advantages unwarranted on other economic grounds provided to companies permitted to hire inmates. If "free market" wage rates
apply, workers in profit-making jobs will make more per hour than
workers in prison work positions make per day or even week. Will
nonprofit prisoner wages be brought up to the level of profit-related
job pay? What impact will this have on corrections costs? Drug
experiments now pay subjects far more than they can earn at other
jobs; animosity develops over access to jobs as subjects, and the
pressure on inmates to show good behavior rises.

Prison Services and Payments for Them

If prison facilities are provided the profit maker, should not
payment be made to prisons? Should not the employed inmates be

charged for the clothing, room, and board provided to them? What
should be done about payments from unemployed inmates? The
more of their pay they must return to the institution, the less motivated the inmates will be to earn. The pharmaceutical industry
now gets free facilities and services from the institutions in which
it experiments. Inmates do not now earn free market wages for
service as experiment subjects and thus cannot, and do not, pay
the institution for personal services rendered.

Competition and Monopsony

The low wages now paid in institutions are possible simply
because the administrations of such facilities are all monopsonistic
employers. If prison authorities authorize new jobs with profit
makers and still assign and limit job access, will they remain
monopsonists? If free access to hire inmates is granted to employers, will prison discipline be undermined? Many drug companies now rely on prison authorities to select subject candidates;
institutions have competed for the right to serve as experiment
locations, acting as monopsonists trying to increase the number of
jobs available.

CONCLUSION

Experience with drug tests on prisoners suggests that, despite claims of training and attitude change outputs, the dominant
outcomes of profit makers' access to inmates will be twofold:
(1) increased profits for the enterprises granted access, and (2)
greater coercion in the institutional setting. Unless this pattern
is significantly changed in a wholly novel scheme for the introduction of private employers into prisons, the presence of profit makers
behind the walls may boost not only the profits of U.S. industry but
also the volume of U.S. crime.

REFERENCES

Avio, K. L.
    1973   An economic analysis of criminal corrections: the
            Canadian case. Canadian Journal of Economics 6: 165.

Diamond, B. L.
    1973   Quality of health care--human experimentation, 1973.
            In U.S., Congress, Senate, Committee on Labor and
            Public, Hearings, before the Subcommittee on Health of
            the Committee on Labor and Public Welfare, Senate, on
            S. 974, S. 878, and S.J. Res. 71, 93d Cong., 1st sess.

Dickinson, D.
    1975   Research on non-inmate human subjects for medical re-
            search experiments. Memorandum dated May 23, to
            Daniel L. Skoler, American Bar Association Commission
            on Correctional Facilities and Services, Washington,
            D.C.

Lenihan, K.
    1974   The financial resources of released prisoners. Report
            prepared for the Manpower Administration, Department
            of Labor, under Grant no. 91-11-71-32. Washington,
            D.C.: Bureau of Social Science Research.

McMahon, F. G.
    1973   Faculty address-research. In Proceedings of the Con-
            ference on Drug Research in Prisons, Airlie, Va.,
            August. Davis, Calif.: Research Center, National
            Council on Crime and Delinquency.

Martin, D. C., et al.
    1968   Human subjects in clinical research--a report of three
            studies. New England Journal of Medicine 279: 1428.

Meyer, P. B.
    1976   Medical Experimentation on Prisoners: Ethical, Eco-
            nomic or Exploitative? Lexington, Mass.: Lexington
            Books.

8
THE ECONOMICS OF
IMPRISONMENT
Martin B. Miller

Ethnographic study of in-prison economic behaviors offers an
alternative view of prisoner subcultures. Licit and illicit behaviors
by staff and prisoners may be rational* economic choices when the
prison is viewed as a microscopic economic system. Sociologists
have traditionally described the prison subcultures and social structure, noting with little enthusiasm for further analysis the few formal, licit economic activities within its boundaries (Clemmer 1940;
Schrag 1944; Sykes 1966; Cressey 1966; Wheeler 1961; Cloward 1960;
Goffman 1961; among others). Psychologists, for the most part,
have been content to study demographic and attitudinal factors in order to differentiate between criminal and noncriminal behaviors
(Sheldon 1949; McCord, McCord 1956; Glueck, Glueck 1950;
Schilder 1944; Gough 1960; among others). Given the intradisci-
plinary metatheoretical assumptions of criminogenesis and the re-
cency of systematic prison research, these foci are appreciated.
Biographical and quasi-fictional prison accounts often describe economic transactions devoid of particular significance (Blake 1971;
Braly 1967; Elli 1966; Pell 1973; Sands 1964; among others). The
interdisciplinary criminologist welcomes timely and refreshing
economic perspectives in the treatment and understanding of organized crime as an economic unit (Schelling 1967), of male crime

---

*The notion that economic choice must proceed from a rational
model is not necessary, nor even desirable. "Not that our behavior
is irrational, it simply turns out to be much more complex and
subtle than those who merely assume rationality are wont to believe.
When we behave rationally, we seek the best available choice or the
best compromise between mutually incompatible considerations;
one can go very wrong, however, in identifying the available choices
and the irrelevant considerations" (Scitovsky 1976: xii).

rates (Baer, Luksetich 1975), of the economic impact of imprisonment (Singer 1973), and of resocialization of the parolee (Colter
1975). This chapter will attempt to integrate some of the author's
researches and personal observations of imprisonment with several
recent, exciting, and serious economic works on contraband and the
functions of the sub-rosa prison economy (Williams, Fish 1974;
Guenther 1975; Davidson 1974). (The classic work in this field, not
reviewed here, is Radford's unique study of the economic organization of a P.O.W. camp [1945].)

TRADITIONALIST PERSPECTIVES

Inmate social structure is viewed as adversarial, caste, and
as an accommodation to the several deprivations of imprisonment
(Hayner, Asch 1939; Clemmer 1940; Goffman 1961; Morris, Morris
1963; Sykes 1966; Sykes, Messinger 1960; Mathieson 1965; among
others). Inmate (argot) roles exemplify crucial axes of prison life
and are adaptive tools of social organization used to cope with the
"pains of imprisonment," for example, the loss of liberty and
autonomy, of certain material goods and services, and of heterosexual relationships. Early studies focused on role differentiation
based on these accommodations--principally, styles of aggression,
leadership, and (mostly) sexual deviances. Demographic variables
were used to replicate studies of prisoner types, attitudes, and
adjustment. Other studies have focused on suffering and time perspective (Farber 1944), importation of prisoner subcultures (Irwin
1970), treatment-custody dimensions (Cressey 1959; McCorkle,
Korn 1954), and prisonization (Wheeler 1961). These have not
seriously challenged earlier perspectives, but have expanded upon
them.

UNTRADITIONAL PERSPECTIVES

Jewell's (1957) study of Mexico's Tres Marias Penal Colony
suggests that microscopic study of prisoner subcultures may be
misleading when compared to broader offender relationships--pri-
marily familial-sexual--and that prison economic structure may be
a unifying concept. Ecological studies of territory and dominance
may bring new insights to the study of prisoner social structure.
Experimental studies may yield crucial theoretical implications for
penology (Zimbardo 1972), for example, the concept that situational
variables transcend personality and character traits. The microscopic studies of Irwin (1970) and Mannocchio and Dunn (1970) give

promise of providing greater understanding across traditional bar-
riers (counselor-prisoner) and among major subcultural prison
societal dimensions (criminal, prisoner, convict). Topical studies--
family relations, sex, race, violence, women's prisons, juvenile institutions, and comparative research--also have the potential for
clarifying discrete issues. However, since most "correctional research" falls within the 1 percent funding allocated for the purpose
of better control of prisoners, it is not surprising that few advances
have been made in these areas.

ECONOMIC PERSPECTIVES

Two general perspectives have emerged: (1) viewing the
prison as an economic unit in transactional relationships within a
larger market (Tabasz 1975) and (2) a microscopic focus on
prisoner-to-prisoner transactions, referred to as "hustling," or
"conniving." This chapter will focus on the second category of
studies, will broaden its perspective somewhat in that there will be
a determined attempt to avoid arbitrary and artificial boundaries
such as contraband/noncontraband goods and licit/illicit services,
and will attempt to analyze staff members' activities whenever they
appear in such transactions, rather than relegate them to a small
set of anomalous events.

Williams and Fish (1974) generally accept the deprivation-
adaptation view of the traditionalists and describe the sub-rosa
economy of the prison in this light, with considerable detail. Their
work is remarkably free of overemphasis of the illicit aspect of
prisoner behaviors, and their descriptions of modus operandi en-
hances the field, notwithstanding some final chapter polemics on
how to cure crime.

Guenther (1975) focuses on contraband. He enlarges the
taxonomy of illicit services and (especially) goods, but bogs down
at the borderland between licit and illicit definitions and fails to
transcend a rather narrow, control-oriented descriptive analysis.

Huff's (1974) dissertation and papers really take another tack,
recounting and accounting for the prisoner-unionization movement.
Although the subject matter has implications for the prison economy,
there are no fresh insights to offer in the analysis of in-prison
economy.

Studies by Strange and McCrory (1974) at Rahway, and Davidson (1974) at San Quentin, are extraordinarily useful as they integrate economic perspectives with emerging views of prison minority
subcultures. Davidson's work reaches further here and strongly
implies a Chicano "Baby Mafia" ("The Family") economic structure

of considerable pervasity and economic strength, with the potential of influencing across-prison-perimeter markets and staff. Unfortunately, Davidson's work is marred by an apparent, excessive enthusiasm for the Chicano, which detracts from his views of the black prisoners and which colors his social class definitions of inmates, convicts, and Family. He defines, rather vaguely, the convict as "aware of who the other convicts are. . . . They talk freely in front of each other. . . . The trust is there. Their unity is in their trust. They know that a fellow convict will not snitch to save himself from punishment." Inmates are snitchers, and snivelers, to Davidson. They are not permitted full role-access to the prison economy. Most Chicanos are convicts; few blacks are convicts. The Family is an enormously pervasive and powerful Mafia-like organization of Chicanos (Davidson's "right guys"). Bowker (1977: 70) also notes that "Davidson paints such a positive picture of Chicano social organization that it is not believable. He also seems to slight Blacks and Caucasians." Nonetheless, his work is rare and therefore useful in analyzing the relationship of ethnicity and prison economic structure.

GENERALIZATIONS

These economically oriented studies advocate the view, generally, that behavioral types respond to needs and values within a (relatively) closed prison market economy. Production, consumption, and distribution of illicit goods and services may be viewed not as individual deviances or rebellion against authority but as predictable consequences of a "stressed" economy. It is one short, but important, conceptual step to consider some assumptions about the economics of imprisonment as they bear upon social structure and to consider some implications arising from this focus, for further study.

The typical U.S. prisoner is taken into the prison system stripped of his material possessions and psychologically traumatized.* His wardrobe, automobiles, furnishings are taken from him; his ability to direct his personal affairs is not called upon; he may not be asked to make more than the simplest of day-to-day decisions about eating, working, playing, or sleeping; communications with his wife (or girlfriend), children, friends, and/or relatives may be

---

*This is more true for the middle-class white prisoner than for the black. See, for example, Brown (1965) and Irwin (1970).

severely limited; he may not be allowed to buy or read all manners
of literature, to see films or art of his choice, or to hear his kind
of music. In short, his former identity is replaced by a prison
"identity kit"--for example, state uniform, state bed, state bedding,
state toilet articles, state soap, state towel, state tobacco, state
medical and dental care, state writing materials, state library
books, state food, state-controlled films and recreational pursuits. *
These goods and services will be, most often, of marginal quality,
minimal in quantity, uncertain as to delivery when requested, and
sometimes absent for considerable periods of time--partially or in
their entirety (Williams, Fish 1974: 49-51).

Prisoners' needs arise out of scarcity of goods and services
endemic to this alien, prison environment. Among the most desired
of these goods and services are clothing, shoes, socks, underwear,
foods high in protein, dairy foods, sweets, all forms of tobacco,
hobby supplies, games, recreational tools, musical instruments and
materials, books, magazines, writing materials and supplies, medical and dental care, nonaddictive medications; also, and especially,
other drugs of all forms, alcoholic beverages, sexual services,
pornographic or erotic materials, admission (fees or bribes) into
institutional programs, weapons, building (or escape) plans, protection or insurance, debt collection, finder's fees, and commissions.
A case may be made that an analysis of these commodities or services is no less useful in understanding social roles in prison than
is argot. They are not merely products of "conspicuous consumption" but clues to the prisoners' adaptive roles, or "compensation"
(Guenther 1975). Guenther emphasizes the potentiality of contraband for violating the security of the prison. For example, he notes:

> 21' length of ladder made from two strands of rope . . .
> 5" homemade pipe bomb . . . Selective Service Reg-
> istration card . . . Virginia Chauffeur's license . . .
> A jar of artist's varnish (for sniffing); arrowheads
> made of aluminum.

However, his categories of "serious" and "nuisance" contraband are
not especially useful in economic analysis (Guenther 1975: 243-54).
It is important that no differentiation be made in this analysis between
contraband and noncontraband commodities, or licit or illicit services.

-----

*The author is aware of the wide variations and several excep-
tions in this generalization of U.S. prisons. Nevertheless, the statement is probably more true than not for most large U.S. prisons.

However, it is relevant that an illicit market is created, most often, from a failure of the formal and legal market to provide goods and services in appropriate quantities, of valued quality, and with timely deliveries. In fact, the more scarcity the greater the probability that an illicit economy will arise (no matter the efforts of security-conscious staff). Larger institutions, and strict regimens, are by their nature to be associated with a well-developed sub-rosa economy. (This model includes psychological needs and costs; in fact, in crises, psychological needs/costs factors far outweigh a simplistic demand/supply-pricing explanation.)

Most prison diets are nutritionally adequate but may be monotonous or unpalatable to some prisoners. They may perceive the need to supplement their diet with more familiar foods, or, by avoiding religious taboos, they require substitutes. They may desire foods more heavy in sweets, protein, or dairy content because of strenuous manual labor, recreational activity, body-building program, or personal/cultural preferences. Davidson writes:

> In the evening, prisoners often buy sandwiches from someone in the block who is making them in volume from food that has been stolen from the mess hall. Several prisoners normally are involved in the collection of contraband that is necessary to make a sandwich. For example, a grilled cheese sandwich requires . . . a hot plate, . . . butter, . . . cheese, . . . bread, . . . and mustard, mayonnaise or catsup. Sometimes sandwiches are made with steak, cheese, lunch meat, and occasionally even bacon and tomato. . . . Sandwiches normally sell for one pack each. The buyer usually has little choice, having to accept the offering of the evening. The fragrant aroma of the sandwiches being prepared often is sufficient advertisement to let the prisoners know that a certain item is for sale that evening. At such times, the shouts of prisoners may be heard as they place their order by yelling out the number of sandwiches wanted and their cell number. (1974: 141)

An inmate may be willing to pay 20 to 30 boxes (of cigarettes-- most often used as currency) for a first-rate set of "choppers" (false teeth), rather than wait six months or longer for his turn in the formal process market. With a low-risk cost factor, his is primarily an economic choice. The risk factor is added cost in the illicit market; that is, risk of incurring disfavor with the staff, risk of a formal breach of prison rules, risk of a formal criminal charge,

risk of negative recommendation for parole, transfer, or admittance
to a program, and the like are each risks with quantitative costs to
be computed in the decision-making process.

These "hustles" may also be in "bonerooing"[*] clothing, hair-
cuts, shoe repair,[†] and the manufacture of alcoholic beverages.

> The production of home brew is extensive. Frequent-
> ly small groups will make it during the day at their
> job for their collective use. However, most home
> brew is produced for sale to others. (Davidson 1974:
> 140-41)

Resourcefulness and ingenuity are well pursued as themes in
economic studies. For example, Williams and Fish quote Tom
Murton:

> During his brief career as a reform penologist at
> Tucker Prison Farm in Arkansas, he was astonished
> to see two inmates driving around the farm in a motor
> vehicle which they had fashioned from a frame, and a
> Wisconsin engine connected to a chain drive. The in-
> mates had constructed the amazing vehicle from waste
> scraps and pieces found around the farm (Murton,
> Hyams 1970: 46-48)

Economic transactions also include staff members' and guards'
(particularly because of their exposure to corruption by prisoners
and their ease of access across prison boundaries) participation in
a wide range of activities, from petty deviances--for example, the
consumption of state food and beverages while on duty--to smuggled
narcotics valued at upward of $100,000. The operations of the
prison canteen and craft shop, prison farms, and factories also fall
within the purview of in-prison economy, and require a more
thorough analysis than offered here.

---

[*]Prisoner argot for special laundering of prison clothing.

[†]Davidson (1974: 140) writes: "The hustle resulting from some
prison jobs may be in direct competition with state-offered services.
Even though the prisoners who do the hustling charge for their services, the superior quality of the prisoner services allows them to
compete successfully with the state's free services."

PRISON LABOR

Prison labor ought to include not only the labor of convicts,
both licit and illicit, but also the occupations of custodial, treatment, administrative, and maintenance staffs. That they interact
with prisoners in the economic market has been traditionally assumed implicitly and uncritically. For example, instant coffee is
sold at most prison canteens, but hot water is not always available
on the cell blocks.

> Therefore many prisoners make and sell "stingers"--
> small electrical coil immersion heaters that are used
> to heat a single cup of water. The stingers enable
> prisoners to make hot coffee almost any time they
> wish. (Davidson 1974: 141)

Staff members are aware of these transactions, consider them petty,
and often participate in them as consumers. Except in the most
general form (Korn, McCorkle 1965; Sykes 1966), these "corrup-
tions of authority," through friendship or economic relationships,
have not been properly analyzed.

The typical U.S. prisoner obtains his job through a classification committee, through a work assignment officer, by being recruited or selected by another inmate, or by seeking out an inmate
with appropriate influence and paying a placement fee for a desirable
job. Jobs may be valued by inmates for their political esteem, their
creature comforts, their potential for escapism, or for the pursuit
of future economic gain. The distribution of these alternatives
among prisons depends upon their individual characteristics. There
is some evidence that all forms of recruitment, selection, and placement are evident, to some extent, within the large prison.

The average American prisoner is paid about 10¢ per hour,
or $15.00 per month, for his labor. In six states he may not be
formally paid at all; in nine other states he may earn more than
$1.00 per day. * He is paid little and generally does not work too

---

*Abstracted from Lenihan (1975: 266-81):

State	Percent Inmates Who Work	Daily Wage
California	45	15¢ to $1.20
New York	95	25¢ to $1.00
Illinois	33	20¢
Michigan	90	20¢ to $2.00
Minnesota	95	50¢ to $1.00
Pennsylvania	95	25¢ to $1.25
Florida	0	None

hard because he is not expected to (by both his colleagues and the prison staff). Work that is difficult or exhausting is defined by the prisoner (and sometimes in penal law) as "hard labor," falling into the category of punishment for the prisoner. No work at all is also punishment of a different sort, for idleness, or empty time, becomes "hard time" in the syntax of the convict. Time for the prisoner, and others as well, ought to be filled with productive, satisfying employment, in order to make time pass quickly, to provide psychological support, and to offer either direct, indirect, or potential income. Work, then, may be both punishment and reward, dependent upon its variable character. Since most U.S. prisoners are underemployed and underpaid, they must seek to satisfy these needs through another means, primarily participation in the sub-rosa economy of the prison.

The U.S. prisoner, on coming into the system, quickly learns that he needs a "gig" (that is, a job), a "contract," or a route. * Some possibilities, which follow, may be legal or illegal. He may:

find a state job with a "pay" number;†
sell his blood, craft work, music, works of art, or literature, if permitted;‡

---

*Williams and Fish point out the differences between a "route" and a "score." The inmate who scores is required, according to the inmate code, to share his loot with closest colleagues or to consume it himself, but not to sell it. "On the other hand, food is regularly stolen from the kitchen on a highly organized and systematic basis. These organized thefts are 'routes' and not 'scores.' A stigma is not attached to the selling of pilfered food obtained on routes" (1974: 44). But this is not as true for a later generation of prisoners. From my interview data and personal observations, the prevailing prison "business" ethic was that one "got nothing for nothing." Everything in prison had its price. There was no stigma attached to selling anything obtained in any manner from "stocks." There was a stigma attached to the selling of goods that were the property of any individual person, including staff or free personnel--the latter, due to the "heat" that could come down from their responses.

†A "pay number" refers to a formal table of organization line-task, performed by a prisoner for a set monthly fee, ranging from $5.00 to $40.00 (in California circa 1968).

‡The California Department of Corrections, for example, severely restricts the potential for prisoner sales of creative works. Most state prison systems forbid or rigidly control the sale of prison-created works. They generally define the prisoner as a ward of the state who may not earn interest or profit during his imprisonment.

earn fees as a medical research subject, which may be risky
(Meyer 1976; Miller 1971);

engage in a needed, but illicit, service, such as a delivery
route for sandwiches, coffee; lend money at interest (not necessarily
usurious); type or write legal or other documents for other prisoners; supply or manufacture pills or "home brew"; sell or provide
protection; take bets; sell, provide, or procure sexual satisfactions;
sell adjunct merchandise to other prisoners for their own consumption or use--for example, picture frames to artists who are permitted to sell them through the "craft shop," by prisoners who are
not permitted to engage in craft shop sales because they lack the
qualifying amount of funds on "the books."

The listing goes on ad infinitum.

For several reasons, the prisoner desires to have funds "on
his account," the most obvious being his desire to draw upon these
funds and to use them for direct canteen purchases. But "money on
the books," as suggested above, also shapes the kinds of occupational activities permitted by prison rules. The economic stratifi-
cation of prisoners is thereby exaggerated by prohibiting prisoners
with no funds to own or engage in activities outside the formal economic structure. They are thereby "invited" to participate in the
sub-rosa economy. There is a kind of self-fulfilling prophecy about
this aspect of prison life, or, at the least, it is akin to the working
of a "debtor's prison" within the prison that prohibits the full participation of impoverished prisoners in the ordinary life of the prison.

Our typical prisoner has brought few funds with him, knows
few persons who are able to deposit more than a few dollars "on the
books" for him, and cannot qualify for either the few work-furlough
placements or the "pay" jobs available in the prison.

Prisoners who deal through the craft shop, or the occupational
therapy program, as it is euphemistically called, also have to ac-
commodate themselves to the dilemma of involuntary contributions
to the Inmate Welfare Fund (this may or may not be a fiction, depending on the institution). That is, inmates must not only make
purchases from approved vendors, at prices that exceed market
prices--or, at the least, at undiscounted prices--but must also permit the state to deduct 10 to 20 percent of the transaction, and often
an additional 10 to 20 percent if the commodity is resold through the
prison craft shop or through the state. A cursory glance at the manner of use of Inmate Welfare Funds, by no means a clearly defined
or agreed-upon policy principally reserved for recreational materials
or for recreational capital improvements, shows little hard evidence
that these funds are used strictly for these purposes (rather than for
maintenance) or that inmates exercise any control over their use.

Some states, more enthusiastically than others, use their inmates as workers in prison industries, on work farms, in mining
and quarrying, on road maintenance and fire lines, and in emergencies. A historical overview of means to which inmate workers have
lent their labors to the several purposes of the states reveals a sec-
tional pattern; that is, the states whose economies have been closest
to the soil cling most tenuously to the antiquated work devices of the
farm and the mine. * The economy of the Northeast, especially,
shaped the tone of prison work to that of the prison-factory. The
anticonvict labor movement has almost completely eroded the prison-
goods market, the use of "lease," "contract," and "piece-rate" systems. Certainly the notion that the state might profit from convict
labor died a hard death. Although there were few redeeming virtues
to these labor practices, at least they avoided the evils of idleness
that has plagued the twentieth-century prison. The "state-use" system, which survives today, is a strange compromise of underem-
ployment, idleness, restricted markets, a proliferation of prison-
taught skills irrelevant to the reintegration of the prisoner cum
parolee; of maintenance needs of the institution, all balanced against
public attitudes opposed to the "rights" of prisoners to work and to
earn market income.

PRISON CUSTODY AND THE SUB-ROSA ECONOMY

The prison staff's overkill approach toward security makes
them complicit in the illicit market economy of the prison. (This
is not so much an indictment as it is a recognition of management
priorities.) Much of the staff's woes in this regard originate from
an unreasonable set of demands placed upon them by the public, by
the legislature, and by the "correctional" bureaucracy who under-
fund and overexpect fulfillment of contradictory prison functions.
Increased custodial demands escalate risk costs to illicit goods and
services. This has a "churning" effect on the prison economy and
may serve to drive out the small-stakes player or "chippie." (In
an ironic parallel, Nelson Rockefeller's stern drug legislation in
New York suffered a similar ignominious fate of escalating risk for
law enforcement, increasing profit to drug distribution, failing to

---

*For a unique analysis of the relationship of punishment and
social structure, see Rusche and Kirchheimer (1939); on prison
labor and the anticonvict labor movement in the nineteenth-century
United States, see Miller (1974).

delimit drug sales, and increasing ancillary crimes partaken to
offset increased retail drug costs.)

SUMMARY AND IMPLICATIONS FOR FURTHER STUDY

Trends toward inmate unionism will intensify the demands for
market wages (Huff 1974, 1975).* High court opinions may continue
to bear upon matters within this area. The use of token economies
suggests that there is therapeutic potential for prison economics.
On the other hand, the implications for a therapeutic milieu--or, at
the least, for any exemplar within the prison, relevant to attitude
change--toward the work ethic and prudent personal fiscal policy
invite a more creative use of "correctional" intervention. Two of
the more recent trends--closing down large, inefficient, close-
custody prisons and construction of small, modular, medium-
minimum custody institutions near major urban centers--will by
their very nature obviate some of the dilemmas of the large prison
environment. The monolithic character of inmate subculture invites
an incisive intrusion into the economy of the prison. As we increase
the pay of guards, as we educate them to the economics of imprisonment, as we remove goods and services from the illicit market to
the legal arena (decriminalization), we reduce the probability of destructive concomitants of the illegal market. This is not to suggest
that such intrusions will seriously modify the dilemma of treating
the prisoner (or parolee, for that matter) as a "less eligible" worker
but that objective, economic foci may hasten the demise of stultify-
ing attitudes. The potential for modifying the inmate culture exists
and may flourish in the positive intrusion of economic perspectives.

REFERENCES

Baer, R., and W. Luksetich
    1975   Labor market determinants of male crime rates. Paper
            read at Iowa Academy of Science, April.

Blake, J.
    1971   The Joint. Garden City, N.Y.: Doubleday.

----

*For a brief, but incisive, glance at Sweden's responses, see
N. Morris (1975: 279-98).

Bowker, L. H.
    1977   Prisoner Subcultures. Lexington, Mass.: D. C. Heath.

Braly, M.
    1967   On the Yard. Boston: Little, Brown.

Brown, C.
    1965   Manchild in the Promised Land. New York: Macmillan.

Clemmer, D.
    1940   The Prison Community. New York: Holt, Rinehart and
            Winston.

Cloward, R. A., et al.
    1960   Theoretical Studies in Social Organization of the Prison.
            New York: Social Science Research Council.

Colter, N. C.
    1975   Subsidizing the released inmate. Crime and Delinquency
            21 (July): 282-85.

Cressey, D.
    1959   Contradictory directives in complex organizations: the
            case of the prison. Administrative Science Quarterly 4
            (June): 1-19.

Cressey, D. R., ed.
    1966   The Prison: Studies in Institutional Organization and
            Change. New York: Holt, Rinehart and Winston.

Davidson, R. T.
    1974   Chicano Prisoners: The Key to San Quentin. New York:
    Holt, Rinehart and Winston.

Elli, F.
    1966   The Riot. New York: Coward, McCann and Geoghegan.

Farber, M. L.
    1944   Suffering and the time perspective of the prisoner. Uni-
            versity of Iowa Studies in Child Welfare 20: 177-78.

Glueck, S., and E. Glueck
    1950   Unravelling Juvenile Delinquency. Cambridge, Mass.:
            Harvard University Press.

Goffman, E.
    1961   Asylums: Essays on the Social Situation of Mental
            Patients and Other Inmates. New York: Doubleday.

Gough, H.
    1960   Theory and measurement of socialization. Journal of
            Consulting Psychology 24 (February): 23-30.

Guenther, A. L.
    1975   The forms and functions of prison contraband. Crime
            and Delinquency 21 (July): 243-54.

Hayner, N., and E. Asch
    1939   The prisoner community as a social group. American
            Social Review 4 (June): 362-69.

Huff, R. C.
    1975   Prisoner's Union: a challenge for state corrections.
            State Government 48 (Summer): 145-46.

    1974   Unionization behind the walls. Criminology 12 (August):
            175-93.

Irwin, J.
    1970   The Felon. Englewood Cliffs, N.J.: Prentice-Hall.

Irwin, J., and D. R. Cressey
    1962   Thieves, convicts and the inmate culture. Social Prob-
            lems 10 (Fall): 142-55.

Jewell, D. P.
    1957   Mexico Tres Marias penal colony. Journal of Criminal
            Law, Criminology and Police Science 48 (November-
            December): 410-13.

Korn, R., and L. W. McCorkle
    1965   Criminology and Penology. New York: Holt, Rinehart
            and Winston.

Lenihan, K. J.
    1975   The financial condition of released prisoners. Crime and
            Delinquency 21 (July): 266-81.

McCord, W., and J. McCord
    1956   Psychopathy and Delinquency. New York: Grune and
            Stratton.

McCorkle, L. W., and R. Korn
    1954   Resocialization within walls. The Annals of the American
            Academy of Political and Social Science 193 (May): 88-91.

Manocchio, A. J., and J. Dunn
    1970   The Time Game: Two Views of a Prison. New York:
            Delta-Dell.

Mathieson, T.
    1965   Defenses of the Weak: A Sociological Study of a Norwegian
            Correctional Institution. London: Tavistock.

Meyer, P. B.
    1976   Drug Experiments on Prisoners, Ethical, Economic or
            Exploitative? Lexington, Mass.: Lexington Books.

Miller, M. B.
    1974   At hard labor: rediscovering the 19th century prison.
            Issues in Criminology 9 (Spring): 91-114.

    1971   Manipulation of the disenfranchised: some notes on the
            ethical dilemma of experimentation using prisoner sub-
            jects. Unpublished paper, School of Criminology, Uni-
            versity of California, Berkeley.

Morris, N.
    1975   Lessons from the adult correctional system of Sweden.
            In Corrections: Problems and Perspectives, ed. D. M.
            Peterson and C. W. Thomas, pp. 279-98. Englewood
            Cliffs, N.J.: Prentice-Hall.

Morris, T., and P. Morris.
    1963   Pentonville: A Sociological Study of an English Prison.
            London: Routledge and Kegan Paul.

Murton, T., and J. Hyams
    1970   Accomplices to the Crime. New York: Grove Press.

Pell, E., ed.
    1973   Maximum Security: Letters from Prison. New York:
            E. P. Dutton.

Radford, R. A.
    1945   The economic organization of a P.O.W. camp. Economica
            (November): 189-201.

Rusche, G., and O. Kirchheimer
  1939   Punishment and Social Structure. New York: Russell &
         Russell.

Sands, B.
  1964   My Shadow Ran Fast. Englewood Cliffs, N.J.: Prentice-
         Hall.

Schelling, T. D.
  1967   Economic analysis of organized crime. In Task Force
         Report, Organized Crime. Washington, D.C.: The
         President's Commission on Law Enforcement, Adminis-
         tration of Justice.

Schilder, P.
  1944   Problems of crime. In Psychoanalysis Today, ed. S.
         Lorand, pp. 345-46. New York: International Universi-
         ties Press.

Schrag, C.
  1944   Social types in a prison community. Unpublished M.A.
         thesis, University of Washington, Seattle.

Scitovsky, T.
  1976   The Joyless Economy: An Inquiry into Human Satisfaction
         and Consumer Dissatisfaction. Oxford: Oxford University
         Press.

Sheldon, W. H.
  1949   Varieties of Delinquent Youth: An Introduction to Consti-
         tutional Psychology. New York: Harper.

Singer, N. M.
  1973   The value of adult inmate manpower. Paper presented
         at the Annual Meeting of the American Society of Crim-
         inology, Toronto, Canada, November.

Strange, H., and J. McCrory
  1974   Bulls and bears on the cell block. Society 11 (July-
         August): 51-59.

Sykes, G.
  1966   The Society of Captives. New York: Atheneum.

Sykes, G. , and S. L. Messinger
    1960   The inmate social system. In Theoretical Studies in the
           Social Organization of the Prison, ed. R. Cloward, pp.
           5-19. New York: Social Science Research Council.

Tabasz, T. F.
    1975   Toward an Economics of Prisons. Lexington, Mass.:
           Lexington Books.

Wheeler, S.
    1961   Socialization in correctional communities. American
           Sociology Review 26 (October): 697-712.

Williams, V. L. , and M. Fish
    1974   Convicts, Codes and Contraband: The Prison Life of
           Men and Women. Cambridge, Mass.: Ballinger.

Zimbardo, P. G.
    1972   Pathology of imprisonment. Society 9 (1972): 4, 6, 8.

9

INDUSTRIAL WAGES FOR PRISONERS
IN FINLAND AND SWEDEN
Peter Wickman

Two different types of industrial or production wage programs have emerged in the Nordic countries of Finland and Sweden. The labor colonies utilizing production wages for inmates emerged in Finland following World War II and thus have developed over a period of nearly three decades, while the payment of production wages to inmates was begun in Sweden, at Tillberga Institution, on an experimental basis in 1972.

The two types of programs vary as to the nature of the societies in which they are found, and they both represent the long-term reform efforts regarding social control that have characterized Nordic correctional systems in recent years. Yet, as is the case with many penal reforms, they represent only a small part of the conventional emphasis on social control in these two countries. They have emerged, however, over a period of time when both countries have been under short-term pressures to institute "law and order" social control policies (Antilla 1974: 9).

The description of these two programs is based largely upon observations made while on a study tour of Scandinavian correctional facilities in the fall of 1974. An attempt was made, through interviews with administrators, policy makers, planners, line staff, and inmates, to ascertain the goals of the various programs and how these were being followed in practice. This chapter then, might be regarded as consisting of informed impressions, somewhat refined by considerable discussion and hopefully untainted by reflection and reading. No attempt will be made here to draw comparisons between the United States and these two countries. This would involve too many variables. It is our contention, however, that even a cursory consideration of these two smaller, rather homogeneous societies, with the larger, heterogeneous United States makes manifest at least one common cultural theme: the work ethic. Leaving further comparisons to the speculative whims of the reader we wish to set forth the following hypotheses:

1. Production wages for offenders as utilized in these two Nordic countries are based on an adherence to the work ethic pervasive in these societies. To the extent that such programs promote a work ethic among their clientele they represent a viable means of reintegrating the offender into the social order of that society.

2. Although recidivism is not significantly lower among those released from open institutions utilizing industrial wages than among those released from closed prisons, such open prisons are nevertheless more economical in terms of benefits provided, both to inmates and society.

Sweden, which has just reached the 8 million mark in population, passed a new Penal Reform in 1974. Swedish penal policy is known for its reformist policies, inter alia ultra modern prisons, the treatment ideology (for example, indeterminate sentences), and a commitment to a work obligation for all able-bodied men (Wickman 1975). Although, according to one American scholar, much of the publicity about the innovative aspects of criminal care applies only to a few institutions and/or a small number of inmates (Ward 1972).

Finland, by virtue of historic ties, shares much of its legal tradition with Sweden, although in the area of criminal sanctions Finland has a more severe sentencing practice than the other Nordic countries. For instance, with about 60 percent of the population of Sweden, Finland had a rate of incarceration of 101 for each 100,000 residents, compared to 50 for each 100,000 for the larger country (Finland had a prison population of 4,706, August 1, 1974, whereas Sweden had 3,817).* It should be noted, however, that Finland was the first among the Nordic countries to abolish the preventive detention for "dangerous recidivists" (Antilla 1974: 9).

In describing the industrial wage programs for prison inmates in these two penal systems I will focus on the following areas of interest:

description of the ways in which such programs are different from
    the conventional security-oriented institution-based programs;
the populations they serve and the types of offenders selected for
    such programs;
the impact of such programs not only on recidivism but in terms of
  reintegration of the offender by virtue of maintaining or building
  ties with "free" society;
the relative cost of such programs.

---

*These figures, and others dealing with the Finnish prison system, were obtained from Kaarina Suomio, Research Office of the VanKeinhoito-osasto (Prison Administration) October 25, 1974.

THE FINNISH MODEL: LABOR COLONIES

The penal institutions called labor colonies emerged in basically their present form in 1946 when there was a shortage of labor in Finland in many sectors of production. In a large part, then, the rationale was economic, but there also was a need to protect certain types of short-term offenders--for example, drunk drivers--from the harsher effects of prison life. These labor colonies present somewhat of a paradox when compared with conventional Finnish prisons, which were the mainstay of the system until the Reform Penal Care Law took effect July 1, 1975--from that date, the emphasis was on production wages throughout the prison system. In the conventional prisons the emphasis is on custody, and, except for scale, the architecture of these prisons is similar to maximum-security institutions in North America. (It should be noted that prison furloughs are available to prisoners in all Finnish prisons, including the labor colonies, except for those 14 incarcerated as dangerous recidivists.)

An important objective of the Finnish prison system is the "normalization" of prison life. As R. J. Långe, the present director, recently stated:

By normalization of imprisonment I mean that in carrying out the sentence the aim is to make the various subfunctions of the term of imprisonment as similar as possible to conditions outside. . . . These sub-functions can be grouped around work categories (or studies), leisure and rest. (Långe 1974: 8)

Work is and has been of prime importance in conventional Finnish prisons, and this work ethic is obvious also in the labor colonies. Lest the reader make an unfair association of the phrase "labor colonies" with Soviet forced-labor camps, it should be noted that Finnish informants took vigorous exception to Conrad's assertion that they are drawn from the Soviet model (Conrad 1970: 121). In fact, they differ drastically from such a model, as they differ from conventional prisons. In conventional prisons the ratio of guards to inmates is about one to four, in the labor colonies there are no guards as such. Likewise, there are no bars or outer walls, and inmates wear their own civilian clothes. Social distance is lessened somewhat in that staff refer to the inmates as "workers." Contacts outside the institution are made easier since there are no restrictions on correspondence, and family visits are allowed each weekend.

Perhaps an overview of the six labor colonies visited would best illustrate the living conditions of the workers, as well as the

types of work in which they are involved. Suomenlinni, located on
an island ten minutes by boat from Helsinki, is a 30-year project
begun in 1971. Here, under the technical direction of the National
Board of Antiquities and Historical Monuments, 84 workers with 20
prison staff are restoring the fortifications and buildings of this
eighteenth-century fortress. The refurbished barracks are being
turned into modern flats, which will be rented to private citizens.
Sipoo is an isolated farmstead where 17 workers are away working
in the forest, supervised by a civilian, while the lone prison staffer
is mulling over workers' accounts. The workers live in a barracks
near the farmhouse where the meals are prepared. Savijärvi is
located by the side of one of the highways leading from Helsinki.
The 66 workers are off working on a highway construction project,
supervised by civilian highway engineers. They live in four barracks, similar to those at Suomenlinni, except these are moved to
new locations as the construction progresses. A staff of seven,
including a bookkeeper, supervises their living area, which is separated from the area occupied by civilian workers by a low fence.
Helsinki Airport and Tikkurila colonies are combined in a large
wooded area adjacent to Helsinki International Airport. Here 230
workers are engaged, half in building a new runway and the other
group in highway construction. They live in the same type barracks
--about 20 to each building. Röykka labor colony is located in a
forested area several hours from Helsinki. Here 18 workers are
running a rather sophisticated sawmill owned by the Forestry Service, while the others cut timber. These six labor colonies are all
under the direction of the Helsinki local prison. One other labor
colony was recently established at Hameenlinna several hundred
kilometers inland. In all, the six labor colonies have a population
of 419 workers. They are supervised by a prison staff totaling 36,
or a staff-inmate ratio of about one to ten.

　　Each of these camps is a self-contained unit in that it has its
own recreation area and dining room, where meals are prepared by
civilian cooks and served to both prison workers and their civilian
coworkers. And of course each colony has its own sauna.

　　Work is outside the perimeter and prison and civilians work
side by side. The men work from 7:00 to 11:00 a.m., and from
12:00 p.m. to 4:00 p.m. They are paid market wages, that is, minimum trade union rates, plus in many instances, piece rates. The
prison administration deducts 25 percent from the worker's base
pay for lodging, laundry, sauna baths, and the like. State and municipal taxes are also deducted, as are family allotments, and
savings of 10 percent are imposed on those who do not have to pay
for more than one dependent. Anything left is for the worker to
spend on himself. One timber worker's account we looked at in

Sipoo labor colony showed a gross income for that month of M2,319 (the markka was worth about $.266). After savings and other deductions he had about M1,029.04, or $273.72 for his own use. From this biweekly amount he pays for meals.

Obviously, then, those 10 percent of the prison population sentenced to these labor colonies are much better off financially than those in the conventional prisons, who are paid about F1 an hour. And, although his out-of-work activities are greatly restricted, his work day is somewhat "normalized."

Prisoners assigned to the labor colonies represent a select category relative to the length of sentence, criminality, and work skills. Specifically, they are drawn from those first offenders serving two years or less, or recidivists with five years between time of last sentence and beginning of the present one. Over 60 percent of those sentenced in 1974 were drunk drivers, and the remaining categories were property offenders and white-collar criminals. About 40 percent came directly from the community. They are given time to set their affairs in order after receiving sentence and before given a bus ticket to the labor colony. The majority, however, are transferred from closed prisons. (Over the 27 years that the labor colonies have been in existence about 70 percent of those eligible applied for such a sentence. About one-third of these were accepted.)

The average age ranges from 18 to 37 years and the average sentence from three to five months. At one camp I noted two representative examples: a 33-year-old driving teacher was serving three months for drunk driving, and an 18-year-old youth was serving nine months for breaking and entering. The average length of sentence in Finland is six months.

How effective are the labor colonies? Recidivism rates may not be the best long-range measure of the effectiveness of a prison term; still, they constitute a direct measure of one of the objectives of the penal sanction, the prevention of new violations.* A cohort of 298 offenders assigned to labor colonies in 1949--but who "did their time" in closed prisons, since the labor colonies were closed due to unfavorable labor market conditions--was compared with 308 men sentenced and serving time in labor colonies in 1950 and 1951.

---

*The rate of escape or "walk aways" from the labor colonies was minimal--two had none, the other four had less than 1 percent. If this occurred, however, or if other severe infraction of rules against repeated drunkenness or fighting took place, they were returned to the closed prison where they began serving their time again, with no credit for time spent in the labor colony.

Using a ten-year follow-up and the Wilkins-Mannheim method, Uusitalo (1968) was unable to find any statistically significant difference in reconviction rates for the two populations. The recidivism rates for ten years after discharge were:

	Percent
Closed prisons	27
Labor colonies	31

In another, less-controlled comparative study of Scandinavian penal institutions in the 1960s, Cline found that a large labor colony in Finland had the lowest antistaff score among the 15 institutions surveyed. On this one index of prisonization, it seems that labor colonies are worth the cost (Cline 1968: 177-79).

What is the relative cost of such programs, both in terms of direct and indirect socioeconomic benefits? Since the budgets of labor colonies have been combined with those of the closed prisons during the 1970s, it was not possible to separate recent figures for expenditures from that of closed prisons. Relying on Uusitalo's earlier study, however, a crucial difference was found in favor of labor camps. The average daily cost to the prison administration, for each inmate, was almost $5 less for the labor camps (Uusitalo 1968: 18). Assuming that this differential remains relatively stable, the prison administration, in cost-benefit terms alone, saved nearly half of its daily cost of $11.01 for each inmate on those 800 sentenced to the labor colonies.

The savings would be even greater if the M25 million paid out to the ministry of transport for machinery and pay for overseers could be balanced against income. Unfortunately, there are no price tags on items such as highway and airport construction and restoration of a fortress for a national monument. Added to these benefits is the support provided families, which decreases the need for social welfare assistance for the dependents of those in labor colonies. From the point of view of socioeconomic benefits it is possible to utilize the labor colony worker more effectively than the inmate of a closed prison. And the indirect costs of prisons are also higher, not to mention the well-known harmful effects of prisons on those incarcerated.

INDUSTRIAL WAGES IN A SWEDISH PRISON:
THE TILLBERGA MODEL

A statement attributed by John Conrad to Torsten Eriksson-- former director of the Kriminalvardsstryelsen (National Correction

Administration), who has done much in his role at the United Nations
to draw attention to the reform efforts of that penal system--also
underscores the work ethos emphasized in Swedish prisons. "First
we build a factory, then alongside of it we build a prison. All Swedes
have to work in order to live and prisoners should be no exception.
They should work to build a better Sweden and they should work to
preserve and increase their skills" (Conrad 1970: 250). The production wage experiment for prison labor, begun at Tillberga in
November 1972, epitomizes this work ethic.

Tillberga is a modern prison built in 1963. It resembles, and
is more comparable to, a modern Swedish factory with an adjacent
compound for its workers. Within the compound, which like the
factory is surrounded by a fence about 15 meters high, are located
the single-story dormitories for the workers, the administration
building, kitchen, and a gymnasium complete with an indoor tennis
court, and the like. Each living unit houses 24 inmates who have
their own rooms and a key to insure privacy. Each unit has a combined lounge and dining area where the men are served their meals.
The gates to the living area, and to the factory, are open during the
daytime. The guard staff and operations center is located in the
administration building to the left of the gate. The institution has
places for 120 inmates, but, as other Swedish prisons in the fall of
1974, it was underpopulated; its population was down to 60 inmates.

I was met by Owe Sandberg, the project director, who is a
psychologist on the Kriminalvårdsstryelsen staff in Stockholm. He
served as my guide during the tour of the administration building,
where I was introduced to the social assistants (social workers)--
who later briefed me on their duties--and the director, Erik Lenhov.
We toured the living area and I was introduced to Lars Eric, chairman of the Inmates Advisory Council, which is called Club Futura
at Tillberga. Lars Eric was my guide through the factory. During
the course of the day I talked with several other inmates, including
the former chairman of the Advisory Council, and renewed acquaintances with several inmates I had met the previous month at
Gruvberget, the vacation village in Northern Sweden. The Advisory
Council seems to be an important network between the inmates and
both the local and national prison administrations. They recently
have negotiated a pay raise of Kr2.60 an hour (the krona exchange
rate was $.2276 in October 1974). Earlier, at the beginning of the
experiment, they had gained the concession of a special leave, the
"Tillberga furlough" from the Kriminalvårdsstryelsen. This was
a special furlough granted once a month to the inmates, in addition
to the regular monthly furlough. Furthermore, the inmate was
eligible to receive the furlough from the second month after his
residency at Tillberga rather than after the fourth month, as in

other prisons. Should the inmate have to travel any great distance
the Kriminalvårdsstryelsen subsidizes his travel. Lars Eric informed me that he received Kr200 a month to underwrite his two
trips to Goteborg.

The factory has two divisions. The metal products division
employs about 20 men, supervised by a foreman and four specialists;
however, it is not as rationalized as the woodworking division. This
division can employ about 80 men. It produces prefabricated houses,
at the rate of three a day at top production, but in October they were
producing nine a week. These houses come in 15 basic models and
are sold on the open market by the Nyckelhus Company. I asked
one of the inmates, and later the project director, "Who gets the
profit from the houses?" Both gave identical replies, "The
Nyckelhus Company." The men are paid minimum wages less one-
third, since no taxes are deducted (by special arrangement with the
Ministry of Finance). Starting rate for production workers is Kr6.20
($1.41) an hour. After the first two weeks they get a raise and go
on piecework, where they can make as high as Kr14.53 ($3.31) an
hour. Lars Eric receives Kr12 ($2.73) an hour for a white-collar,
clerical-type job. He orders all the small parts for the houses, a
task formerly done by a civilian and an inmate clerk. Nonproduc-
tion workers--that is, cooks, cleaning men, and the like--receive
Kr8 ($1.82) an hour.

Budget planning is an integral part of the program at Tillberga.
Each man is required to make out a budget, in consultation with the
social assistants, during his first two days. The several assistants
discussed this process emphasizing its importance and their thor-
oughness. The inmate is allowed to keep 25 percent of his earnings,
but the rest is budgeted. He must set aside Kr300 for his furlough,
and arrange for monthly payments on fines, damages (for law violations), and other debts. He is also responsible for purchasing his
own meals. Should the inmate have faulty memory regarding how
much he owes for these items, a social assistant checks with an
agency that keeps a record of such debts. The most he is expected
to pay on such debts is Kr400. The average pay is about Kr1,600,
so he is encouraged to save and send money to his wife or girlfriend.
Tillberga income is not deducted from Social Service payments,
should his family be on welfare. "The meaning of the experience,"
I was told, "is not that he support his wife . . . [but] that he learn
to earn money and spend it wisely."

Productivity and its rewards are the name of the game at
Tillberga. Commitment to the work ethic was evidenced by the
following comments:

Lars Eric's response, when I asked why the Advisory
Council did not meet during work hours: "We could, but

you see," pointing at his desk, "I have too much work to
do." A foreman asked a Kriminalvårdsstryelsen official
"Do workers outside have time off for group therapy?"
The director answered, "Work is the best treatment we
have--therapy should be used as a complement to work."
A man 20 years of age, serving a youth term, had
transferred to Tillberga but wanted to go back. Said he:
"Men here are not interested in talking, just in their
work and what they are going to do on furlough. They
are not together here."

How are the men selected? To be eligible they must be suit-
able for placement in an open institution, fit for work, and interested
in industrial work. They must also be willing to cooperate with the
staff to put their finances in order. Over the first two years of the
experiment about 700 men applied and about 40 percent were accepted.
Inmates have transferred to Tillberga from closed prisons such as
Kumla and Österåker. A few are assigned directly. The average
stay is four and a half months, compared to the average sentence of
two months in Sweden. Lars was serving six years and hoped to get
off at half or two-thirds time.

How effective has the Tillberga experiment been? There have
been no studies comparable to that carried out by Uusitalo in Finland.
But a one-year follow-up had just been completed of the 63 men released in the spring and summer of 1973 (there were no escapes or
"walk aways" from Tillberga). Eight of these had been returned to
prison, a recidivism rate of 13 percent. Four of these had requested
to be transferred to Tillberga--the greatest advantage seen was the
extra weekend leave they received (the number "messing up" on
furlough was only 4 percent, compared with 10 percent in other
prisons). The concept of production wage was generally received
favorably, but some thought they had worked too hard for the money
received (they are employed as carpenters, truck drivers, welders,
and clerks). The general reaction was positive, however.

Generally, then, the results are favorable, so much so, from
the point of view of the Kriminalvårdsstryelsen, that plans were
under way to adapt production wages to a closed prison. At Skogome
prison workers who provide laundry service to outside hospitals were
to have gone on production wages by January 1975. Perhaps an interesting study of production wage results in a closed prison compared with those of an open prison will be forthcoming.

The cost of Tillberga is considerable when compared with U.S.
standards, or even with the labor colonies. But it should be noted
that in Sweden the cost of maintaining an inmate averages about
$12,000 a year. The small number of inmates at Tillberga, com-
prising only about 2 percent of the prison population, contribute

more than their share of the Kr70 million income garnered by the
Kriminalvårdsstryelsen in 1973 (out of a total budget of Kr459 million). Also, prisoners in Tillberga are paying part of their cost of
maintenance--such as, food--while those in other institutions receive Kr2 an hour and make no such contribution. If social benefits
are considered, then it would seem that inmates at Tillberga are
helping to build a "better Sweden," at least in the area of housing.
While society is profiting financially from goods produced, it is also
doubtless benefiting from the lessening of stigma due to penal sanction. As Lars Eric stated, "I'm just like any other man, I work
and I go home twice a month to visit my family and friends."

With their penchant for experimentation in correctional programs, the Swedes have developed a rather sophisticated model
within which prisoners are paid production wages. Obviously, this
model would be considered too costly for wide adaptability to other
systems; and it would not be adaptable to the large-scale maximum
security prisons in the United States. However, the less costly,
and less sophisticated, Finnish model seems to have greater potential for adaptation to North America. It certainly suggests an
alternative form of sanction for the many thousands of misdemeanants
sitting in our jails.

Both of these models rely on--and reflect, to some extent--the
work ethic of their respective culture. Both provide more equitable
remuneration for work provided by the sentenced offender. Work is
thus more meaningful, within the context of such economic benefits
to the prisoner, and such programs may very well lessen the effects
of prisonization. The economic and social benefits may far outweigh
their costs. Since it cannot be argued that the pay-off is greater in
terms of recidivism, such industrial prison programs might serve
as viable models at least to the conservative reformer. It should
be noted that neither the Finnish labor colonies nor Tillberga make
any pretense at vocational training. That is, they both select capable
men who are willing and able to work. Their value, then, is for
those offenders already somewhat integrated with society. For these
men they provide a means for continuing and strengthening a work
capability and ethic that they already possess. The situation for the
many unemployables in maximum security in Finland, or for the
nearly 400 recidivists serving indeterminate sentences in Sweden,
remains unchanged. Thus, although the two models present viable
examples of alternatives to incarceration in closed prisons, they do
not alter the fate of those incarcerated in other institutions--partic-
ularly those without work skills.

A final caveat. Both these societies share an awareness of
the reality that modern industrial societies operate under within a
mixed economy. They do not pay lip service to the myth that "pure"
capitalism exists. This seems to be an important state of awareness

that will have to be attained before the United States can move toward the utilization of industrial wages in our penal systems.

REFERENCES

Andenaes, J.
    1968   The legal framework. In Scandinavian Studies in Criminology, ed. N. Christie, vol. 2. London: Tavistock.

Anttila, I.
    1974   Current Scandinavian Criminology and Crime Control. Helsinki: Research Institute of Legal Policy.

    1971   Conservative and radical criminal policy in the Nordic countries. In Scandinavian Studies in Criminology, ed. N. Christie, vol. 3. Oslo: Universitetforlaget.

Cline, H. F.
    1968   The determinants of normative patterns in correctional institutions. In Scandinavian Studies in Criminology, ed. N. Christie, vol. 2. London: Tavistock.

Conrad, J.
    1970   Crime and Its Correction. Berkeley and Los Angeles: University of California Press.

Långe, R. J.
    1974   Penalization and sanctions. Paper presented at the conference, "Carcerce Societa," Venice, Italy.

Uusitalo, P.
    1968   Recidivism after release from closed and open penal institutions. Unpublished paper (English translation), Helsinki.

Ward, D.
    1972   Inmate rights in Sweden and Denmark. Journal of Criminal Law, Criminology and Police Science 63: 240-55.

Wickman, P.
    1975   Criminal Care in Sweden: Impressions of a Visiting Sociologist. Translated into Swedish and forthcoming in Kriminalvård. Stockholm: Kriminalvårdsstryelsen.

10

THE "MENTALLY DISORDERED OFFENDER":
A CAPTIVE OF THE STATE?
Renée Goldsmith-Kasinsky

INTRODUCTION

We are witnessing the emergence of the conflict perspective in the study of deviance and crime. The power conflict model of criminal behavior challenges the apolitical, value-free perspective. This model views crime as a natural phenomenon and social conflict that must be viewed within a socioeconomic framework in relation to the political power of the state. In the mid-1960s the labeling perspective of deviant behavior made a breakthrough in enabling us to see that the categories of deviance were a product of agencies of social control rather than a characteristic of the individual so labeled. Howard Becker, a major proponent of this perspective, defined deviance in terms of the relationship between the rule makers and the rule breakers.

> Social groups create deviance by making the rules whose infraction constitutes deviance and by applying those rules to particular people and labeling them as outsiders. From this point of view, deviance is not a quality of the act the person commits, but rather a consequence of the application by others of rules and sanctions to an "offender." The deviant is one to whom that label has successfully been applied: deviant behavior is behavior that people so label. (Becker 1963: 9)

Seen from the perspective of labeling, this paradigm of deviant behavior is as much a political issue as it is a sociological or criminological one.

The radical theorists have recently taken a further step in making more explicit the nature of the social conflict. * They argue that deviance is only rule violation in the limited sense, that it involves violating the rules in the context of relative power. This power is derived mainly from the mandate to define others into categories that make them subject to the operations of the definers. In our society the law is usually viewed as an instrument for curbing nonconformity. However, the law also can be seen as functioning to create and define criminality and deviance. The application of the law by the ascription of motives and deviant labels is indicative of the dominant conceptions of deviance that are held at any one time by the rulers or powerful members of the society (Taylor, Taylor 1970: 77).

Liazos (1972) utilizes the term "covert institutional violence" to characterize those forms of oppression that the ruling class utilizes to control socially powerless groups in our society. The therapeutic or medical model implemented through the instrument of institutional psychiatry is one method, according to Szasz (1970: 67), of keeping poor persons in a childlike state and depriving them of all civil rights and human dignity. From this point of view, "mental illness" as a social fact is brought about by the institutionalized practices of psychiatric agencies and institutions. They are utilized by those in power for the social control of particular powerless groups in the society. It is important for a thorough understanding of deviance and criminal behavior to document the power conflict and the role of the state in creating deviance, using specific empirical case studies.

In this chapter we will see how this form of covert institutional violence is being utilized to keep a class of those persons labeled as mentally disordered offenders in a security wing of a provincial mental hospital in British Columbia in a state of preventive detention through the use of civil commitment procedures and an indeterminate sentence.[†] This label is applied by the rule

---

*For a radical perspective on deviance, see I. Taylor, Walton, and Young (1973) and other articles published by them that grew out of the English National Deviancy Conference. Also, see A. Platt (1974).

[†]The data for this study were obtained in 1973 while the author was a consultant to the Health Security Programme Project, which undertook an examination of the total health care system in British Columbia. For a review of the literature in the field as well as specific recommendations, see Goldsmith-Kasinsky (1974: chaps. 4, 5).

makers in the context of a power conflict. I will analyze these commitment procedures and the implications of the indeterminate sentence for the "total institution" as well as for the inmates. The
ideological underpinnings of the therapeutic model and the interest
group it serves will be explored.

In British Columbia the person classified as a mentally disordered offender finds himself in a no-man's-land, cast between the
authority of the attorney general's Department and that of the Ministry of Health. The label "criminally insane" is misleading. Most
of these offenders have not even been convicted of their alleged criminal offense. For example, 92 percent (N = 88) of the order-in-
council inmates were detained at Riverview Hospital in the Lower
Mainland of British Columbia between 1922 and 1973 (on medical
evidence) and have never stood trial to determine their guilt or innocence.* Only seven persons were detained as incompetent to
stand trial by judicial determination; the rest were judged to be mentally incompetent and committed. Murderers spend 11 years in jail
on the average; but a plea of "not guilty by reason of insanity" could
bring an indeterminate sentence resulting in life imprisonment.
This state of affairs is more reminiscent of Lewis Carroll's Through
the Looking Glass than it is of a modern social institution.

> There's the King's messenger. He's in prison now,
> being punished: and the trial doesn't even begin til
> next Wednesday and of course the crime comes last
> of all.

And what is the crime? Why, being declared criminally insane, of
course. That crime comes last of all.

---

*Since the fieldwork for this article, there has been a major
policy reversal on the issue of accused persons held in Riverside indefinitely, on the strength of a cabinet order without due process of
law. This policy change resulted from the outcome of a test court
case on behalf of J. John Sayle in March 1974. Justice F. Craig
Munroe granted Sayle a writ of habeas corpus, ruling that his confinement contravened the Canadian Bill of Rights and Criminal Code.
Munroe ruled that every person has the right "not to be deprived of
his liberty except by due process of law" (Ex Parte Sayle 1974, 18ccc
56 [S. C.]). After the Sayle decision, the Department of the Attorney
General has instigated court proceedings to determine fitness to
stand trial. Yet, in many ways, in the opinion of the author, these
legal deliberations resemble a kangaroo court.

Kenneth Donaldson, who spent 15 years involuntarily incarcerated in Florida State Hospital, prompted a landmark United States Supreme Court ruling on behalf of mental patients. According to Donaldson, "My disease was that I refused to admit that I was ill. From what I've seen and heard, that is the worst disease you can have--refusing to admit that you have a disease" (Time Magazine 1975). In the O'Connor v. Donaldson case, the Supreme Court declared that a state may not "fence in the harmless mentally ill solely to save its citizens from exposure to those whose ways are different" (O'Connor v. Donaldson 1975). This decision is indicative of the recent judicial rulings in the United States in the past decade that support the patient's constitutional rights to both receive and refuse treatment. It may have major implications for those U.S. state mental institutions holding approximately 750,000 patients, half of whom were originally committed without their own consent (New York Times 1974).

The United States Supreme Court ruled that every mental patient in the United States who is held involuntarily has the right to be either treated or released. "A finding of 'mental illness' alone cannot justify a state's locking a person up against his will and keeping him indefinitely in simple custodial confinement," wrote Justice Potter Stewart in the Donaldson case. * Critical questions remain to be answered by future cases, such as, What constitutes adequate treatment? and What are considered fair standards for commitment?

PREVENTIVE DETENTION FOR SOCIAL NUISANCES

Let us take a closer look at these persons who are confined in the Riverside unit by an executive order-in-council and labeled by psychiatrists and correctional authorities as "mentally disordered offenders." The senior medical staff have described Riverview Hospital as part of the community dumping syndrome, and the Riverside Security Unit for the criminally insane is Riverview's "port of last resort" according to the head nurse. Originally, mental hospitals like Riverview were more accurately referred to as poorhouses. The disproportionately high number of patients who are poor, uneducated, and of minority status suggests differential enforcement of the commitment procedures against those of the lower class,

---

*The background to Donaldson's case is detailed by his lawyer, Bruce Ennis (1972: chap. 5). Donaldson describes his experience in his book, Insanity Inside Out (1976).

since there is no hard evidence that mental illness occurs less frequently among those of the upper class.

The types of charges of order-in-council inmates also support this thesis. The vast majority of charges included those of breaking and entering, theft, mischief, and other lesser offenses such as vagrancy. A large percentage of these persons have never been tried for these charges; the others have been found not guilty by reason of insanity.

The net effect of the total system seems to be to detain and hold in custody at Riverside, for an indeterminate period, society's social nuisances. Interestingly enough, this finding is similar to what has been pointed out as the chief consequence of Canada's habitual offender legislation in terms of the characteristic population entrapped in its net (Klein 1973: 421-23). A review of the issues involving the use of the therapeutic model will shed some light on how this system works.

THE THERAPEUTIC MODEL: USE AND ABUSE
OF THE INDETERMINATE SENTENCE

An analysis of the historical and philosophical roots of the therapeutic model and its enforcement through the use of the indeterminate sentence will allow us to understand, within a broader theoretical framework, the functions and malfunctions of the present system in British Columbia.

The therapeutic model is to a large extent replacing the criminal model as the major system of social control for particular deviant groups.

Traditionally, the criminal law has been the major power of the state for enforcing conformity upon those who refused or were unable to abide by it. In its origins, however, the criminal law failed to differentiate among the various classes of nonconformist. To be poor, to beg in public, or to be mentally abnormal was as much of an offense as to commit a violent crime. All those charged with deviant status or acts were grouped together for equal treatment in the criminal process.

In recent years, however, there has been a formidable departure from the use of criminal penalties and sanctions as the major system of social control for particular deviant groups. In its place has been substituted a different model of control, described as "civil" or "therapeutic." Within this system, little or no emphasis is placed upon an individual's guilt for a particular crime, but much weight is given to his/her physical, mental, or social shortcomings. In dealing with the deviant under this new system, the state is said to be acting in a parental role or "parens patriae"--a term derived from the English concept of the King's role as father of the country. The therapeutic model seeks not to punish but rather to change or to socialize the nonconformist through treatment and therapy.

Therapeutic Model	Criminal Model
Little emphasis on individual guilt	Individual guilt
Emphasis on criminal actor's mental or social problems	Emphasis on criminal law and crime committed regardless of actor involved
State acting in parens patriae to socialize criminal through treatment	State sanctions criminal in form of punishment

Since the emergence of the therapeutic revolution beginning with the use of juvenile court, there has been what Nicholas Kittrie (1971: 4) has described as a "process of divestment" whereby criminal law has been relinquishing its jurisdiction and sanction over many of its traditional subjects--namely, the drug addict, the juvenile, the alcoholic, and the mental patient. This process of divestment has not been motivated, on the whole, by societal willingness to begin tolerating the conduct or condition previously designated as criminal, but by a new shift of societal concerns. Divestment has been carried out in the name of the new social emphasis upon therapy, rehabilitation, and prevention--as contrasted with the criminal law's emphasis upon retribution, incapacitation, and deterrence.

That the concept of treatment has not been completely motivated by benevolent intentions is widely recognized. J. W. Mohr, sociologist of the Canadian Law Reform Commission, introduced a workshop in Toronto on the "Philosophy and Empirical Justifications of the Treatment of Criminals in the Penal Process" by warning us:

> Let us not forget that treatment in the criminal justice system is an afterthought to cover up the embarrassment we are left with, when the use of capital punishment declined, when corporal punishment and deportation dried up. Prisons and other holding institutions are historically clearly the outcome of this process, since if you can neither kill people nor shame them or send them away, the only avenue that is left is to hold them somewhere and do nothing. . . .

> On this continent, from the early Quaker and
> Auburn systems, treatment meant no more than the ap-
> plication of current ideologies. Although there was
> much good will and good intention in all these develop-
> ments, the basic element of "bad faith" was never
> squarely faced and the problem of ambiguity and am-
> bivalence remains as one of the consistent features in
> the "treatment of criminals." (Mohr 1972)

The increasing function of the state in this contradictory
parens patriae role raises serious questions regarding both the
conceptual framework of the therapeutic state and the procedural
safeguards that apply to the exercise of the state's parens patriae
powers. Psychiatrist Thomas Szasz has been the most searing
critic of his own psychiatric fraternity. "The impediment I want to
consider is restraint on persons exercised by psychiatrists by virtue of the powers vested in them by laws. For those oppressed by
psychiatrists, liberty means freedom from psychiatric coercion"
(1964: 67). From the point of view of the legal profession, Nicholas
Kittrie raises the fundamental issue of the basic balance between
society's right to protect and improve itself and its members
through preventive measures and the individual's right to be different and to be left alone. The use of the indeterminate sentence
speaks to this basic dilemma.

The Indeterminate Sentence

The enforced-treatment philosophy of the therapeutic model
was structured on the basis of the indeterminate sentence. Sentences would not be fixed at commitment, but would be based upon
an inmate's "progress." Proponents of the indeterminate sentence
have linked it to the concept of rehabilitation.

However, even when it was first proposed in the nineteenth
century, its use as a potent psychological instrument for inmate
manipulation and control was recognized. At the 1870 meeting of
the First American Prison Congress, Z. R. Brockway, warden of
the Detroit House of Correction and a leading penologist of his day,
proposed the indeterminate sentence as a progressive step forward
for "the protection of society by the prevention of crime and the
reformation of criminals." While ardently proclaiming the humanitarian aims of this system, prison administrators never lost sight
of its punitive value. Warden Brockway (who was eventually relieved
of his post for excessive corporal punishment) wrote in the American
Reformatory System:

> The indeterminateness of the sentence breeds discon-
> tent, breeds purposefulness and prompts to a new ex-
> ertion. Captivity, always irksome, is now increas-
> ingly so because of the uncertainty of its duration;
> because the duty and responsibility of shortening it
> and of modifying any undesirable present condition of
> it devolves upon the prisoner himself, and again, by
> the active exactions of the standards and criteria to
> which he must attain. (Mitford 1974: 81-82)

In the past two decades, the indeterminate sentence coupled
with treatment has been carried to its greatest sophistication in the
state of California. In her study of U.S. prisons, many of which
were in California, Jessica Mitford described the indeterminate
sentence as "the perfect prescription for at once securing compli-
ance and crushing defiance, because the prisoner is in for the maximum term and it is theoretically up to him to shorten the time
served" (1974: 82). In order to oversee the fixing of release dates
and the remodeling of prison behavior, California in 1944 created
the Adult Authority. This panel of "skilled experts in human behavior" alone has the discretionary powers to judge prisoners'
progress and set release dates for prisoners with no interference
from prisoners and no right of appeal. The Adult Authority's reputation for arbitrary use and abuse of their enormous discretionary
powers are well documented (Irwin 1970).

In the 1970s the effects of the indeterminate sentence have
taken their toll in California--in unusually long prison sentences
and widespread violence, sometimes culminating in death. * After
being heralded with such hope only two decades earlier, the indeterminate sentence is now being questioned by scholars, administrators, and inmates alike. Since 1969 many of the treatment programs
have been abandoned. The main reason for present disillusionment
with the therapeutic model is that the inmates regard it as a form of
"cruel and unusual punishment." As John Irwin, exconvict and
author of The Felon put it, indeterminate confinement is "a grand
hypocrisy in which custodial concerns, administrative exigencies
and punishments are all disguised as treatment" (1970: 51).

---

*It was at O-Wing, the Soledad Prison Adjustment Center, that
the 1970 slaying of black inmates serving an indeterminate sentence
gave rise to the Soledad Brothers case and the bloody chain of events
surrounding George Jackson (Jackson was serving an indeterminate
term for robbery).

Consequences of the Indeterminate Sentence
for the Inmates in British Columbia

A leading California forensic psychiatrist, Bernard Diamond
(1962: 203), referring to California hospitals such as Atascadero,
comments, "Such hospitals for the criminally insane may often be
only prisons in disguise--barbaric institutions operating under a
false front of medical responsibility in which there is not even a
pretense of adequate therapy." The functions of Riverside unit in
British Columbia can best be understood beginning with this basic
assumption.

From the perspective of those persons who feel they are
languishing away abandoned as deadwood in Riverside, there are no
euphemisms that can shelter them from the reality of their experiences. For them, it is not a hospital but a prison; they are
not patients but prisoners, prisoners who are sentenced to an indeterminate period on the grounds that they might be dangerous to
society. These persons, who have not received any judicial verdict,
feel that they are on a merry-go-round of commitment, medication,
discharge, bail, cessation of medication, relapse, and recommit-
ment.

The inmates of Riverside unit conducted their own two-hour
meeting (never before done in the history of this institution) specifically to inform me of how they experienced their confinement
and the failings of the system. The moderator of the meeting
poignantly summed up their sentiment in a nutshell:

> I would have much preferred to go to the penitentiary.
> They got a parole system and you know what you're
> striving for. Here you're striving for something but
> you never know whether it exists or not, you see, and
> this can destroy one's mind. You get like a dog chas-
> ing his tail. Eventually you just lay down and say to
> hell with it. I'm not chasing it no more. And this is
> what some of them do.
>   I've seen men hang themselves here--very,
> very close friends of mine. And there's no need for
> it. Absolutely no need. It's because there's no pro-
> gram for them. They feel that they're just going on
> in a vicious circle. And there's just no way out of it
> for them. . . . And the environment--looking at men
> who have been here 30, 35 years.

This inmate has served eight years in Riverside. He is attempting
to support his wife and three children and keep them off welfare by

selling copper artwork, which he does as a "hobby." He is not allowed to go off grounds on weekends to visit with his family, although he is living in an open ward.

These men feel like Kafkaesque characters; men to whom no
clear-cut social standards are applicable. They suffer from a supposed mental disorder and are indefinitely committed for an offense,
often unproved, that would impose only a mild sentence on others.
They feel they are being unjustly held captive and hold a cynical
view toward the so-called treatment rationale given to them by their
bureaucratic administrators. Their psychiatrist is placed in the
position of both judge and jury. Such administrative procedures
make a mockery of justice and rehabilitation.

This is precisely why Szasz likens institutional psychiatry
practiced on those involuntarily confined to mental hospitals to the
inquisition movement. He agrees with Diamond that hospitalization
for mental illness is worse punishment than imprisonment in the
penitentiary.* The degraded status of being labeled a mentally disordered offender is deeply felt by the majority of inmates at Riverside. An inmate summed up the insidious control of the institution
over him in a letter to me:

> I am a foreign born, Hungarian, 1924, Canadian citi-
> zen with good references. I have no police records.
> A crime was committed against me, resulting to
> psychiatric captivity by miscarriage of justice. Be-
> ing sentenced by Order-in-Council for an indeter-
> minate period for threatening. I was unable to find
> legal remedy since 1968. I had no interest to be men-
> tally ill and I was never mentally ill. I was harmed by
> unwanted psychiatric intervention.

In the early 1950s the treatment model, first tested on California inmates, held some promise for them. However, by the
late 1960s disillusionment had already set in. Inmates recognize

---

*Szasz (1965) details the consequences of being an involuntary
patient. "He suffers a serious loss of civil rights. In many jurisdictions he is automatically considered legally incompetent: He
cannot vote, make valid contracts, marry, divorce. . . . [He]
must suffer invasions of his person and body, cannot communicate
freely with the outside world, usually loses his license to operate
a motor vehicle, and suffers many other indignities as well."

that treatment programs are a sham and are just another way of exercising total control over their behavior. The view it fosters of them as "sick patients" makes it difficult for them to maintain any dignity and self-respect.

Like most hospitals and prisons in North America, those of British Columbia cannot boast of genuine treatment programs. They are merely custodial institutions that make use of rehabilitation rhetoric.

CIVIL COMMITMENT PROCEDURES AND
HOW THEY WORK IN CANADA

The mentally disordered offender is created by the application of new types of "borderline" commitment procedures and sanctions that are lodged between civil and criminal law. Let us now examine some of these procedures to see how the state begins to exert social control over this category of persons.

The mentally disordered offender is likely to move into a medical process, or out of it, in a fairly haphazard manner. A determination of competency to stand trial or determination of civil commitment are two separate measures that may be initiated by the state. These measures do not require the defendant's acquiescence, and may bring them commitment for an indeterminate period. Proceedings for the determination of competency to stand trial are already being used to a disturbing degree as instruments of preventive detention. They may be used against persons whose offenses are so minor that they would never think of raising the insanity defense on their own behalf and who may not even be sufficiently ill or sufficiently dangerous to warrant civil commitment. Law enforcement agencies are increasingly utilizing civil commitment processes to deal with those they label as mentally ill, sexual psychopaths, defective delinquents, narcotic addicts, and alcoholics.

In Canada there are two civil commitment routes that by-pass the criminal process. * The first is authorized under Section 527 of the Criminal Code. Mentally disordered persons may be charged with an offense and kept in a place of safekeeping under an order of the lieutenant-governor of a province, yet never be brought before a court of law. There is no limitation imposed upon the lieutenant-

---

*Barry Swadron (1964: 332) describes the legal problems connected with civil commitment procedures in Canada as they relate to the mentally disordered offender.

governor of a province with respect to the type of evidence of an individual's mental condition that may be satisfactory to him. Medical certificates, however, are not equipped for an order made under Section 527. This ruling is used primarily as authority for the transfer of persons under sentence from prisons to mental hospitals if they should become mentally disordered. It is also used, however, to confine for an indefinite period those persons in various pretrial stages who are merely charged with an offense, those in custody awaiting trial, or those declared to be "unfit to stand trial."

The second procedure is authorized under the 1964 Mental Health Act of British Columbia. A person who is thought to be mentally disordered can be certified as such by two medical certificates made out directly to the superintendent of the hospital. Such an individual can be detained for years upon renewal of the certificates. The 1964 act also makes provisions for the apprehension of a person believed to be mentally disordered under a magistrate's warrant. Prisoners in jails, lock-ups, or training schools may be removed to mental health facilities upon order-in-council of the lieutenant-governor based upon two medical certificates.

Admissions to Riverside: The Politics
of the Order-in-Council

In British Columbia in 1975, almost all of the mentally disordered offenders were processed by an order-in-council authorized under Section 527 of the Criminal Code rather than under the Mental Health Act. There are four major procedures whereby those charged with criminal offenses are initially committed to the Riverside Security Unit of Riverview Hospital (Battersby, Rigg 1972: 4-5).

1. A magistrate or judge, on evidence of one doctor that the accused is mentally ill, can order a person sent to Riverside for observation for a period of not more than 30 days. This action is done under Section 543(2) of the Criminal Code and can be done at any time before verdict or sentence, though it is frequently done at preliminary hearings. At Riverside, tests are conducted to determine the accused's fitness to stand trial. If the psychiatrists feel that he is fit, they will have him sent back to court where it is still possible to try the issue of his fitness. Should the psychiatrist at Riverside not feel a person is fit to stand trial, it has become standard procedure for the accused to be held in Riverside as an order-in-council patient. He is held "at the pleasure of the lieutenant-governor" at the issuance of an order-in-council, until such time as the lieutenant-governor feels that the person is fit to stand trial. The

grounds by which the lieutenant-governor obtains the right to order someone held before trial are unclear, but seem to derive from Section 546, which authorizes the sending of prisoners to mental hospitals. While this seems like an abuse of this section, it is frequently used.

2. A person may be committed to Riverside during trial if he is found unfit to stand trial, and this decision can be made at any time during the trial. In particular, it can be made before the decision of whether the accused is guilty or not. A person found unfit during trial is sent to Riverside under 543(6) and kept there until the lieutenant-governor sees fit to send him to trial again.

3. A person may be sent to Riverside if he is charged with a crime and found not guilty by reason of insanity as provided under Section 542 of the Criminal Code. If one is sent to Riverside under this section, he or she is also kept there by an "order-in-council" at the "pleasure of the lieutenant-governor."

4. A person may be convicted of a crime, incarcerated, and subsequently sent to Riverside as provided in Section 546 of the Criminal Code.

There is only one route out of Riverside: a recommendation for release by the review board and subsequent release by an order-in-council. (The British Columbia review board for mentally disordered patients does not conform to the standards recommended in the Criminal Code amendment of Section 527[a] of June 1969. For a discussion of the British Columbia review board procedure, see Goldsmith-Kasinsky [1974: 46-56].)

Let us now examine in greater detail the various commitment procedures that create different classes of mentally ill persons. The exercise of discretionary powers by the police, the courts, and the hospital staff function to deprive the committed persons of their civil liberties and relegate them to a state of preventive detention. The following sections analyze the commitment procedures for classes of persons known in legal parlance as the 30-day remandees (those persons who are awaiting trial or found unfit to stand trial), for those persons found to be not guilty by reason of insanity, and for those mentally disordered prisoners.

The 30-Day Remandees

Beginning in 1972 the largest proportion of all 30-day remand cases throughout British Columbia received psychiatric assessments at the Lower Mainland Regional Correctional Centre. It is a grossly inadequate facility in which there is no assessment unit or psychiatric staff in the remand area. An "observation" is limited to one psychia-

trist who comes in several days each week and in 30 minutes examines all those persons needing assessment.

Those persons who are found to be mentally ill are transported
to Riverside by a prison guard or a city policeman. They are usually placed in handcuffs, although there have been cases of persons
appearing at Riverside in shackles. If a person who has been admitted from prison after his trial has been found fit to stand trial,
he will either be returned to prison or released, depending on
whether or not his stay in Riverside has exhausted his sentence.
The medical records for 1970 show that, of the 109 men* admitted
on remand, 91 were returned to trial and 18 were detained on a subsequent order-in-council. However, during the same period, only
two men were admitted on a warrant of committal following a judicial determination of "unfit to stand trial." Therefore, of all those
20 accused persons committed to Riverside during 1970 by order-
in-council, 18 of them, or 90 percent, were detained indefinitely
without a trial.† Comparing these figures to those provided by the
attorney general's department between 1922 and 1973, we find that
88 persons were detained at Riverside by order-in-council on medical evidence alone and only seven persons had their unfitness to
stand trial judicially determined.

An examination of the Riverside patient files together with
interviews with judges, prosecutors, lawyers, and Riverview
psychiatric staff revealed that it is the practice to obtain order-in-
council for accused persons in custody under Section 527 of the
criminal code in connection with the 30-day warrant. This section
allows the lieutenant-governor of the province "upon evidence satisfactory to him" (in practice, two medical certificates) to remove
any person who is "insane, mentally ill, mentally deficient or
feebleminded" while in custody in a prison to a "place of safekeeping." Section 527 together with the wide discretionary powers
utilized by the police and court in connection with the 30-day remand is the usual mechanism employed to commit an accused for
an indefinite period of time to Riverside.

---

*In 1975 there were 12 women who were order-in-council
persons in Riverview Hospital. They were located in the Eastlawn
unit where they were integrated with the rest of the hospital's patients, rather than placed with the men, who were segregated in
the Riverside unit.

†The case studies and statistical information presented are
based upon Richardson, Smilsky (n.d.).

In practice, both the police and the courts are allowed wide discretionary practices, which on occasion directly contravene both legal and civil libertarian principles.

Before a warrant may be issued, the justice must have at least an affidavit of a medical doctor stating his belief that the accused is mentally ill. However, according to Riverside staff, the police sometimes have no affidavit and no doctor as a witness in court, yet they manage to convince the justice to issue the warrant for observation by saying they will drop the charge or enter a stay of proceedings after the accused is examined at Riverside. The police recharge him, since they now have their medical report. It is common practice for the courts to send some 30-day remandees to Riverside while the police investigate the evidence.

However discretionary, police power could also be exercised under the Mental Health Act unless clear guidelines become available. * The 1964 act allows a police officer to take a person into custody if he or she is thought to be a danger to himself or to others and is apparently suffering from a mental disorder. In 1973 an amendment to Section 27 of the act increased the likelihood of abuse by broadening the power of a police officer to take a person into custody on the basis of "information received by him."

When an accused is sent to Riverside for examination, the hospital usually receives a list of charges against him and the magistrate's signature. Lacking is any record of the circumstances leading up to arrest and the behavior of the accused at the time of arrest. If there has been a court appearance, request for court transcripts have been treated as an affront to the dignity of the court.

The issue of competency can be raised by the court, the accused, and the prosecution at any time in the pretrial or trial stages. The prosecutor will sometimes raise the issue as an expedient way to be rid of harmless social nuisances such as vagrants or alcoholics. Once this process is initiated, the behavior of the psychiatrists, as well as the procedural regulations surrounding the order-in-council

----

*Little research has been done on the use of police discretion in relation to the apprehension and commitment of mentally ill persons. This is probably due to the low visibility of this form of policy activity and the attendant difficulties related to outside observation. An examination of the exercise of police power under Section 10 of the Mental Health Act of Ontario provides some interesting data. See Fox, Erikson (1972).

patients, serves to reinforce the initial decision that resulted in the commitment.

Although the psychiatric staff at Riverview displayed their traditional distrust of the legal process, their role was also supportive of the status quo, serving to reinforce the initial judicial decision that began the commitment procedure, and conforming to the procedural regulations surrounding the order-in-council patients. They adhered to paternalistic sentiments fostering overprotectiveness toward their wards. This observation agrees with McGarry's (1969) findings at the Bridgewater Hospital for the Criminally Insane in Massachusetts as well as that of Hess's study of Ionia in Chicago (1961: 1079). In essence, the psychiatric staff became the gatekeepers of this prison.

Let us examine some specific cases in point: of persons who on 30-day remand find themselves classified as order-in-council patients. They best illustrate the problematic aspects of the application of commitment procedures invoking Section 527 of the criminal code. All cases illustrate the political nature of the order-in-council.

A man charged with vagrancy was examined by doctors in Oakalla while on a 30-day remand on May 20, 1969. On May 22, satisfactory evidence of mental illness having been produced, he was transferred to Riverside under an order-in-council pending complete or partial recovery and competency to stand trial. On May 30, without the knowledge of the hospital, charges were dropped. Yet notice was not given to Riverside (by the prosecutor in the particular jurisdiction where the alleged "crime" occurred) until January 18, 1971--fully two years later. Consequently, the patient was civilly committed under the Mental Health Act. Had this been done originally, or at least when the charge was dropped, he would not have been detained for two years in a state of psycholegal limbo. Instead, he had been placed in facilities for treatment that are not supported by the same financial resources as are facilities for the civilly committed. In 1971, two years later, the same patient was in Riverside because of administrative difficulties in transferring an "undesirable" patient from unit to unit. If he had been civilly committed in May 1969, he would not have been in the hospital two years later.

A man charged with trafficking in marijuana, upon being found competent to stand trial, was further detained by obtaining a minister's order-in-council certificate. The patient had already recovered to the required level of competence in order that he might be tried, but in the delay he began to deteriorate. Subsequently, the normal term of imprisonment expired, but, as he had deteriorated to the extent that he was incapable of caring for himself, it became necessary to detain him as an involuntary patient under Section 23 of the Mental Health Act. Letters of complaint were written by hospital staff to the minister, but the patient's detention continued under the order-in-council. Since no one may have access to an order-in-council patient without the lieutenant-governor's permission, any appeal to an outside psychiatrist had to await a stay of proceedings. As one staff member commented, "When we try to fight for a patient we run up against a wall."

The case of a 36-year-old Danish man charged with possession of a concealed weapon for "having a hatchet under his sweater" also is a flagrant example of the abuses that can result from invoking the order-in-council procedure. This man was originally remanded for a maximum of 30 days observation period. Subsequently, two medical reports certifying the doctor's opinion that he was "mentally ill and in need of treatment" were sent to the remand court and then on to the attorney-general's office. On December 7, 1965, this man's status was changed completely exparte and nonjudicially to indefinite custody by an order-in-council. In order to be released back to court for a complete or partial recovery, a further order-in-council was required. Five years later, the hospital's attempt to obtain a release from the order-in-council revealed what they referred to as "a surprising fact." A stay of proceedings by the courts had initially been granted in 1965. Therefore, according to this judicial determination, proceedings should not have continued with his case, and the order-in-council status was inappropriate.

All three examples are representative of the order-in-council persons who are social nuisances rather than serious threats to the social order. It illustrates the abuse of the remand process. It also illustrates the psycholegal limbo created, which serves to deprive those persons classed as mentally ill of any civil liberties and due process. This order-in-council procedure seems to be utilized as an instrument of social control.

A research report commissioned by the Canadian Law Reform Commission (1973) recommended that judges or magistrates, rather than lieutenant-governors or provincial cabinets, should decide on the disposition of persons unfit to stand trial. Although this recommendation, if implemented, would not attempt to solve the basic problems surrounding the complex issues of persons considered legally incompetent, it would at least insure a judicial determination of the issue, rather than a total reliance on administrative procedures with no safeguards.

Persons Not Guilty by Reason of Insanity

The legislation that allows for the use of indeterminate sentencing with commitment procedures (order-in-council) for mentally disordered offenders (as well as habitual and sex offenders) was created in large measure in an effort to find alternatives to capital punishment and to protect the public from the dangerous mentally disordered offender. It would seem that there would be little need for the use of the insanity defense since the virtual abolition of capital punishment coupled with the decreasing severity of sentences and the introduction of parole and probation (Canadian Law Reform Commission 1973).

From the statistics of the Department of the Attorney General, we find that between June 1971 and July 1973 a total of 143 persons were subject to order-in-council in Riverside, of whom 53, or approximately 26 percent, were found "not guilty by reason of insanity." What is the result of a finding by the court that an accused is not guilty by reason of insanity? The criminal code (Section 523) states that the accused shall be in "strict custody . . . until the pleasure of the Lieutenant-Governor of the province is known."

Let us compare the time spent by two individuals who have been convicted of noncapital murder--one sentenced to life imprisonment; the other charged with murder, found "not guilty by reason of insanity," and sent to Riverside. The individual sentenced to imprisonment in jail will spend approximately 11 years, including the time spent pending appeals. Four patients presently in Riverside Hospital, charged with murder, have spent, to date, 39, 24, 17, and 15 years, respectively (Auxier 1972). At the time of this study, 42 percent, or 67, of the Riverside population have spent from one to ten years, and eight persons have spent 11 to 39 years. Almost all of these persons would not have been incarcerated such a long time had they been sent to a penal institution. And some might never have been incarcerated.

The Sentenced Mentally Disordered Offender

If a prisoner has a breakdown or appears to prison authorities to be mentally ill, he may be sent under order of the lieutenant-governor to Riverside. Should a sentenced inmate be in Riverside after his sentence has expired and the psychiatrist thinks he is still mentally ill, he will be transferred to the part of Riverview Hospital for civil admissions and held as an involuntary admission under Sections 23 and 24 of the Mental Health Act. Thus, he can be detained indefinitely if the authorities want him inside the gates, by one procedure or another.

Let us briefly examine the Baxstrom v. Herold (1966) United
States Supreme Court decision in order to focus more closely on the
issues of due process in relation to civil commitment procedures
and psychiatric predictions of dangerousness.

Johnnie K. Baxstrom was discovered to be mentally ill while
serving a sentence in a New York State prison. After being declared
mentally ill, he was transferred and civilly committed to Dannemora
State Hospital, a facility of the New York State Department of Corrections for "insane criminals." Baxstrom brought successful suit
against this action. The Supreme Court held that the law providing
for Baxstrom's civil commitment to Dannemora was in violation of
the equal protection clause of the Fourteenth Amendment in the U.S.
Constitution, because he was not given the right to the jury review
available to all other persons civilly committed in New York, and
because civil commitment beyond the expiration of his prison term
was made without a judicial determination that he was dangerously
mentally ill--a determination that is afforded to others so committed. (The brief filed in 1966 with the United States Supreme Court
in Baxstrom v. Herold gives us an insight into the role of counsel
in commitment cases. Statistics documented in the brief indicate
that, when counsel had been assigned to those alleged to be mentally ill, commitment was successfully resisted in about 20 percent
of the cases [Kittrie 1971: 93].)

As an immediate consequence of this decision, 969 persons in
the same situation ("Baxstrom patients") were transferred during
1966 from the hospitals under the New York State Department of
Corrections to the state civil hospitals under the jurisdiction of the
Department of Mental Hygiene. These patients were passed over
for many years (a mean rate of 15 years) by psychiatrists as inappropriate for civil hospitalization. A follow-up study of these
patients one year later (Hunt, Wiley 1968: 124) noted that there were
no significant problems with the Baxstrom patients. Only seven had
been certified as too dangerous for a civil hospital. All the others
had been absorbed into the general patient population--many resided
on open wards--and over 200 had been released. Sociological explanations of these results focused on the conservative, social control function of the psychiatric role (Steadman 1972). This experience
stimulated other administrative and legislative reforms. Following
the Baxstrom decision a shift occurred in concept of dangerousness
and the numbers sent to civil hospitals increased threefold over
civil commitments in the previous year.

In conclusion, the use of order-in-council and commitment
procedures, which have created a class of persons we have referred to as "mentally disordered offenders," can be criticized on
the grounds that they utilize the mental health powers of the state

to invest judicial power over so-called criminals, without the safe-guards of the court procedures. Norval Morris, a Chicago crim-inologist, points out that this approach represents a confusion of purposes between the medical and social welfare functions of the state, on the one hand, and police and correctional functions, on the other. He points to the institution for "defective delinquents" in Bridgewater, Massachusetts, where men were held "for a combina-tion of crime and retardation much longer and in grossly less at-tractive circumstances than they would have been had these labels not been combined."*

We have seen that the majority of the mentally disordered of-fenders in British Columbia do not represent a serious threat to the public safety, but can be more aptly characterized as societal nui-sances. The order-in-council administrative procedures for the handling of these alleged offenders have been utilized by the state as a political instrument for the control of the lower classes. The net result has been to abuse the state's power in the name of "re-habilitation" in order to relegate society's nuisances to a state of preventive detention. Certainly, this is an example of the use of covert institutional violence by the state.

CONCLUSION: PIECEMEAL REFORM
OR RADICAL CHANGE?

As we have already pointed out, the therapeutic model and its concomitant indeterminate sentence are presently being reexamined by vastly different interest groups, ranging from administrators and correction officials to prisoners' unions and inmates in the United States and England. Yet, despite the convincing evidence of the failure of the therapeutic model and use of indeterminate sentence elsewhere, the Canadian penitentiary service in the mid-1970s is just beginning to embark on comprehensive regional psychiatric treatment centers. Their description of the function of these cen-ters contains all the rhetoric and programmatic aspects of those in-stitutions for the mentally disordered and dangerous offenders that in California have already been acknowledged to be a total failure.

There is very little evidence that Canada has benefited from the experiences and mistakes of other nations in the criminological field. For example, Canada passed its own habitual offender

---

*Morris (1966) cites other legislation suffering from a simi-lar confusion of function, namely the sexual psychopath law and juvenile court legislation.

legislation only after it was pronounced a failure and repealed both
in England and the United States.* And, as we have demonstrated,
its treatment of the mentally disordered offender utilizing a treatment model and the indeterminate sentence is just beginning to gear
up to full use at a time when other developed nations are abandon-
ing it.

My observations, together with those of other scholars, suggest that there is a deliberate Canadian policy to suppress powerless social nuisances through the use of state power and the exercise of discretion by administrators.

The Canadian society can either attempt to improve its manner of dealing with mentally disordered offenders or to restructure
the issue in such a way that it no longer classifies persons and
processes them into a special group of problems requiring special
institutions and attention. The author has opted for the latter type
of solution. Reforms dealing with "total institutions" and their
clients in North America can be viewed as falling into one of three
general perspectives.

First are those reforms that, in Jessica Mitford's (1971) words,

> call for more money for Corrections, more . . . re-
> searchers, more experts, more utilization of the latest
> scientific know-how in "treatment" of prisoners, build-
> ing new correctional therapeutic communities to re-
> place the old fortress prisons.

This is the standard bureaucratic type of reform; if the system does
not work, pile on more of the same in the hope that quantity will
make up for the lack of creative approaches. It is a dangerous approach, especially because it fails to take into account the sense of
despair prevailing among the victims of the present system, namely,
the inmates in preventive detention. Such "reform" is likely to lead
to more anomie, more suicides, and perhaps outright rebellions.

Second are those reforms designed to make the system more
accountable and responsive to the needs of the inmates. Thus, both
Judge Bazelon (1974: 230), of the U.S. Court of Appeals, and Professor Kittrie (1971: 400-04) suggest that the major thrust of a reform ought to be building more legal safeguards into civil commitment procedures so that they would not be open to such flagrant
abuse. Kittrie goes further by recommending a therapeutic bill

---

*See Klein (1973) for a critique of this legislation. See also,
Canadian Committee on Corrections (1969).

of rights for inmates that would allow them to shape the conditions
of their own rehabilitation, something the therapeutic model was
supposed to do but, in fact, never did in fear of losing social control over the inmates.

Third are those types of reforms that would lead eventually to
the abolition of the present system of incarcerating the mentally disordered offender in large institutions. These reforms usually originate with the inmates themselves and are designed to reduce the
discretionary powers of authorities, permitting the patients to organize to fight injustice within the system. These are the reforms
that seem to point in the direction of a fundamental restructuring of
the system as it presently exists. It would appear that the system
as it is presently constituted is designed to thwart the very rehabilitation it proclaims as an ideal. The inmates should be able to organize the medical and legal expertise that would, in fact, assist
them in rehabilitating themselves. Inmates throughout North America
have been organizing around three major objectives: (1) abolition of
the indeterminate sentence and all its ramifications; (2) establishment of workers' rights for the prisoner, including the rights to organize collectively and to bargain as in a trade union; (3) restoration
of civil and human rights for the prisoner. *

Reform in administrative procedures governing commitment
procedures and the movement to eliminate "total institutions" in
favor of community-based services have just begun in this decade.
The pioneering step of Jerome Miller--as commissioner of the Department of Youth Services in Massachusetts, beginning in 1969--
has demonstrated that it is possible to make radical changes in official ideology and policy that will radically reform treatment programs, given proper commitment and structural conditions, in a
relatively short period of time. (The Massachusetts experience
provides us with an interesting case study of the problems inherent
in major structural and ideological reforms. Some of these issues
are discussed in Ohlin, Coates, Miller [1974].)

Many observers of total institutions over the years have noted
that the health of a society is often reflected in its response to its
social deviants. By this yardstick, our creation and handling of the
mentally disordered offender continues to remind us that those
prison bars are not separating the sane from the insane, but rather

---

*There is a growing literature on prisoners' rights and the
prisoners' union movement in North America and Europe. Two recent articles with good bibliographies and notes on this subject are
Price (1974) and Reason (1974).

the powerful majority from a powerless small minority. This is a situation that will lead to neither justice nor rehabilitation, but only perpetuates a system of covert institutionalized violence.

The concept of due process has raised issues relating to a "right to treatment" as well as a "right to be let alone." We must begin to create a new care system for the mentally disordered and mentally ill in Canada and elsewhere that is based upon the types of reforms that insure the basic human, legal, and civil rights of the client it serves. Such a system should contain mechanisms and channels that deal effectively with clients' grievances and guard against arbitrary and unnecessary treatment.

REFERENCES

Attorney General's Department
    1973   Statistical Data. British Columbia.

Auxier, J., and L. Ramsay
    1972   A ten year review of persons in British Columbia found not guilty of murder by reason of insanity. Unpublished paper.

Battersby, M., and C. Rigg
    1972   Mental patients and the law. The People's Law School.

Baxstrom v. Herold
    1966   383 U.S.

Bazelon, D. L.
    1974   Psychiatrists and the adversary process. Scientific American 230 (June).

Becker, H.
    1963   Outsiders. New York: Free Press.

Canadian Committee on Corrections
    1969

Canadian Law Reform Commission
    1973   Criminal law: fitness to stand trial. Ottawa, May.

Diamond, B. L.
    1962   From McNaghten to Currens, and beyond. California Law Review 2 (May).

Donaldson, K.
   1976   Insanity Inside Out. New York: Crown.

Ennis, B.
   1972   Prisoners of Psychiatry. New York: Harcourt Brace
          Jovanovich.

Fox, R., and P. Erikson
   1972   Apparently suffering from mental disorder. Centre of
          Criminology, University of Toronto, September.

Goldsmith-Kasinsky, R.
   1974   The issue of the mentally disordered offender; and Treat-
          ment programs for mentally disordered offenders. In
          Health Security for British Columbians, ed. R. G.
          Foulkes, vol. 5, pp. 27-57, 59-85. British Columbia:
          Queen's Printer.

Hess, J. M., et al.
   1961   Competency to stand trial. Michigan Law Review 58
          (May): 1078-1100.

Hunt, R. C., and Wilby, eds.
   1968   Operation Baxstrom after one year. American Journal
          of Psychiatry (January).

Information Canada
   1973   The general program for the development of psychiatric
          services in federal correctional services in Canada.
          Office of the Soliciter General, Ottawa.

Irwin, J.
   1970   The Felon. Englewood Cliffs, N.J.: Prentice-Hall.

Kittrie, N.
   1971   The Right to Be Different. Baltimore: Johns Hopkins
          Press.

Klein, J.
   1973   Habitual offender legislation and the bargaining process.
          The Criminal Law Quarterly.

Kutner, L.
   1967   The illusion of due process in commitment proceedings.
          In Mental Illness and Social Processes, ed. Thomas
          Scheff. New York: Harper & Row.

Liazos, A.
    1972   The sociology of the poverty of deviance: nuts, sluts and
            preverts. Social Problems 20 (Summer): 103-20.

McGarry, A. L.
    1969   Demonstration and research in contemporary for trial
            and mental illness: review and preview. Boston Law
            Review 49.

Mitford, J.
    1971   Kind and Usual Punishment. New York: Knopf.

Mohr, J. W.
    1972   Philosophy and empirical justifications of the treatment
            of criminals in the penal process. Unpublished paper.

Morris, N.
    1966   Impediments to penal reform. University of Chicago Law
            Review 33: 627-38.

New York Times
    1974   October 22: 1.

O'Connor v. Donaldson
    1974   95 S. Ct. 2486.

Ohlin, L., R. Coates, and A. Miller
    1974   Radical correctional reform: a case study of the Massa-
            chusetts youth correctional system. Harvard Educational
            Review 44 (February).

Price, R.
    1974   Bringing the rule of law to corrections. Canadian Journal
            of Criminology and Corrections 16 (July).

Reason, C.
    1974   Racism, prisoners and prisoners' rights. Issues in
            Criminology 9 (Fall).

Richardson, J., and P. Smilsky
    n.d.   Mental incompetence to stand trial in British Columbia:
            a study of admissions and discharge at Riverside Hospital.
            Unpublished paper, University of British Columbia Law
            School.

Rubin, S.
    1965   Psychiatry and Criminal Law. Dobbs Ferry, N.Y.:
            Oceano.

Steadman, H. J.
    1972   The psychiatrist as a conservation agent of social control.
            Social Problems 20 (Fall).

Swadron, B.
    1964   Detention of the Mentally Disordered. Toronto:
            Butterworths.

Szasz, T.
    1970   Ideology and Insanity. New York: Doubleday.

    1965   Psychiatric Injustice. New York: Macmillan.

    1964   Law, Liberty and Psychiatry. New York: Collier.

Taylor, I., Walton, and Young
    1973   The New Criminology. London: Routledge and Kegan
            Paul.

Time Magazine
    1975   July 17.

    1974   October 22.

11

DANGEROUSNESS AMONG INCOMPETENT FELONY DEFENDANTS: A TENTATIVE ASSESSMENT OF PREDICTIVE VALIDITY

Henry J. Steadman and Joseph J. Cocozza

There has been a steady increase in the tempo of critiques of the rehabilitative model in corrections (Kaufman 1973; Smith, Fried 1974; and Morris 1975). More generally, there have been a number of recent criticisms of the appropriateness of the entire medical model to criminal justice services (Wilkins 1974; Carlson 1975). One area that these analyses have not touched upon, but which is central to the models being criticized, is the various roles played by psychiatrists in the criminal justice system, particularly their roles as predictors of dangerous behavior. In probation, sentencing, parole, and diversion, there has been a steady increase in the use of, and dependence on, psychiatrists as estimators of the potential for future dangerous behavior. The use of psychiatrists to make such estimations and the very concept of dangerousness itself appear to have some attractive dispositional features. However, as we have noted elsewhere (Steadman 1974), these allurements may be analogous to the mythical Greek Sirens, whose songs beckoned the unwary to disaster.

To obtain some indication of this attractiveness one has only to survey the range of uses of dangerousness throughout the criminal justice system.

USES OF DANGEROUSNESS

The use of dangerousness in the criminal justice system is related in some instances primarily to correctional settings. However, in most instances, uses of dangerousness involve both

This research was supported in part by PHS Grant No. MH20367, funded by the National Institute of Mental Health, Center for the Studies of Crime and Delinquency, Washington, D.C.

correctional and mental health institutions. On the primarily criminal level, dangerousness is related to the sentencing process (compare the Model Sentencing Act) and to parole decisions. On the
second level, dangerousness is a crucial concept in statutes dealing
with sexual psychopaths, defective delinquents, defendants not
guilty by reason of insanity, and incompetent defendants.

The first two areas, sentencing and parole decision making,
relate primarily to the criminal use of dangerousness. For example, a very significant section of the 1972 Model Sentencing Act
proposed some specific criteria and procedures for sentencing the
dangerous offender. This type of offender was defined as one:

> being sentenced for a felony in which he (a) inflicted or
> attempted to inflict serious bodily harm or (b) seriously
> endangered the life or safety of another and he was pre-
> viously convicted of one or more felonies not related to
> the instant crime as a single criminal episode, AND
> (c) the court finds that he is suffering from a severe
> mental or emotional disorder indicating a propensity
> toward continuing dangerous activity [emphasis added].

This criminal disposition involves the mental health system specifically through psychiatric estimations of propensities toward continuing dangerous activity.

Another predominantly criminal justice system decision related to dangerousness, but considerably more covert than the
recommendations of the Model Sentencing Act, is that of parole. In
a study of two Midwestern parole boards, J. E. Scott, and R. D.
Vandiver (1974) found that the single most important factor in the
board's decisions was the inmate's current offense. Regardless of
the institutional adjustment or sociodemographic characteristics of
the inmate, the most significant factor for the parole boards he
studied was the seriousness of the inmate's current charge. This
finding suggests that in the evaluations for parole a major concern
is with societal protection and that a major factor in the estimates
of the danger a parolee may pose is his current offense. As such
this is one type of prediction of dangerousness regularly employed
in the criminal justice system.

When we talk of sexual psychopath laws and defective delinquent statutes, we move into areas that overlap and confuse criminal
justice and mental health questions. These overlaps occur both
through the agents involved in the decision making and in the institutions to which individuals may be committed. However, one especially significant feature of all the psychopathy laws, as reviewed
by N. Kittrie (1971), is that in every case he cites--and in the Ohio

statute discussed by H. E. Allen, C. F. Simmonsen, and M. S. Gordon (1973)--commitment depends on conviction, mental disability of some sort, and some demonstration of danger to society. In every instance, the estimation of the probability that the individual will engage in some type of conduct that is defined as dangerous is central to the dispositional process.*

The two final areas of criminal justice dispositions involving the use of dangerousness result in direct diversion into the mental health system. They are the judicial findings of NGRI (not guilty by reason of insanity) and incompetency to stand trial. The NGRI determination in most jurisdictions does not necessarily imply any decision involving dangerousness. However, in the District of Columbia, after the criminal court arrives at an NGRI verdict, there is a special hearing to determine whether the individual is mentally ill and dangerous and therefore requires mental hospitalization. In contrast to these procedures, implicit predictions of potential danger are employed to detain patients in mental hospitals under involuntary civil or criminal commitment standards during the hospitalization that necessarily follows an NGRI finding in most states.

Take, for example, the New York case of Bruce Sherman, who in May 1972 was found NGRI in the shooting death of his wife. The dangerousness issue arose in Sherman's case when the civil hospital to which the court committed him requested his release less than three months after his trial. The hospital's release committee, in July 1972, concluded that Sherman showed "no evidence of being mentally ill or in need of continued hospital care." Subsequently, two court-appointed psychiatrists agreed with the hospital release committee. In addition, these psychiatric examiners concluded that, while Sherman had an "explosive personality" that could be set off by his drinking and while there was no way they could

---

*In fact, it is the extreme, and as yet unsolved, difficulties surrounding the use of dangerousness in these psychopath statutes that provided the forum for two of Judge David Bazelon's major decisions. In Millard v. Cameron and Cross v. Harris, Bazelon went into an unusual, but needed, specification as to what was required for commitment under the Washington, D.C. sexual psychopath laws. What Bazelon's decisions accentuated was the abysmal absence of any sound basis for either defining or predicting dangerousness, this despite the wide use of the concept of dangerousness as exemplified by the 29 states and the District of Columbia (Kittrie 1971), which currently have special legislation for psychopathic offenders and defective delinquents.

assure the court he might not under such influences attempt to kill his father, he had no treatable mental illness.

Sherman remains in a civil mental hospital because the judge decided it was the hospital's obligation to protect the community from this dangerous person, even if he did not have a treatable mental illness. So, although a determination of dangerousness had no part whatsoever to play in Sherman's criminal disposition, his continued criminal court-ordered detention was quite dependent on the court's estimation of the danger he posed to the community.

The second direct diversion to the mental health system from the criminal justice system involves incompetent defendants, a group 10 to 15 times larger than defendants found NGRI. The common law standards for competency deal with the defendant's ability to understand his charges and the court process and to cooperate with an attorney in his own defense. Therefore, no question of dangerousness is involved in a judicial determination of fitness to proceed with a trial. However, in New York, from 1971 through 1974, the location to which the incompetent indicted felony defendant was sent depended on the court's determination of dangerousness. If the defendant were found dangerous, he went to a correctional mental hospital, which was assumed to be more secure and better able to control "dangerous" persons; if not dangerous, he went to a high-security, civil mental facility. It is these events and issues that are a focus of our current research and to which we will now turn.

NEW YORK STATE'S CRIMINAL PROCEDURE LAW-- SECTION 730.50

September 1, 1971 was the effective date of New York's Criminal Procedure Law (CPL). Section 730.50 of this statute mandated that in the case of all indicted felony defendants found incompetent to stand trial a determination be made as to whether the defendant was a dangerous incapacitated person. Such a person was defined in the statute as "an incapacitated person who is so mentally ill or mentally defective that his presence in an institution operated by the department of mental hygiene is dangerous to the safety of other patients therein, the staff of the institution or the community."

Seizing upon the opportunity presented by the implementation of this tautological statute, bereft of guidelines, we undertook a prospective study of all indicted, male felony defendants who were found incompetent during the first 12 months of the CPL. Among the many issues we hoped to address was the accuracy of predictions made by the two court psychiatrists in such cases and by the

court where the ultimate decision rested. As it turned out, there
was an 87 percent concurrence rate between the psychiatrists and
the court, so for the most part our data on predictive validity focus
on psychiatric predictions of dangerousness made within the criminal dispositional process. One of the attractive features of this
natural experiment was the contrast it offered to prior research in
this area, which for the most part lacked such definable, specific
psychiatric and judicial predictions. Usually, research subjects
were selected because of availability, expected high risk, or special
policy interest, and then retrospectively studied. In most cases,
actual predictions of dangerousness had to be inferred, making criteria for this determination difficult to sort out and to utilize for
tests of predictive validity. However, the research we are reporting here did probe, prospectively, very specific predictions of
dangerousness by both psychiatrists and the court. Let us now turn
to our findings.

FACTORS ASSOCIATED WITH DETERMINATIONS
OF DANGEROUSNESS

There were 257 indicted felony defendants found incompetent
between September 1, 1971 and August 31, 1972. Of these, 154
(59.9 percent) were found dangerous by the court psychiatrists.
There is a vast range of questions these data address, but in this
chapter we will limit ourselves to two. First, we will look at
sociodemographic, criminal history and prior hospitalization characteristics as they were associated with psychiatric findings of
dangerousness. We reported initial findings in this regard previously (Steadman 1973), before we had the much wider range of
variables that we now have at our disposal. In addition, in the following section we will examine, for the first time, a second major
topic--the accuracy of these predictions based on a number of outcome measures.

Viewing the data in Table 11.1, it is apparent that there is
very little that distinguishes the defendants found dangerous from
those found nondangerous by the court psychiatrists. Both groups
were a little over 30 years old on the average, with ninth grade
education, and of approximately the same physical dimensions,
5' 8" to 5' 9" and just over 160 pounds. There were some slight
differences on racial and marital status variables, with the blacks
and Puerto Ricans more often dangerous than whites and currently
married more often seen as dangerous than the nonmarried. Similar slight differences occurred in history of addiction, but the difference in history of alcoholism between the two groups was

statistically significant, with defendants having such a history more often found dangerous. For the most part, however, on these background factors there was little to distinguish defendants found dangerous from those found nondangerous.

TABLE 11.1

Background Characteristics of Indicted Male, Incompetent Defendants in New York, between September 1, 1971 and August 31, 1972

	Not Dangerous	Dangerous	Number
Average age at admission (years)	30.8	30.7	
Race (percent)			
White	44.6	55.4	83
Black	41.9	58.1	117
Puerto Rican	31.4	68.6	51
Other	16.7	83.3	6
Marital status (percent)			
Never married	45.0	55.0	129
Divorced, separated, widowed	36.7	63.3	79
Currently married	34.1	65.9	44
Average education (grade)	Ninth	Ninth	
Average height	5' 9"	5' 8"	
Average weight (pounds)	165	162	
History of alcoholism (percent)			
None	44.0	56.0	141
Some	34.2	65.8	111
History of drug abuse (percent)			
None	41.5	58.5	135
Some	38.7	61.3	119

Note: Out of a total number of 257 defendants, 59.9 percent were found dangerous, 40.1 percent not dangerous.
Source: Compiled by the authors.

Turning to Table 11.2, we see that a similar pattern occurs with criminal and hospitalization history characteristics as with the sociodemographic ones. Both groups had approximately four prior arrests and two prior convictions. Those with histories of juvenile delinquency were somewhat more often found dangerous. Looking only at violent prior convictions, the two groups are the same, with 60 percent of those with and those without prior violent convictions being found dangerous. The Legal Dangerousness Scale Score reported is a Guttman-type summary scale of seriousness of criminal history that we developed in our Baxstrom research (Cocozza, Steadman 1974; Steadman, Cocozza 1974). In the current research population, there was practically no difference on this summary measure among those found dangerous and nondangerous by the psychiatrists. The measure of prior hospitalizations reported in Table 11.2, average months of prior hospitalization, is quite alike for both groups. It appears that there was almost no association between all types of background characteristics (sociodemographic, criminal history, and prior hospitalization) and findings of dangerousness by the court psychiatrists. This is not to say, however, that it is impossible to demarcate what was related to these psychiatric determinations for the court. In fact, if we move to Table 11.3 it is clearly evident one fact that was.

TABLE 11.2

Criminal and Hospital History of Indicted Male,
Incompetent Defendants in New York, between
September 1, 1971 and August 31, 1972

	Not Dangerous	Dangerous	Number
Juvenile delinquency (percent)			
None	41.3	58.7	208
Some	33.3	66.7	48
Average number prior arrests	4.0	3.6	
Average number prior convictions	2.3	2.1	
Violent crime convictions (percent)			
None	40.5	59.5	173
Some	39.3	60.7	84
Average legal dangerousness scale score	4.6	4.7	
Average number months in mental hospital	24	21	

Note: Out of a total number of 257 defendants, 59.9 percent were found dangerous, 40.1 percent not dangerous.
Source: Compiled by the authors.

TABLE 11.3

Psychiatric Findings of Dangerousness,
by Alleged Offense

Type of Alleged Offense	Psychiatric Finding		
	Not Dangerous	Dangerous	Total
Violent against person			
Number	25	74	99
Percent	25.3	74.7	100.0
Potentially violent against person			
Number	37	42	79
Percent	46.8	53.2	100.0
Property			
Number	23	27	50
Percent	46.0	54.0	100.0
Sex			
Number	7	5	12
Percent	58.3	41.7	100.0
Drug			
Number	5	3	8
Percent	62.5	37.5	100.0
Other minor			
Number	6	3	9
Percent	66.7	33.3	100.0

Note: $X^2 = 17.27$ p $< .01$.
Source: Compiled by the authors.

There is a consistent and significant association between the
current alleged offense of these incompetent defendants and psychiatric findings of dangerousness. This was the finding of our initial
report on the issue also and, even with the substantial increase in
the number of background variables examined here, we were unable
to locate any factor that was more highly related to this determination. In fact, it is the current alleged offense that partially explains
the small association between race and findings of dangerousness.
Among these incompetent defendants, blacks were more often
charged with violent crimes against persons, and defendants with
violent crimes against persons as the alleged offense were more

apt to be found dangerous. Of all such factors examined, it was current alleged offense that appeared to most heavily influence psychiatric estimations of dangerousness.

It is striking how this finding compares with that of Scott and Vandiver mentioned above. Just as conviction offense was the prime determinant of parole board decisions, so, too, in our population, did current alleged offense that involved violence against persons lead to a strong likelihood of a psychiatric determination of dangerousness, regardless of almost any other factor.

The next logical step in this type of research, one that Scott's and Vandiver's data did not enable them to do, is determining the validity of predictions of dangerousness that rely so heavily on such a factor.

LEVEL OF PREDICTIVE VALIDITY

Just as there was little on which to distinguish the dangerous defendants from the nondangerous on background characteristics, there is little that distinguishes them on outcomes. Regardless of whether they were seen as dangerous or nondangerous by psychiatrists, both groups were almost as likely to be assaultive while hospitalized, rearrested, and rearrested for violent offenses. On certain measures one group is somewhat higher, while on other factors the other group is higher. Overall, however, there are no consistent substantial differences.

As Table 11.4 shows, there was a substantial difference in the length of time that the defendants determined dangerous spent hospitalized immediately after judicial determination. For the dangerous--who were sent to a correctional mental hospital--the average stay was 46 weeks, while for the nondangerous--sent to a mental hygiene maximum-security facility--the average stay was 37 weeks. However, for those who were then subsequently transferred to regular security mental hospitals rather than back to court, the dangerous patients stayed 17 weeks before discharge compared to 22 weeks for the nondangerous.

Still looking only at outcomes in terms of processing through the two systems, we see some differences between the final criminal dispositions of the two groups. For the nondangerous defendants, 65 percent were convicted of a felony, compared to 51 percent of the dangerous. The two groups were similar on percent dismissed, 5 percent nondangerous and 7 percent dangerous, on misdemeanor convictions, 5 percent nondangerous and 6 percent dangerous, and in NGRI dispositions, 5 percent nondangerous and 2 percent dangerous. The other major difference, which closely

TABLE 11.4

Outcome Measures of Indicted Male, Incompetent Defendants
in New York, between September 1, 1971
and August 31, 1971

	Not Dangerous	Dangerous
Average number weeks hospitalized immediately after finding of incompetency	37	46
Average number weeks in civil hospital after transfer	22	17
Disposition of CPL charges (number)	83	121
Guilty, felony (percent)	65.1	50.8
Guilty, misdemeanor (percent)	4.8	5.9
Dismissed, acquitted (percent)	4.8	6.8
NGRI (percent)	4.8	1.7
Pending (percent)	20.5	34.8
Percent assaultive--initial incompetency hospitalization	36.0	42.0
Average number per person	0.9	1.0
Percent assaultive--civil hospitals of transfer	0.0	8.3
Average number per person	0.0	0.2
Percent with one or more rearrest	54.0	49.0
Average number per person at risk	1.3	1.1
Percent with one or more rearrest for violent offense	16.0	14.0
Percent rehospitalized	44.0	39.0
Percent rehospitalized for violence	6.0	8.0
Percent assaultive after rehospitalization	18.9	28.6
	.6	.6

Note: Out of a total number of 257 defendants, 59.9 percent were found dangerous, 40.1 percent not dangerous.

Source: Compiled by the authors.

relates to the discrepancy in the percentage convicted of felonies, is
the percentage pending: 35 percent of the dangerous defendants'
cases were still pending on September 30, 1974, while only 21 percent of the nondangerous cases remained pending. This is not surprising given the longer initial hospitalizations of the dangerous
defendants. Thus, the dispositional experiences of the two groups
may be expected to be almost the same.

What about outcome measures that might be used as criteria
of dangerous behavior? The answer is that on all those we employed, and which are displayed in Table 11.4, there are practically
no differences. There was as much assaultiveness in maximum
security hospitals and in civil hospitals to which transfers occurred,
as high a rate of rearrest and rearrest for violent offense, and as
much rehospitalization and rehospitalization precipitated by violent
incidents and assaultive behavior after rehospitalization.

As is evident in Table 11.4, 36 percent of the nondangerous
and 42 percent of the defendants determined psychiatrically dangerous had at least one assault in the high security facilities to which
they were initially sent after judicial determination of incompetency,
although the number of assaults per person in the the two groups was
about the same (0.9 and 1.0, respectively). Of the 19 nondangerous
patients transferred to civil hospitals before return to court, none
were assaultive, whereas 4 (8 percent) of the 48 dangerous patients
were assaultive.

Of the 103 nondangerous defendants, 70 (68 percent) were released to the community at some time during the three-year follow-up
period, opposed to 96 of the 154 dangerous patients (62 percent).
Among those released, those in the nondangerous group were slightly
more often rearrested, 54 percent and 49 percent, respectively.
Similar very slight differences favoring the dangerous group occurred for rearrest for violent crimes--16 percent of the nondangerous group and 14 percent of the dangerous.

The other remaining indicator of violent behavior is violent
behavior leading to rehospitalization. This is important since there
were some indications in our prior research (Steadman, Cocozza
1974) that there is differential handling of violent acts by police when
the person alleged to have committed that act is known to be an ex-
mental patient; that is, rehospitalization is substituted for arrest.
On this indicator, there is a very slight tendency in the direction
opposite that of the rearrest data. Of the 52 dangerous defendants
who were rehospitalized, and for whom we have information, 4 (8
percent) were rehospitalized because of violent behavior, whereas
2 (6 percent) of the 36 nondangerous patients were rehospitalized.
After these readmissions to mental hospitals, the nondangerous
group did have a smaller percentage (19) than the dangerous group

(29) with assaults while hospitalized, but the average number per person was exactly the same (0.6), indicating that while a smaller percentage of the nondangerous were assaultive while subsequently hospitalized, those that were had a greater number of assaults.

In sum, on the entire set of criteria factors for subsequent violent behavior, there are negligible differences between those defendants who were determined by court psychiatrists to be dangerous and those that were evaluated as nondangerous. This was true both in the more immediate situations of the hospitalization following these determinations and for the more distant indicators of behavior in the community resulting in rearrest, rearrest for violent offenses, and for rehospitalization associated with violent behavior. Had this entire group of 257 incompetent defendants been randomly put into two groups, the level of accuracy obtained by the psychiatric predictions would have been reached. Given the actual base rate of behavior for the total group of 257 defendants, there was no predictive validity in the psychiatric predictions made for this group of defendants beyond that obtainable by chance. The psychiatrists were wrong as many times as they were correct.

CONCLUSION

The data we have reported in the latter portions of this paper concerning the initial assessments of the predictive validity of these psychiatric estimations of dangerousness provided to the court are quite consistent with the corpus of literature on the psychiatric prediction of dangerousness in other settings. There has yet to be a demonstration of abilities, either clinically or statistically, to predict with sufficient accuracy to have any practical utility. In the instance examined here the level of predictive expertise demonstrated was that expected by chance. These findings and their consistency with prior research again raise the question of why there is the growing trend toward use of psychiatric estimations of dangerousness throughout the criminal justice system when no special psychiatric expertise in these regards can be empirically demonstrated.

Our conclusions from these initial analyses of our data certainly must be considered tentative. Much additional analysis coupled with more vigorous controls are required and will be forthcoming. However, it appears unlikely that our basic finding of psychiatric inabilities in this area of such serious and broad policy dimensions will be voided. This finding is especially important given the unusual definitiveness of the predictions examined that produced study groups that had been clearly labeled dangerous and nondangerous. Our data on these two groups and prior empirical evidence suggest that, at this time, expectations of accurate predictions of future dangerous behavior by psychiatrists in any criminal justice or mental health setting appear unwarranted.

REFERENCES

Allen, H. E., C. F. Simmonsen, and M. S. Gordon
    1973   Operational research in criminology: an examination of the decision-making process for commitment under sexual psychopath statute for apparently unrelated offenses. Paper presented at the Annual Meeting of the American Society of Criminology, New York.

Carlson, N. A.
    1975   The federal prison system: forty-five years of change. Federal Probation 39 (June): 37–42.

Cocozza, J. J., and H. J. Steadman
    1974   Some refinements in the measurement and prediction of dangerous behavior. American Journal of Psychiatry 131 (September): 1012-14.

Kaufman, E.
    1973   Prison: punishment, treatment or deterrent? Journal of Psychiatry and Law 1 (Fall): 335-51.

Kittrie, N. N.
    1971   The Right to be Different: Deviance and Enforced Therapy. Baltimore: Johns Hopkins Press.

Morris, N.
    1975   The Future of Imprisonment. Chicago: University of Chicago Press.

Scott, J. E., and R. D. Vandiver
    1974   The use of discretion in punishing convicted adult offenders. In Crime and Delinquency: Dimensions of Deviance, ed. M. Ridel and T. Thornberry, pp. 191-208. New York: Praeger.

Smith, J., and W. Fried
    1974   The Uses of American Prisons: Political Theory and Penal Practice. Lexington, Mass.: Lexington Books.

Steadman, H. J.
    1974   Dangerousness in law and mental health: Greek siren or
            treatment/dispositional aid? Paper presented at the
            Annual Meeting of the American Society of Criminology,
            Chicago.

    1973   Some evidence on the inadequacy of the concept and de-
            termination of dangerousness in law and psychiatry. The
            Journal of Psychiatry and Law 1 (Winter): 409-26.

Steadman, H. J., and J. J. Cocozza
    1974   Careers of the Criminally Insane: Excessive Social Con-
            trol of Deviance. Lexington, Mass.: Lexington Books.

Wilkins, L. T.
    1974   Current aspects of penology: directions for corrections.
            Proceedings of the American Philosophical Society 118
            (June): 235-47.

12

THE JUST COMMUNITY APPROACH TO CORRECTIONAL REHABILITATION: A BREAKTHROUGH PROGRAM IN PENOLOGY
Peter Scharf

THE PROCESS AND CONTENT OF
DEMOCRATIC VALUES

Democratic society is, in theory, committed to the notion that its prisons will resocialize its inmates toward more democratic social values. In reality, prisons produce a quite different effect. Most inmates return to society more embittered, alienated from society, and cynical about its institutions than when they entered prison.

Critical to understanding the impact of prisons is differentiating between the process and content of social values. The process of values refers to the underlying reasoning of a political belief or ideology. The content refers to its specific orientation. For example, two people with similar conservative political beliefs might justify these similar orientations with strikingly different reasoning patterns. Research indicates that the process of thinking tends to remain stable across situations. That is, people will use very similar reasoning processes to solve a wide range of social problems. Political contents are far more easily reversed and changed as people move among different situational environments.

Developmental theory as found in such writers as George Herbert Mead, Jean Piaget, and Lawrence Kohlberg offers a dynamic approach to understand the evolution of the process of social ideas. During the past 25 years, for example, Kohlberg has posited a theory that conceptions of society and law evolve through an invariant developmental sequence. This theory, documented by both cross-cultural and longitudinal research, posits six stages of moral development, evolving sequentially in all societies (see Table 12.1).

Each moral stage contains a qualitatively discrete conception of the relationship of law to individuals and society. A correlation between Kohlberg's moral stages and legal reasoning has been empirically documented in a recent study of legal socialization (Tapp,

Levine 1974). Broadly speaking, social institutions play a critical role in determining both the rate of moral growth and the final stage of moral reasoning. Institutions that encourage open dialogue, moral conflict, and democratic interaction are usually associated with rapid sociolegal development.

TABLE 12.1

Kohlberg's Stages of Legal Perspectives

Stage 1	Law conceived in terms of concrete prescriptions. Wrongdoing implies automatic punishment.
Stage 2	Law defines guidelines as to what will be tolerated by authorities. Laws have no moral value, except as is instrumentally useful to particular individuals.
Stage 3	Laws are shared consensus as to right action. The law has force as an expression of group opinion and feeling.
Stage 4	Law is defined in terms of fixed generalized laws or rules. Laws are to be obeyed in order to preserve social order and to maintain respect for society and its institutions.
Stage 5	Law seen as being defined from legitimate, voluntary social contract. Laws are valid when symbolically agreed to and when they perform utilitarian functions.
Stage 6	Law seen as embodying implied justice principles of social contract. Illegitimate laws seen as not prescriptively valid.

Source: Compiled by the author.

PRISONS AND MORAL REASONING

Traditional prison environments offer few opportunities for rapid moral growth. Inmates in a variety of custody, as well as psychotherapy, prisons were found to perceive their prison environments as hostile to their growth and development as well as unfair. Inmates were seen as "conning" and "scheming"; correctional officers were perceived as being arbitrary and unfair. In some prisons, inmates were found to actually regress, in terms of their stage of moral reasoning, during an age period where developmental theory would predict a substantial advance in terms of moral maturity.

   A recent study compared the reasoning of delinquents of different ages with matched controls from comparative social environments. The results of the six samples reveal that delinquents tend
to be markedly less mature than the controls. These observations
imply that delinquents tend to be less morally mature than are typical peers from similar environments. While this does not mean
that being in a lower stage in any single case causes delinquency,
it does suggest that most delinquents are recruited among less
morally mature youth. It further implies that the consequences of
being labeled delinquent lead offenders to remain in poor moral en-
vironments--for example, prisons, foster care, and the like (see
Table 12.2).

TABLE 12.2

Comparative Moral Stage Levels of Delinquent
Youth and Controls

| Setting | Ages 12 to 13 | | Ages 15 to 17 | | Ages 18 to 20 | |
	Delinquent	Control	Delinquent	Control	Delinquent	Control
Indiana	--	--	224	293	--	--
Connecticut						
Reformatory	--	--	--	--	260	319
Connecticut						
Treatment	164	230	--	--	--	--
Texas	--	--	208	252	--	--
Scotland	--	--	219	286	--	--
England	208	275	203	289	--	--

Source: Compiled by the author.

   To illustrate these findings, we offer some examples of inmate responses to the dilemma as to whether a man should steal a
drug to save his wife, who is dying of cancer. One inmate displayed the following Stage 1 comments:

   No, he shouldn't. That's stealing. I wouldn't do no
   time for nobody, no matter what. I don't care if it
   was my wife. It doesn't matter. . . . He will get
   bagged if he does that.

The reasoning here fails to differentiate even rational interests
from a fear of punishment. Unfortunately, being afraid of punishment only rarely deters crime. This youth, for example, was arrested more than a dozen times during the next five years.

An example of Stage 2 reasoning provides perhaps a typical offender response to the dilemma:

> Yah. Because if my wife was dying I'd want to save her. She's with me. I would want to keep her around. I need her.

This subject's Stage 2 hedonism is replaced by a morality of concern at Stage 3. Here, the criterion of rightness becomes a matter of mutual expectations, rather than simply a calculation of hedonistic interest:

> Yes, I think he should have done it because his wife was dying and he needed the drug. And if there was some sort of law, or some way he could have got the money--besides, him and his friend couln't raise the money. So I feel that he did the right thing--the only sensible thing--the only thing that he had left to do.

While roughly half our sample of 16- to 20-year-old delinquents had some Stage 3 thinking, a far smaller proportion had developed what might be clearly seen as substantial Stage 4 thinking. One exception in our study was found in the interview with a 19-year-old safecracker who somehow emerged from a two-year prison sentence with a recognizably Stage 4 moral ideology. When asked if he thought it was right or wrong for Heinz to break in and steal the drug, he answered:

> I think Heinz was wrong, even though he was in a peculiar situation where it was actually a matter of life and death. He was still stealing from a man who had developed this thing, and it was his right [the druggist's] to keep it because it was his possession. Heinz violated the man's rights by taking it.

The rarity of Stage 4 inmates and the near total absence of Stage 5 reasoning indicated that few released offenders understood either the logic of Stage 4 concrete democratic norms or the principled Stage 5 ideals of a constitutional democratic society. This is obviously important, considering both high recidivism rates for most (if not all) prison programs as well as the political alienation frequently observed among many exoffenders.

THE PRISON ENVIRONMENT: INTERACTION
WITH DEMOCRACY

The bleak history of corrections, in terms of producing democratic citizens, has some exciting exceptions. In the early nineteenth century, there was a wave of reform predicated on the notion that prisoners could be taught democratic values by participating in a controlled democracy behind prison walls. The most notable experiment in prison democracy was that instituted by Thomas Osborne, from 1913 to 1916, in the Auburn and Sing Sing prisons.

Osborne (1916) offered a civic education rationale for the democratization of prison life. His ideology contained elements both of a Jeffersonian democratic faith in the human potentiality for rationality as well as a Deweyite belief that democratic experience begets democratic attitudes. In his Prison and Society, Osborne declared:

> Outside the Walls, a man must choose between work
> and idleness. . . . (Why not let himself teach these
> lessons before he goes out?). . . . Such things are
> best taught by experience. So inside your walls you
> must have courts and laws to protect those who are
> working from the idle thief. And we must rest assured that the laws would be made and the laws enforced. The prison must be an institution where
> every inmate must have the largest possible freedom,
> because it "is liberty that fits men for liberty."

Osborne was seemingly influenced by the work of Charles Cooley, and possibly George Herbert Mead, in providing a theory base for his work. Democracy required democratic thinkers, and only by experimenting with democracy could one learn the logic of the constitution. In a 1924 work published shortly before his death, Osborne used Cooley's notion of learning through experimental role playing to justify giving inmates experience in democratic life:

> In some prison schools will be found a class in civics.
> That is very well--all knowledge is useful; but it has
> little relation to real training in citizenship. As every
> boy knows, the only way to learn to play baseball is to
> play it. An attempt to make pitchers, catchers, batters
> and base-runners by studying the rules and reading a
> history of the game would be so ridiculous that even
> penologists have not suggested it; even in prisons
> where it is permitted, they actually play ball instead

of studying. So with citizenship: to know how to be a
good citizen--to do one's duty to the community and
encourage one's fellow-citizens to do theirs; to claim
one's own rights without infringing upon the rights of
others; to learn by one's mistakes; to trust and not
be discouraged when deceived; to be trusted and stand
up under it--to learn how to do even a part of these
and other necessary things, a man must actually do
them. Fortunately, it is not impossible--even in
prison.

In the Mutual Welfare League experiment, the Sing Sing
"screws" shifted their role from that of hostile warders to something akin to the modern, counselor-correctional officer. Osborne
(1924) noted that "it is good that you should . . . be on such good
terms with the men . . . while the system has freed the prisoners,
it has also freed the guards." He added that the guards were "friends
trying to help these men try to take their proper places in society."
Fredrick Dormier, Sing Sing's "Principal Keeper," observed:

Under the old system I felt it my duty to be harsh
and severe. . . . But it used to get on my nerves.
I scolded my children and kicked my dog. . . . Now
it's different. I enjoy my work at the prison.

A whole range of activities were introduced into the prison.
Knitting, singing, and playing in the prison band became popular
recreational activities. The men also organized sanitation and fire
departments. (The inmate fire department on numerous occasions
was credited with the saving of prisoner lives.) A bank, with assets
of over $30,000, was organized "by inmates for inmate benefit."
    The League court was responsible for nearly all disciplinary
infractions committed in the prison. At Sing Sing, five inmate-
judges served for five months each. The hearings were open to all
members of the League, and appeals might be made to the warden
(Osborne 1916). At the appeals hearing, the inmate-judges would
be forced to explain the justice of their decision. Often, more than
a hundred inmates would attend an appeals hearing.
    Conviction by the League inmate-jury typically meant the loss
of an inmate's citizenship in the Mutual Welfare League. This was
usually sufficient to deter wrong action in that it returned the offender of the League constitution to his condition before the League
went into effect, that is, into a system of unilaterally imposed prison
discipline. More severe punishments included banishment to a "non-
League" prison (for example, Clinton prison).

THE NIANTIC JUST COMMUNITY PROJECT

Following Osborne's example, we sought to create a prison environment that would actively stimulate democratic reasoning. The goals of the proposed alternative were to create a setting that would be perceived as legitimate by inmates and staff and that would actively stimulate the social thinking of the individuals involved.

The experimental project was undertaken in a single cottage at the Niantic, Connecticut, State Farm for Women. There had been a near riot at the institution, and feelings between staff and inmates were generally hostile. In spite of these antagonisms, inmates, staff, and administrators all expressed a willingness to at least explore the possibility of working together to create a new set of institutional rules. As an initial step, we proposed a "constitutional" meeting where inmates and staff could "air" differences and, most important, begin to explore possible bases for mutual collaboration and cooperation. Though both inmates and staff expressed a reluctance to attend the "conventions," nearly the entire staff and half the inmates attended the first meeting.

After a number of months of conflict, there evolved a definition of a program and common rules that were acceptable to most of the staff and inmates. The inmates would control discipline within the cottage through community meetings; in turn, they would receive many privileges that had not previously existed on the farm. Inmates agreed to make some accommodation with staff and also agreed to try to settle grievances and conflicts through the proposed democratic structure. Community meetings were established as the central political forum of the cottage. The entire group would decide joint disciplinary action to be taken against particular members (either inmates or staff). It would also determine important policy issues for the cottage. Common topics included interpersonal conflicts and tensions between inmates, alleged violations of institutional or cottage rules, and protests regarding prison policies and restrictions. In each type of action, the critical element involved granting inmates a large degree of actual control over the particular decision to be made. This was true even where the meeting might arrive at a decision that violated the expectations of staff members or administrators. In few cases (even those dealing with a serious incident, such as contraband or assault) was the community meeting decision overruled by the prison administration. To offer an example of these meetings, we provide an excerpt from a community meeting dealing with an inmate named Pudgey, who had violated a rule of "confidentiality":

Carole: She talked about the cottage, and she talked about everything that this place stands for, like it was nothing; we were dogs, man, and I don't feel like I had to sit and listen to that garbage; and it all stemmed from the fact of what Pudgey told . . . this afternoon when she talked to her.

Pudgey: How do you know it all came from me?

Carole: Because she said it did. . . .

Marla: I didn't say that you did; I am saying the conversation that went on from when this thing started, when you got called down for her clothes or some old garbage like that. And then the whole thing went on and on, and the three of them are sitting there, talking about us, and Joe, like he was nothing; and I don't feel like I had to be subjected to this bullshit because you opened your mouth about something you shouldn't have mentioned. . . .

Jackie: Pudgey, why do you think we sit here and say and do the things we do to you?

Pudgey: I don't know.

Jackie: It must be something; people like to listen to records and watch TV without spending our time on you, so that is the way I would feel. Like, we are giving up what we like to do to talk to you, and it's not just because it is for something to do, either.

Pudgey: I don't. . . .

Marlene: I want to ask you, Pudgey, why you really wanted to come over here. Why?

Pudgey: . . . .

Jackie: Tell the group why.

Pudgey: I wanted to come because I wanted to be able to relate to people more, because maybe I would be able to express myself better.

Pat: Do you feel disappointed in the house? You said you wanted to come in the cottage and see how it was; you just said this, or something. Do you feel like nothing is happening, like we are at a standstill. . . . Do you feel bored?

Pudgey: No.

Marlene: She couln't possibly, because ever since we started she has been the one on the floor; everything we had, Pudgey has been on the floor. It's always Pudgey; why did she do this, or Pudgey this, or Pudgey that; and Pudgey's not the only one who got a problem.

In dealing with Pudgey, the other inmates sought to bring
moral pressure on Pudgey to change her ways. It was assumed
from the outset that she was guilty of the offense of "talking outside
of group," and that the meeting represents more a means to reem-
phasize the norms of the community than it was a means to establish Pudgey's guilt or innocence. Throughout the meeting, the other
inmates invited Pudgey to reenter the "moral community" of the cottage. They asked her repeatedly "if [you are] sincere" or if "[you
are] disappointed in the house." These gestures were seen as invitations for Pudgey to recant, admit her offense against "the house,"
and, most important, to rejoin "the cottage community." Though
the group involved a violation of a house rule, Pudgey was never
punished. Simply calling her (and other inmates') attention to the
rule is deemed punishment enough.

More serious violations of cottage rules often involved punishment as well as group disapproval. The actual penalties imposed by
the community meeting were assessed by a discipline committee,
mandated to meet with the community meeting. Appeals were made
to the community meeting, which had the power to overturn or modify
the decisions of the board. This provided a means to ensure that the
cottage democracy would be forced to respect most appeals that
might conflict with the immediate "will" of the group. The most
common disciplines assigned by the board tended to be imaginative.
For example:

For disrupting a meeting	Pat must lead every meeting for the next week.
For playing the radio too loud	Robin must sing for her supper the next three nights.
For being out of place	Carol loses recreational privileges for one week and must write an essay on "Responsibility."
For persistent use of abusive language	No one in the unit is to speak to Chris for two days.

The Just Community program offers what we might call a
political therapy. Inmates are encouraged to exert political decision-
making influence. The hope was that this would result in inmates'
assuming the authority perspective of a single social community,
something many of them had never before done in any real sense.
It was hoped that this role taking of one community would extend to
a more general capacity to take the perspective of society at large.

Prison personnel were trained in facilitating democratic group processes and adopted collective group responsibility techniques used both in Russian (Makarenko 1935) and Israeli (Rabin 1957) education projects.

Research Hypothesis

Given our objectives in the Niantic Project, we sought to heuristically test the key assumptions of the project.

First, could we create a prison moral atmosphere that inmates would accept as fair and legitimate? The importance of this problem lies in the assumption of most observers of prison life (for example, Mitford 1973) that offenders will feel themselves morally alienated from any prison environment. This view assumes that the very fact of incarceration creates an adversary relationship between prisoner and warden in which the offender will perceive almost any treatment as coercive. In contrast, our assumption was that the prison justice structure could be modified so most inmates would agree to the fairness of the rules of the setting.

Second, we sought to discover if an environment perceived as just would in fact stimulate sociolegal thinking among offenders. While it had long been assumed (Kohlberg 1974) that an environment perceived as just would stimulate higher stage thought, this had never been tested, neither in a natural environment nor with an offender population. This second hypothesis can be understood both as a heuristic test of the relationship between the perceived moral tone of an environment and moral reasoning and as an exploration of possible use of prison moral climates in the reeducation of the offender.

Subjects

Twenty-four model cottage inmates were selected at random from the model cottage project. A group of 12 subjects from a traditional cottage in the same institution was matched (as a group) according to age, race, crime, and length of sentence.

Instruments

A new method of scoring environmental perceptions was developed (by the author of this study) called the Moral Atmosphere Scoring System (MASS). The instrument involves a two-hour interview probing inmate perceptions of program goals, rules, inmate role, and staff norms. Fixed criteria were developed for each aspect of moral atmosphere to determine if the inmate accepts, rejects, or is ambivalent toward a particular aspect of moral atmosphere.

Effects of environment upon moral reasoning were measured, using Kohlberg's Moral Maturity Interview. This measure scores the logical structure underlying moral judgments. Legal reasoning can be measured independently by rating legal issues separately from other moral topics.

Our effectiveness in terms of postrelease life adjustment was measured by a recidivism count of program graduates as well as a qualitative open-ended interview dealing with a number of aspects of postrelease adjustment (for example, family, job, societal attitudes, and the like). Interviews were analyzed qualitatively with the goal of inductively deriving the critical variables determining offender recidivism. (Interview schedules and rating procedures for the three instruments are available from the author.)

Procedures

Trained interviewers were used in gathering the data for the study. Several of the interviewers were former inmates from federal institutions, as it was felt that former inmates with no affiliation with the experimental project would have the best chance of acquiring candid interviews from the project. Interviews were recorded on tape and transcribed. Trained scorers from the Laboratory of Human Development at Harvard University analyzed the transcribed data. The interviews were scored blind and scorers had no identification with the experimental project. An interjudge reliability of .81 was achieved among moral atmosphere raters, while a .92 reliability was achieved by the moral judgment scorers.

Results

Our scoring of the prison moral atmosphere indicated an acceptance of the rules and decision-making structure in the model cottage. Overall, 75 percent of the model cottage inmates were scored as accepting the fairness of the political structure of the cottage. Inmates saw themselves as "authors" of the rules, and they generally thought the rules were fairly enforced by their fellow inmates. One inmate stated:

> In here you make the rules, it's not like someone is
> putting them down on you from above. The girls make
> them and make sure that they are fair to both sides,
> staff and women.

Even discipline decisions were generally perceived as just when decided by the group as a whole: "It's different when the group comes
down on you than when the pigs do it." As well, inmates voiced a
high degree of acceptance of the constitutional framework established
by the group (see Table 12.3).

TABLE 12.3

Female Inmate Rules Perceptions: Democratic
and Control Institutions

	Traditional Female Cottage		Model Female Democratic Cottage	
	Number	Percent	Number	Percent
Inmates accepting program as just	4	33	18	75
Inmates divided or ambivalent	5	42	4	17
Inmates rejecting program	3	25	2	8

Source: Compiled by the author.

The model cottage perceptions differed quite strikingly from
those of the female custody prison. Where inmates in the model
cottage perceived an "authorship" of the cottage rules with a certain
degree of collective ownership, the control cottage was characterized by an inmate "acceptance" of the rules as a part of moderately
benign imposed matriarchy. One inmate offered:

> In here they take care of you pretty good; but if the
> guard sees you doing something, she tells you about
> it and makes you do what she wants. . . . They
> don't beat you or nothing, but the rules is for the
> guards and what they want you to do.

While the MASS represents a first effort to score prison environments in developmental terms, we offer that the results indicate preliminary trends in the perceptions of prison rules. This tends to support our contention that inmates will respond to fairness of treatment, even if they reject the larger injustice of the judicial process that sent them to prison. Where this by no means implies that we are seeking to "pacify" inmates in terms of the broader structural issues of the legal system, it does imply that the internal justice structure of a prison can be reorganized so that inmates might respond positively to the justice of the correctional setting's rules.

Analysis of pre- and posttest moral judgment interviews indicated differences of 39/100ths of a moral stage from pre- to posttest (five months apart) among inmates under 24 years of age. This group was considered to be on target, as longitudinal studies (Kohlberg 1974) indicate that moral reasoning tends to stabilize after the age of 25. This was seen as a sizable change since nearly one-third of the group shifted more than half a moral stage (for example, Stage 2 to 2-3). As well, it compared favorably with similar moral education efforts run with noncriminal populations (Kohlberg 1974). The differences were significant when compared with matched control groups in both male and female prisons, and with "treated controls" using intensive moral discussion groups (meeting six hours per week) in the traditional male prison. Analysis of variance procedures indicated significant differences at the .01 level (see Table 12.4).

TABLE 12.4

Changes in Moral Reasoning Levels

	Pretest	Posttest	Change
Model cottage inmates, under 24 years of age (n = 17)	260	299	39
Control women's prison (n = 10)	270	268	-2
Control men's prison (n = 18)	254	256	2
Control using moral discussion groups without democratic moral atmosphere, males (n = 19)	251	268	17

Note: Scores are represented in terms of Mean Moral Maturity Scores. One stage = 100 MMMS points; that is, Stage 2 = 200.
Source: Compiled by the author.

These results indicate that an intervention designed to allow inmates democratic control within an institution could facilitate moral change among inmates. Qualitative analysis of inmate interviews (specifically on legal issues) indicated even more mature thinking in control groups. Of 17 inmates, 12 were scored higher on legal issues than on their cumulative moral judgment scores. This made us optimistic that our prison democratic intervention could affect inmate thoughts about larger societal legal issues.

The moral atmosphere interviews of the inmates who changed in terms of moral judgment form a striking contrast with the interviews of inmate "regressors." For example, in inmates who changed in terms of moral maturity and attitude, we find a general acceptance of the cottage program. Barbara sees herself as having been personally transformed by the program:

> I know it was the cottage, but a lot came from me. If
> I had been in another cottage, I would not be responsible
> as I have been. Here I knew if I did something, I was
> not just hurting myself [but] it would affect everybody
> . . . like just staying out of work. . . . In the be-
> ginning I started taking days off . . . and then I thought
> of what it would do to the cottage if everyone started
> taking days off, staying home. . . . People would say:
> "Barbara is staying home, so why can't I ?" . . . It's
> not because I would get punished; it's because I care
> more.

Jeanie is even more eulogistic than Barbara. She notes:

> I found something in this cottage I was looking for a
> long time, and that was understanding. Like, I did a
> few things I got caught for, but there wasn't anybody
> condemning me, like the police. . . . When I got
> caught we talked it over, and I found a lot of under-
> standing. . . . I found love in this house; not with
> everybody, but with a certain few.

Most of the changers see themselves as "authors" of the cottage rules. Sue argues:

> Pat and I sat for two days going over the rules of the
> cottage and how we felt we wanted to be treated, and
> that we didn't want to be treated as a prisoner; we
> wanted to be treated like human beings. . . . I feel
> this is the goal, and it has helped me quite a bit.

These results on moral change provide some evidence that a prison may be used as a potential means to alter the structure of inmate values. This is methodologically interesting, as earlier experiments with milieu therapy lacked a research tool to document changes in the process of moral thinking as opposed to moral content. This distinction is critical since, while it is easy for the inmate to fake changes in the content of his values (for example, "I don't believe in ripping-off no more"), changes in the process of thinking are much more difficult to counterfeit.

Initial recidivism rates are optimistic, but should be viewed cautiously. Several graduates are doing well in college; several have attempted to organize exoffenders in a variety of self-help projects. Overall preliminary results indicate a program recidivism rate of 14 percent after a mean of two years in the community. However, it is still premature to judge the efficacy of the Just Community program in terms of the adjustment of its graduates. Until a carefully matched control group is followed for five years after release, comparisons must serve only heuristic rather than evaluative purposes. Even if a carefully controlled experiment were to be available, recidivism data must be scrutinized carefully, with its implications evaluated cautiously. A prison program experience, as any educational program, represents only one input into a complex life process. Just as it would be silly to expect four years at Harvard or six years in Summerhill to retrieve an otherwise damaged life pattern, so, too, it is slightly ridiculous to expect a program in prison to successfully assume responsibility for the permanent redirection of its graduates' lives. Any major life change is a complex social process. Family, peers, faith, meaning, work--all become reevaluated. Consider, for example, what it would mean for the average doctor, lawyer, college teacher, or banker to become a pimp, hooker, con man, or booster. Social alliances would have to become rejected, new skills and ties developed. Any such change obviously requires the constant support of persons willing to welcome the "changer" into a new life-style. When such support is not available, it is unrealistic in the extreme to expect any meaningful alteration in criminal behavior. The Just Community offered a beginning for inmates to assume new meaning in their lives, as well as new ties and a sense of community. Where future ties and community were available and accepted, the inmates' changes became permanent ones. Where they were unavailable or rejected, the Just Community program was a transitory (though possibly positive) experience.

In the future, though, we hope to make more community options available. A program restaurant along the lines of the Delancy Street project has been proposed, but at this point we must regard the experience as just one life experience among many. We feel

that the success of the program should not be judged by its success
in recidivism alone. In that inmates seem to accept the community
as legitimate, and its treatment fair as judged by their own values,
it perhaps may be legitimized--if inmates do no worse than do other
inmates in other programs following graduation.

SUMMARY

This chapter is a progress report on a long-term intervention
experiment to use cognitive developmental theory as a guide toward
the democratic reform of the prison. The use of cognitive-develop-
mental theory offers, at once, a philosophical and psychological
guide for experiments in democratic prison management. Its emphasis upon staff and inmate political collaboration in democratic
management suggests a new role for custody personnel.

While we have focused here on the positive aspects of our experiment, as Merton and others have aptly noted, prison democracy
faces overwhelming constraints. The Osborne experiment lasted
less than three years, Macconochie's Australian "mark system" experiment, less than six. In each case, the prison bureaucracy soon
became pitted against the democratic prison experiment. The demands of order soon superseded those of social rehabilitation or
justice.

While our project has faced similar pressures, I believe the
idea deserves merit as a concept, if not a pragmatic reality, in the
near term. For prisons to become democratic, and democratic
citizenship to be an accepted goal of corrections, many things must
change. Inmates must become conceived as "legal" citizens, pos-
sessed of rights, and granted a modicum of dignity. Other changes
must include a redesign of the prison as an architectural entity and
the reintegration of the prison into economic life.

In spite of this, the "Just Community Approach to Correctional
Rehabilitation" offers an alternative to the rather grim field of
penology and corrections. In addressing the process of reasoning
rather than content we feel we offer a therapy that differs from other
"persuasional" therapies presently used with offenders. Similarly,
its emphasis upon fairness as well as democratic participation offers
an approach consistent with the revival of concern for inmate rights
as well as a mechanism to engage in the legitimate reeducation of
the felony offender.

REFERENCES

Dewey, J.
  1930   Democracy and Education. New York: Macmillan.

Hartshorne, H., and M. May
  1930   Studies in the Nature of Character. New York:
         Macmillan.

Kohlberg, L.
  1969   Stage and sequence. In Handbook of Socialization Theory
         and Research, ed. D. Goslin. Chicago: Rand McNally.

Kohlberg, L., K. Kauffman, P. Scharf, and J. Hickey
  1974   Just Community Approach to Corrections. Cambridge,
         Mass.: Harvard Graduate School of Education Press.

Langer, J.
  1969   Theories of Development. New York: Holt, Rinehart and
         Winston.

Makarenko, A. S.
  1967   Collective Family. Garden City, N.Y.: Anchor.

Mead, G. H.
  1934   Mind, Self and Society. Chicago: University of Chicago
         Press.

Merton, R.
  1957   Social Theory and Social Structure. New York: Free
         Press of Glencoe.

Mitford, J.
  1973   Kind and Usual Punishment. New York: Knopf.

Osborne, T.
  1924   Prisons and Common Sense. Philadelphia: Lippincott.

  1916   Prison and Society. New Haven, Conn.: Yale University
         Press.

Piaget, J., and B. Inhalder
  1960   Psychology of the Child. New York: Basic Books.

Rabin, A. I.
1957   The Israeli Kubbutz as a laboratory for testing psycho-
        dynamic hypotheses. Psychological Records 7.

Scharf, P.
1973   Moral Atmosphere and Intervention of the Prison. Doc-
        toral dissertation, Harvard University. Xerox University
        Microfilms, Order 74-11, 332.

Studt, E., et al.
1969   C-Unit: Search for Community in Prison. New York:
        Russell Sage.

Sykes, G.
1958   The Society of Captives. Princeton, N.J.: Princeton
        University Press.

Szasz, T.
1963   Law, Liberty, and Psychiatry. New York: Macmillan.

Tapp, J. L., and F. J. Levine
1974   Legal socialization: strategies for ethical legality.
        Stanford Law Review 24: 1-74.

13

SOME POSITIVE CHANGES IN
THE PAROLE PROCESS
Don M. Gottfredson

For the purpose of fostering debate in a discussion of the
"successes and failures of parole," I was asked to describe some
positive changes in the present parole process. I claimed to know
of two positive changes relevant to such debate and said I would try
for three.

The first positive change has to do with development of a national data base, which now can enable discussions such as this to be
held more on the basis of evidence and less on pure speculation. The
second concerns an increasing interest by paroling authorities in
articulating and examining their paroling policies. In trying for the
third, I will present what I can in the area of evidence for the effectiveness of parole as one alternative mode of release from prison.

NATIONAL DATA BASE

It has been about 35 years since the presidential crime commission study known as the Wickersham Report described accurate
data as "the beginning of wisdom" and decried the lack of statistical
reporting systems in criminal justice. It has been eight years since
the more recent President's Commission on Law Enforcement and
Administration of Justice lamented that the situation was unchanged.
The commission stressed the need for reliable statistical information on parole and its results, along with the same need for every
other sector of criminal justice (President's Commission on Law
Enforcement and Administration of Justice 1967a: 60, 1967b: 123;
Lejins 1967). Long before, paroling authorities had expressed
widespread concern with this problem--for example, in 1956, at the
National Conference on Parole. The wheels of criminal justice
statistics development, however, do grind slowly. In 1964, the
Advisory Committee on Parole of the National Council on Crime
and Delinquency called for an exploratory project to demonstrate

procedures for compilation of comparable data on parole. As a
result, in December of that year a feasibility study was started
under the auspices of the National Parole Institutes (Gottfredson
et al. 1970).

Eleven years of collaboration by research workers and paroling authorities have resulted in the present system. Those who
have collaborated in the program include 55 paroling agencies in
50 states, the federal government, and Puerto Rico. Data based
on agreed-upon definitions, intensive deliberation, careful reliability studies, and systematic collection procedures is now available
for about 250,000 persons paroled in the various U.S. parole jurisdictions. All these quarter of a million persons have been followed
to determine parole outcomes--all for one year, substantial numbers for two and three years, and some for four years.

My intent here is not to summarize the results of analyses of
these data on parole. The most recent report of that project seeks
to do this in one volume, and it lists 57 reports of analyses issued
by the project staff (Neithercutt, Moseley, Wenk, 1975). Rather,
it is to assert that one positive change in the parole field is the
present availability of information from this reporting system.
This is unique in the criminal justice system. There are yet no
comparable, offender-based national record-keeping systems for
courts, jails, probation, or prisons, following up each adult offender to determine outcomes; neither are there any for the
juvenile justice system.

This data resource has several important implications for
discussions of alternatives to parole or of its abolishment. One is
that the program can describe the extent of use of parole and the
outcomes of the process.* Another point shown by this system is
that parole is by these data demonstrably different in many ways
among the various jurisdictions in the United States. The states
and the federal system are extremely diverse in sentencing structures, paroling philosophies, paroling procedures, the use of
parole as a mode of release, and kinds of persons paroled. A study

---

*Over the last eight years for which data is available (through
1972) the use of parole as a mode of release steadily increased.
Across the country in 1972, about two-thirds of releases (66 percent) were parolees. The most recent data for parolees with three-
year follow-up show that, of 17,654 persons studied, 71 percent
were nonviolators; 8 percent (1,415) were recommitted to prison
with a new major conviction. See National Council on Crime and
Delinquency Research Center (n.d.).

of reports from this program should humble anyone prone to quick
generalizations about parole--about its nature or its results. A
further implication is that an important, unique resource is available as an aid to testing the consequences of the institution of alternatives to present parole practices. The results of parole, as
measured by the present reporting system, can help somewhat in
forecasting the results of radical change; more important, they
provide a readily available fund of information for measurement of
such consequences--including changes in time served in institutions
as well as in correctional outcomes. Surely it is time that we at
least look as we leap. Given the availability now of this data resource, it seems reasonable to require that any radical change in
paroling practice be accompanied by assessment of its consequences.

This argument relates mainly to issues of effectiveness, however, and ultimately it must be based on premises concerning such
aims of the criminal justice system as reduction or control of
criminal behavior. Important as that may be, it can only partially
address issues of fairness or equity, and it is these concerns that
lie at the heart of many criticisms of present parole (and sentencing)
structures. The second positive change is closely related to these
issues.

ARTICULATING AND EXAMINING PAROLING POLICY

In a recent review, Kay Harris sorted the increasing criticism
of parole systems into three categories: critics' focus on procedural
failings, asserted counterproductive aspects of the process, and
claims of ineffectiveness. She states:

> Many critics focus on procedural failings, contending
> that present parole procedures lack the safeguards
> necessary for fair and accurate decision-making.
> Other critics believe that the present parole system
> creates a level of anxiety and frustration among con-
> fined populations that is counter-productive in terms
> of institutional management and the correctional
> process. A smaller, but growing, number of critics
> are questioning the wisdom of having a parole system
> at all, contending that the system is not, and perhaps
> cannot be, effective in achieving its stated goals.
> (Harris, n.d.)

The first concern focuses on issues of procedural due process,
but also on concerns for equity. It includes arguments that paroling

decisions are arbitrary, capricious, or reflect the exercise of unfettered discretion without due care.

The second criticism, that the parole process is counterproductive, asserts that it arouses a high level of tension and frustration in prisoners and "epitomizes for most inmates a system of whim, caprice, inequity, and nerve-wracking uncertainty" (Kastenmeier, Eglit 1975). Thus, this criticism is related to the first except for the "nerve wracking uncertainty." It reflects either humanitarian concern or the rehabilitative idea or both.

The third sort of criticism addresses the problem of effectiveness of treatment. There is a general disenchantment across the land with the rehabilitation ideal, a cry for abolishment of the "myth" of treatment, and a return to a punishment philosophy-- renamed as "just deserts." This study was not intended to debate this issue; but it is inextricably intertwined with issues of parole, related as it is to the philosophical basis for indeterminate sentencing. I should only like to note an important distinction between (1) a general finding from many studies that the treatment programs studied do not reduce recidivism and (2) claims that nothing works, or will work. The latter require a tremendous conceptual leap, which may qualify as the greatest overgeneralization in the history of criminology.

Attention is invited now, however, to the first two criticisms (of unfairness and uncertainty). Then I will offer some evidence on the parole process as a crime-control mechanism.

The concept, "fairness" is not the same as the concept, "justice." There may be, however, reasonable agreement that justice requires fairness, that fairness is not necessarily justice, or that "justice includes fairness but is more demanding"(Wilkins 1975: n. 6, 154). Similarly, it seems that fairness includes the concept, "equity," which may be taken to mean that similar persons are dealt with in similar ways in similar situations.

If models of parole decision making can provide increased equity, hence fairness, at the same time providing explicit statements of policy and reducing uncertainty as to sentence length, these models would seem pertinent to the first two types of criticism. The concept of paroling "models" calls attention to the two general classes of decisions made about parole by paroling authorities: individual case decisions and policy decisions. The latter, which may be assumed to set the framework within which the former are made, generally are not stated explicitly.

Studies completed in collaboration with the U.S. Board of Parole showed that the implicit policy could be made explicit through an analysis of practice. Judgments on offense severity, parole risk, and institutional performance were found to account for most of the variance in parole decisions (Hoffman 1972). Accordingly, "guidelines" were developed to combine these dimensions as a statement of general policy (Gottfredson et al. 1975). Thus, for persons with average institutional adjustment, assignments to offense severity and parole prognosis (by an experience table) indicate the expected range of time to be served in prison before release. When the time is set outside the expected ranges, specific reasons are required of the decision makers. Provision has been made for periodic review and revision of the policy guidelines.

There is widespread interest among paroling authorities in the development of articulated policy along similar lines. Presently, parole boards in California, Louisiana, Minnesota, Missouri, New Jersey, North Carolina, Virginia, and Washington are actively participating in projects with this aim. Paroling authorities in 17 other states have volunteered to participate as observers.

Numerous advantages accrue from an explicit, clearly stated policy. Discretion is not removed, but it is structured in a way that can enhance equity, facilitate the giving of reasons, and expose decision policy to public debate and criticism. An explicit policy model provides a tool for periodic examination of fairness, and it should substantially reduce the uncertainty felt by inmates under indeterminate sentences.

COMPARING MODES OF RELEASE

Comparisons of effectiveness of parole versus discharge from prison would be most readily made on the basis of an experimental design. This would imply random allocations of inmates to these different modes of release and follow-up by a common procedure to determine the extent of new crimes. Lacking such a design, we may at least compare outcomes if the follow-up data are available. Since the groups paroled and not paroled may not be equivalent in risk of new convictions, aside from mode of release, we may seek to correct statistically for demonstrable bias in the comparison. In the study of decisions by the U.S. Board of Parole, mentioned above, records of the Federal Bureau of Investigation were made available for follow-up study.

During that study, a random selection of subjects about to appear for parole consideration was made, with a variety of data extracted from the case files. At the time of the analysis to be reported here, a total of 1,833 persons in this larger group had been released from prison at least two years before. Of that number, there were 1,223 adult males with sentences of 14 months or more for whom FBI records were located. (Of the 1,833, persons with sentences of 13 months or less were excluded [106]. Of the remaining subjects [1,727] the FBI record was not located for 41; these cases were excluded. Of the remainder, there were 1,594 males and 92 females. Of males, 1,223 were adults and 371 were juveniles--by commitment status). *

If a successful outcome is defined as absence of any conviction during the two-year follow-up period, the success rates for the three modes of release differed rather markedly. Men paroled (450) succeeded 89 percent of the time. For mandatory release (473), the rate was 74 percent; for discharge at expiration of sentence (300), it was 68 percent. That is, parolees were convicted less often of new crimes, with mandatory releases coming in second in success rate. Persons released at the expiration of their sentences came in last, with nearly a third having new convictions before two years.

For other purposes of the project and to provide a correction for demonstrable differences in risk of new convictions among type of release groups, prediction instruments were developed. All subjects were randomly divided into a study sample (607) or a validation sample (616). One such instrument was comprised of a listing of 28 offender attributes associated with the new conviction criterion. Scores obtained by unit weighting of these items were associated in the validation sample with new convictions. †

An analysis of covariance was done, with absence of new convictions as the dependent variable, with subjects classified by mode of release, and with these prediction scores as the covariate. The proportions of success, corrected for known differences in risk for persons released by these three means, were: parole, 83 percent; mandatory release, 77 percent; and expiration, 71 percent. (The obtained F for the test among adjusted means was 7.65, which, for

---

*The analyses described here were completed by William Brown and Guy Pasela.

†The point biserial correlation coefficient was .30. A multiple linear regression equation was found also, in an attempt to reduce the number of items. Beginning with 67 items as potential predictors, an initial screening resulted in selection of 16. Nine items accounting for the most variance in the criterion were then used in a multiple regression. The multiple r was .35; in the validation sample, however, the point biserial r was only .22. Thus, the more valid 28-item scale with unit weighting was used in the comparison of modes of release. The same analysis, with the regression-derived base expectancy as the covariate, had similar results.

2 and 1219 degrees of freedom, is significant at the 1 percent level
of confidence for a one-tailed test.)

These differences must be associated with either unknown
selection factors or the different modes of release, or both. If unknown selection factors account for the differences, then the board
is quite astute in its decision making; that is, it does better than
the statistical prediction in the selection of good risks. If, on the
other hand, mode of release accounts for the differences, then
parole is the most effective mode, followed by mandatory release,
with release at expiration of sentence still last.

It should be noted that persons on parole or mandatorily released under supervision may be returned to prison for "technical"
violations, in which case they would be less exposed to the risk of
new convictions due to confinements. If the aim of the process is
reform, or rehabilitation, or reintegration, this issue is very relevant to the test of effectiveness. If the only aim is the restraint of
crime, it is not. It may be asserted, then, by supporters of parole,
that this reflects merely one purpose of the process, and that the
test of effectiveness of release procedures is to be found in the
subsequent conviction rates of persons released by different means.
This seems to be an argument only from the restraint perspective;
perhaps it is of interest, however, since arguments for abolition of
parole sometimes adopt this view--rejecting reform, rehabilitation,
or reintegration as appropriate goals.

Before confidence in a correct interpretation of these results
and their implications--in terms of other correctional goals--
could be assumed, a number of further questions must be raised.
How many of the "successes," by this criterion, were back in
prison as technical violators, for how long, and for what? How
many of the technical violators were returned to prison in lieu of
prosecution for new offenses? How do the groups compare under
conditions of equal exposure to the risk of new convictions? What
other aspects of the parole process account for the observed differences? These, and perhaps other, relevant questions need to
be addressed. My point is simply that these issues may be examined empirically and that such evidence should be considered in
discussions of effectiveness of, or alternatives to, the present
paroling process.

CONCLUSION

Two positive changes pertinent to debate on the successes and
failures of parole have been described. The first is the availability
of a national data base on parole permitting more rational planning

about release procedures from a basis of evidence than is now possible in other sectors of criminal justice. Such evidence should be
entered into the debate. The second positive change is the development of more clearly articulated paroling policy, which addresses
issues of fairness and of inmate uncertainty and at the same time
provides a basis for more rational policy development.

As a third contribution to the discussion, some results of
federal parole decision making were described. These results show
that persons paroled are subsequently convicted of fewer crimes,
even when a correction is made for the selection of the identifiably
better risks for parole. The observed differences may be due to
unknown factors in parole selection or to mode of release. In
either case, if an objective of the parole process is crime control,
these results should give pause to the critic who would abolish that
process.

REFERENCES

Gottfredson, D., P. Hoffman, M. Sigler, and L. T. Wilkins
    1975   Making paroling policy explicit. Crime and Delinquency
            (January).

Gottfredson, D. M., M. G. Neithercutt, P. S. Venezia, and
E. A. Wenk
    1970   A National Uniform Parole Reporting System. Davis,
            Calif.: National Council on Crime and Delinquency.

Harris, M. K.
    n.d.   Disquisition on the need for a new model for criminal
            sanctioning systems. West Virginia Law Review 77:
            263-326.

Hoffman, P.
    1972   Paroling policy feedback. Journal of Research in Crime
            and Delinquency 9 (July).

Kastenmeier, R. W., and H. C. Eglit
    1975   Parole release decision-making: rehabilitation, exper-
            tise, and the demise of mythology. The American Uni-
            versity Law Review 22: 477-88. Reprinted in W. E.
            Amos and C. L. Newman, Parole: Legal Issues,
            Decision-Making, Research, p. 82. New York: Federal
            Legal Publications.

National Council on Crime and Delinquency Research Center
    n.d.   Three year follow-up analyses--1970 parolees. News-
           letter, Uniform Parole Reports, Davis, Calif.

Neithercutt, M. G., W. H. Moseley, and E. A. Wenk
    1975   Uniform Parole Reports: A National Correctional Data
           System. Davis, Calif.: National Council on Crime and
           Delinquency Research Center.

President's Commission on Law Enforcement and Administration
of Justice
    1967a   Parole and aftercare, chap. 6. Task force Report:
           Corrections. Washington, D.C.: U.S. Government
           Printing Office.

    1967b   Criminal statistics--an urgently needed resource,
           chap. 10. Task Force Report: Crime and Its Impact--
           an Assessment. Washington, D.C.: U.S. Government
           Printing Office.

Wilkins, L. T.
    1975   Some philosophical issues: values and the parole deci-
           sion. In Parole: Legal Issues, Decision-Making,
           Research, ed. W. E. Amos and C. L. Newman. New
           York: Federal Legal Publications.

14

SOME SOCIAL POLICY IMPLICATIONS OF THE COMMUNITY-BASED CORRECTIONS CONCEPT
Herbert Roll

INTRODUCTION

Behavioral scientists and intuitive observers agree that
although the harm prisons do is hard to measure, whatever good they do is too elusive to discern.

John Conrad

Critics of penal institutions appeared to have arrived on the
scene as soon as those programs began operation in the latter part
of the eighteenth century. One can read of descriptions of conditions in our early workhouses, houses of corrections, jails, and
penitentiaries and readily understand why such conditions moved
many interested individuals and groups to early prison reform efforts. For nearly 200 years we have been painfully aware of the
failures of our penocorrectional system. We have been told that
the prison environment is overly regimented, characterized by harsh
discipline, patterns of inmate-inmate and staff-inmate exploitation;
that they are breeding grounds for homosexuality and other unnatural
acts; that the prison experience is both psychologically and socially
destructive to the inmate; that they are "colleges of crime," that
prison inmates are exposed to unique antisocial subcultures, ad
infinitum. Such criticisms have been clearly stated and reiterated
by Clemmer (1958), Sykes (1958), Cressey (1961), Goffman (1961),
Galtung (1958), Menninger (1966), Mitford (1971), and so on.
Perhaps the most seminal treatise on the negative effects of
the large, isolated penal institution was John Irwin's (1970) The
Felon. He not only provides us with insights into the development
and history of criminal careers but, most important, he sensitizes
us to the "reentry problem" experienced by all offenders who are
released into the community. We shall see later in this chapter
that this problem, perhaps more than any other, has far-reaching
implications for correctional reform.

Even those institutional programs that have utilized special "treatment techniques," such as group counseling, have not given us much occasion for optimism. Indications from the literature reveal that such programs do not do much better, if at all, than traditional correctional programs. Bailey's (1966) well-known evaluation of studies of correctional outcome was most discouraging. Of the 100 reports analyzed, he found that positive (program) results were indicated in only one-half of the studies.

Thus, while the results of correctional research have often been inconclusive, contradictory, and, in some cases, next to useless, there does seem to be general agreement, among critics, that such institutional programs, by their very nature, can have very little in the way of positive influence on an inmate's future behavior.

Presently being offered as an alternative to traditional institutional programs and other programs of incarceration is the concept of "community-based corrections." While prison reform has been a controversial issue in this country since its founding in the late 1700s, the concept of community-based correctional programs has its historical origin in the last half of this century. It may be appropriate at this point to distinguish between the two concepts. Prison reform is, of course, the broader, more inclusive concept and may or may not be limited to efforts made to improve conditions in our existing prisons, reformatories, and other institutions. If the concept refers to more substantive reform than simply changing institutional conditions, it generally has included efforts directed at the reduction of prison sentences, the increased use of standard probation and parole programs, and the like.

Community-based corrections, on the other hand, is a far more radical and controversial concept. By definition, the concept implies the use of alternative correctional policies to institutionalization for all but the most dangerous and hardened of offenders. In its most idealistic formulation, nearly all offenders would be kept in the community to be rehabilitated. The underlying rationale here is that since the crime was committed in the community--the offender and victim are members of the community, and this is where his family, job, and other resources are--the best course of action is to rehabilitate the offender in the community.

For the purpose of this study, the community-based corrections concept will include such programs as halfway houses, work release and training release programs, furlough programs, stipend programs, prerelease guidance centers, community corrections centers (mini-prisons), probation subsidy programs, diversion programs, and so on. (For a more complete description of these programs, see Glossary at the end of this chapter.)

This policy, argue its proponents, does not isolate the offender from society, the community, his family or friends; does not expose him to the debilitating conditions of large isolated institutions; and minimizes the reentry or reintegration problem for the offender. In addition, proponents argue that community-based programs are much cheaper than institutional programs by as much as six or seven times.* Labeling theorists also argue that the degree to which the offender penetrates the criminal justice system and the longer he is exposed to its stigmatizing effects, the more likely he will develop a deviant self-concept and identity. The community-based corrections concept, then, also makes good theoretical sense as an alternative to policies of incarceration and institutionalization.

Allen and Simonson (1975: 485) caution that many community programs have not been able to fulfill the inflated claims made by their supporters. Nevertheless, they state that inmates placed in such programs do no worse (in terms of recidivism) than those inmates placed in traditional prisons, training schools, or reformatories. They conclude:

> Even if the results are only equal, the cost of community
> corrections is so much lower than institutionalization
> that its emphasis can be justified on economics alone.
> And if the costs were the same, the community programs
> would be worth consideration on humanitarian grounds.

Alper (1974: 204) makes a similar plea for the use of community-based programs:

> Even granting that the rate of recidivism for persons
> placed in such community settings may prove to be no
> lower than those released from the traditional institu-
> tutions, the former may be viewed as preferable because

---

*Estimates of the costs of these programs vary over time. Some argue that an offender can be supervised in the community in a traditional probation program for $400 to $600 a year. Recent estimates of incarcerating an offender in an institution ranged from $7,000 to $20,000 per year. Others argue that "start up" or initial outlay costs of (residential) community-based programs will be higher than that now estimated for traditional institutional programs. However, there appears to be general agreement that, over the long run, even residential community-based programs will be far less costly than institutional programs.

persons confined to prisons are rendered worthless in
their own eyes. Treatment in the community cannot possibly degrade them to a like degree. There is the additional advantage that community dealings with the trouble-
maker from their midst helps to bring home the responsibility which the neighborhood has for both criminogenic
conditions as well as for the individual offender.

The community-based corrections concept has also received
official sanction from such august bodies as the President's Commission on Law Enforcement and Administration of Justice, in 1967,
and the National Advisory Commission on Criminal Justice Standards
and Goals (1973). The report by the latter committee sounded especially encouraging:

> The Commission considers community based corrections
> as the most promising means of accomplishing the
> changes in offender behavior that the public expects and
> in fact now demands of corrections.
>   Dissatisfaction with incarceration as a means of
> correction has grown to a point where some states have
> almost completely abolished incarceration for some
> classes of offenders. In other states, experimental
> programs have been successful enough that once-over-
> crowded prisons and reformatories now are unused.
> Clearly, the future lies with community based cor-
> rections.

Good progress toward achieving those goals appeared to be
well within reach when this latter report was being formulated. By
the mid-1960s, probation and parole programs had been implemented
in all states, and many such services had even been established at
the lower (misdemeanant) court level in many jurisdictions. Work
release and training release programs that had been developed in
Wisconsin and North Carolina also achieved considerable widespread
acceptance. Such innovative concepts as bail reform and pretrial
diversion were also gaining national attention, due to the efforts of
the Vera Institute in New York.
     When it came to correctional reform, however, the most
dramatic, and perhaps controversial, example occurred in the state
of Massachusetts between 1969 and 1973. During that time, Commissioner Jerome Miller closed all of the State Department of Youth
Services reform schools and replaced them with community-based
programs operated primarily by private groups. While these efforts were not met without considerable resistance, substantial

correctional reform did occur as a result of limited planning and a good public relations campaign.

Even as late as 1975, in the state of Washington, Governor Daniel Evans proposed a reorganization of the state's correctional system. The governor's plan called for construction of seven "secure" and eight "moderately secure" small corrections centers, while reducing the populations at the Monroe Reformatory and the Washington State Penitentiary. These corrections centers are to be located in or near urban centers and their populations are to be small enough so that, as Department of Social and Health Services Secretary Morris put it, "corrections staff will be dealing with individuals rather than a mob." This radical plan did not occur overnight, nor did it occur in isolation of equally controversial changes in correctional policy. Washington State, a recognized leader in corrections, had been long involved in such programs as halfway houses, group homes, work and training release programs, probation subsidy programs, and so on.*

THE PROBLEM

Thus, as we entered the 1970s the pattern appeared to be quite evident. The concept of community-based corrections had been officially sanctioned as the programming model for the future; progressive jurisdictions were adopting that model for their own attempts at correctional reform; and, furthermore, the concept had the widest possible support from theorists in the social sciences. The trend was clearly toward a "tearing down of the walls" and the focus was on the problem of "reintegrating" the offender into the community. But has the adoption of this policy been as widespread as expected? Is the nation clearly moving toward a state of massive and substantive correctional reform? The evidence would indicate otherwise. For the past several years we have witnessed the swing of the pendulum from left to center, then further and further to the right. As one recent article described it, "Those hardliners are

---

*In 1974 LEAA launched a rather limited effort in community-based corrections programming in the following areas: Duluth/St. Louis County, Missouri; Orlando/Orange County, Florida; Baton Rouge/East Baton Rouge Parish, Louisiana; Salt Lake City/Salt Lake County, Utah; San Mateo/San Mateo County, California; and Vancouver/Clark County, Washington. All of the programs in this demonstration project were based on a model program developed in Des Moines, Iowa.

back." Advocates for capital punishment have been quite successful in restoring the death penalty in several states, and others call
for "flat time" and an elimination of individualized treatment. Still
others advocate a call for swift and sure punishment. Most disturbing of all, however, is the recently renewed debate of punishment
versus rehabilitation, that is, the debate is addressing itself to the
issue of either punishment or rehabilitation.* While liberal correctional administrators and governmental officials advocate the adoption of the community-based corrections concept, middle America
appears to be heeding the call of "law and order." This, of course,
implies a return to the days when maximum use was made of incarceration and imprisonment and criminals and delinquents were out
of sight and out of mind.

     Thus, when we consider the future of the community-based
concept, we are faced with a dilemma. At a time when community-
based corrections are being proposed as alternatives to traditional
methods of processing offenders, there is a rising fear, among the
public, of crime and criminals.

     How can we explain this dilemma? Why is it that a concept
that seemingly provides an answer to our needs stands a very good
chance of never being adopted on other than a very limited basis?
Some would answer that this is not a new dilemma, that it has always
been an inherent problem of American criminal justice policy, and
that the problem is based on fundamental ideological or philosophical
differences held by those who wish to rehabilitate the criminal and
those who wish to protect society by punishing the criminal. It is
tempting to succumb to this explanation for it is reasonably sound
and may, in fact, be partially valid. Other more subtle explanations
can be found if we are willing to be more critical in our analysis.

     While ideological orientation may indeed be an important con-
tributing variable in the understanding of resistance to correctional
reform, the relationship between ideology and resistance to reform
does not appear to be necessary and sufficient.

     According to Cressey (1968), the following sources of resis-
tance to correctional reform exist:

     There are four principal and interrelated sources of re-
     sistance to innovation in the field of corrections. These

_____

*One such conference held in Seattle, Washington, on Decem-
ber 18, 19, and 20, 1975, had over 1,500 persons in attendance.
The conference was jointly sponsored by the King County Prosecutors Office and the Law and Justice Planning Office.

are: conflicting theories regarding efficiency of measures for maximizing the amount of conformity in the
society; the social organization necessary to adminis-
tering correctional programs; the characteristics and
ideologies of correctional personnel; and the organization of correctional clients to each other and to correctional personnel.

All of the above are indeed important sources of resistance
to correctional reform. However, a fifth, and perhaps the most
important source of resistance, has not yet been identified. To this
list we would add the resistance of the community. If we were considering the broader topic of prison reform, then community acceptance or resistance would not be so important a factor. The
success of such efforts are not so dependent upon community acceptance. It would seem imperative, however, that efficient implementation of any community-based program will require administrators and program planners to enlist the support and involvement
of the community. A major thesis of this chapter is that we have
failed in many of our attempts at correctional reform because we
have not taken the time or effort to involve the community, and thus
to gain its support.

The President's Commission on Law Enforcement and Administration of Justice recognized the necessity for involvement in its
1967 report:

Failure to involve important elements of the correctional
community can jeopardize not only the creation of new
community programs but the survival of those which
prove successful. . . . It is also essential that representatives of allied service agencies such as welfare and
mental health be involved in the planning for community
programs. . . . Finally, one of the most critical problems in developing new community programs is to secure the involvement and participation of the community
itself.

In spite of this earlier recommendation, the field of corrections has all but ignored the importance of community involvement
in program planning and implementation. Correctional agencies
have not only isolated themselves from each other, they also have
managed to isolate themselves from other components of the criminal justice system, or should we say, "nonsystem." More important, with few rare exceptions, correctional agencies have maintained a policy of noninvolvement with the community and have

expected the same in return. The general public, on the other hand, has maintained a policy of "out of sight, out of mind" for its criminal and delinquent offenders. All indications are that the public would rather not have direct contact with delinquent and criminal offenders, and that it characteristically leaves such contacts to its formal agents of social control.

This unfortunate situation has resulted in three major obstacles to correctional reform:

1. The general public lacks adequate information about the correctional system and thus suffers from an inaccurate perception of its operation.

2. The general punlic lacks adequate information about correctional clients and thus suffers from an inaccurate perception as to the danger they pose to the community.

3. Correctional agencies do not have an accurate perception of how the public views them, their clients, or their practices.

A major problem for research, then, is that such programs are characteristically planned and implemented with little or no input from the community, and without empirical knowledge of the degree of support among various community groups. This is most unfortunate since the experience with such programs in the Netherlands and in Scandinavia suggest that such participation and support is absolutely necessary to ensure their effectiveness and continuation. (For an excellent discussion of these programs, see Conrad [1970].)

Alper (1974: 203) speaks of the need for a closely coordinated planning effort:

> The sources and types of likely opposition, financial aspects, timing, public information, legislative support-- all of these need to be documented and analyzed for the benefit of others who may now be willing to embark on the new course. Existing information from the theoretical and applied research and the vast range of available alternatives should now be made available to correctional authorities, juvenile institutions and agencies, universities and other research bodies.

But we, in America, have just discovered that body of knowledge and skills known as "criminal justice planning"; and even though we might be aware of its existence, we have yet to fully appreciate its potential. This is quite apparent when an outsider reviews the workings of our nonsystem of criminal justice that I mentioned earlier. In contrast, our colleagues who have been affiliated with the fields of mental health and mental retardation have obviously made good use of planning and community organization skills. Faced with similar obstacles, both fields have made a smoother transition from institutional programs to community-based programs than we are now experiencing.

As Conrad (1965) has pointed out, the correctional administrator will never be in a position to design his services to his heart's desire. Nor is it conceivable that the day will ever come when offenders can be processed through a correctional program with only those things done for him that need to be done. Any comprehensive reform effort that is as controversial as the proposed transition from institutional to community-based corrections must be based on a series of compromises. What we are saying is that we have failed to fully utilize an already existing body of knowledge, skills, and techniques in the planning and implementation of community-based programs.

We know, for example, that community resistance to such programs is often based on fear of personal safety, fear of loss of material possessions, and feelings that the neighborhood reputation, and thus property values, will decline (Yablonsky 1967; Empey, Erickson 1972). However, we do not know who is likely to feel this way, or why they take this position. Furthermore, we do not know if community-based programs are more successful in some kinds of neighborhoods than others, whether they are more effective with some offender types, and not others, and so on.

The sociological literature contains a paucity of information about the community-based corrections concept. Not only is information lacking concerning the programs per se, it is almost entirely lacking regarding public attitudes toward the community-based corrections concept. The singular exception would be Alternatives to Prison: Community Based Corrections (Perlstein, Phelps 1975). Unfortunately, this contains very little about the problem of public   resistance to the community-based corrections concept.

Of the few studies mentioned in the literature, several having relevance for this chapter are the national surveys conducted by Louis Harris and associates for the Joint Commission on Correctional Manpower and Training in 1968-69 (Harris 1968a, 1968b, 1969).

Unfortunately, none of these studies dealt exclusively or even extensively with the community-based corrections concept. A partial explanation for this was that, at the time of the Harris surveys, the community-based corrections concept was still being developed and was relatively unknown. Nevertheless, some of the responses to items contained in these early studies had far-reaching implications for present-day correctional programming. It is unfortunate that we did not pay more attention to them at that time.

The first study (Harris 1968a) found that community-based corrections were looked upon with an air of distrust, and the public was reluctant to see its use expanded. This was in spite of the fact that by a two-to-one margin there was a general feeling that not enough help was being given to offenders released from prison. The survey disclosed that, despite its awareness of the reentry problem, the public was personally reluctant to have close or frequent contact with such offenders who had served time for violent crimes. Furthermore, desire for the most severe penalties and the greatest degree of uneasiness about contact with offenders were found among the lower-income and less educated groups. It is a tragic irony that most convicted offenders come from these same groups and that many correctional administrators feel that community-based programs must be located in areas containing such groups.

This study also revealed considerable community resistance toward the concept of the "halfway house." While most people (77 percent) felt that the halfway house idea was a good one, when they were asked if they would personally favor a halfway house being established in their neighborhood, their support dropped to 50 percent. When further asked how they felt most people in their neighborhood would feel about such programs, opposition increased to a two-to-one margin.

The second Harris study (1968b) was designed to measure the attitudes of correctional personnel toward three substantive areas: the criminal justice system, education and training as preparation for current job, and attitudes toward present job and agency. Most correctional personnel felt that true rehabilitation required equal attention to individual treatment of the offender and to influencing and changing community patterns that create the conditions in which crime flourishes or reintegration of the offender becomes all but impossible. However, less than three in ten believed that past counseling efforts have been very successful. Nevertheless, there was recognition of their potential value and overwhelming support for their continued use.

With respect to the reentry of the offender into the community, community acceptance was considered a major problem to be overcome. Further questioning by the research staff indicated that it was in this area that correctional personnel felt they were giving the least help.

When asked about their suggestions for improving corrections, a majority of the correctional workers felt that the community must be more involved and that there should be an increased use of both probation and parole. They did not believe that restraint was incompatible with rehabilitation. While these attitudes were clearly in support of the community-based corrections concept, it was recognized that such programs faced major problems in the areas of community acceptance, lack of trained personnel, lack of adequate funds, and so on.

The third Harris survey (1969) did not contain any items related specifically to volunteers' attitudes toward community-based corrections programs. This was surprising in view of the fact that an earlier Harris survey concluded that "one approach to achieving community acceptance and involvement is through the employment of volunteers in the correctional process."

A 1973 study by Berk and Rossi was designed to assess the receptivity of change in adult corrections among a sample of "elites" in Washington, Florida, and Illinois. These elites were defined as persons occupying a position that necessarily involved them in the formulation, approval, or administration of correctional policy.

Berk and Rossi (1973) found that the elites in their sample were very receptive to progressive correctional reform, but seemed convinced that such reforms would probably be resisted by the general public. A major conclusion of this study was that policy makers, regardless of their personal predispositions, would probably formulate policy that was felt to be consistent with the attitudes of their constituents. (The results of this study are not in keeping with the "low profile approach" used by many administrators in implementing such programs as group homes and halfway houses. Users of this approach first get the program in operation, then attempt to get the neighborhood and community to accept and support it.)

Riley and Rose (1975) conducted a similar survey of Washington State citizens. Using many of the same topics as Berk and Rossi, this study focused on the general area of "prison reform." While most attitudinal items were oriented to assessing the public's attitudes toward reforms in prisons and other correctional institutions, the study included three items that surveyed general attitudes toward the community-based corrections concept. Riley and Rose found general support for these programs, although the effect of program information upon attitudes toward program reform was found to be negligible (a major hypothesis of the study).

Roll (1975) is conducting a public opinion survey of attitudes toward the community-based corrections concept in the state of Washington. Utilizing a random sample of 500 Spokane, Washington, households, the study is focusing on four major classes of variables: demographic, ideological, social distance, and program support. Available theory and research would lead us to believe that demographic variables are highly influential in determining an individual's ideological orientation. This, in turn, will determine the degree to which he is willing to be in close proximity to offenders (social distance), and this relationship will affect the degree to which the

respondent will support community-based correctional programs.
Analysis and interpretation of the data could not be completed in
time for inclusion in this study. However, preliminary analysis of
the pretest data would indicate that most respondents will approve
of community-based corrections programs as long as they are not
located in their neighborhoods.

CONCLUSION

We are not so naive to believe that knowledge of public attitudes
toward these programs alone will guarantee that community programs
will be adopted in a given area. As pointed out by the National Advisory Commission on Criminal Justice Standards and Goals (1973),
we cannot gear our programs toward existing attitudes under the
assumption that attitudes never change. Such a policy necessarily
limits the degree of our innovation to existing levels of public acceptance.

What we are saying is that the public opinion survey can be a
valuable tool in the planning process for community-based corrections. Knowledge of such community attitudes can identify sources
and kinds of resistance, estimate the strength of that resistance,
and help us determine what kinds of programs are likely to be tol-
erated in a given area. We feel strongly that possession of such
knowledge can make the difference between success and failure of
many community-based corrections programs.

Boydell and Grindstaff (1971) state that the disparity between
executive policy and public attitude may be due to the fact that the
general public simply does not have access to the same information.
In those instances where change is being initiated at the executive
level, those supporting the revision in policy have the responsibility
of disseminating such information.

From our earlier discussion, we concluded that public perception of correctional clients and programs was, in fact, grossly dis-
torted. We attribute these inaccuracies to the perpetuation of popular myths and to the overdramatization of criminal behavior by the
mass media. Such stereotypical thinking will continue to pose an
obstacle to correctional reform until we take definitive action to
dispel it.

We also feel that we have little reason to recommend community-
based corrections programs when we do not have adequately trained
personnel to operate them efficiently. With few exceptions, the typical probation officer, parole officer, or corrections counselor lacks
the necessary advocacy and community organization skills. These
roles are foreign to many correctional workers, who have deliberately maintained a "low profile" in the community.

Thus, another planning consideration is that we must not only involve ourselves in the community but also involve the community in corrections. Many correctional administrators see volunteer programs as the answer to community involvement. However, this conception of community involvement is too narrow if the community-based corrections concept is to be successful. Citizens must be involved in every phase of program planning, implementation, and administration of community-based programs.

Finally, we must be painfully aware that community-based corrections programs are not appropriate for all offenders. Continued and extensive use of probation and parole programs for the past two decades has resulted in changing the composition of the populations of many of our large penal institutions. Some institutions receive only the most hardened and dangerous offenders. It may be inaccurate today to argue that "only ___% of our institutional population is really in need of maximum security." Residence in a maximum security institution should not automatically exclude an inmate from participation in community-based programs. On the other hand, it is apparent that some inmates should never be considered for such programs. High standards for screening and selection must be developed and maintained. To do otherwise not only endangers the community; it endangers the future of correctional reform as well.

GLOSSARY OF COMMUNITY-BASED
CORRECTIONS PROGRAMS

Community Corrections Centers (Mini-Prisons)

Small minimum- to moderate-custody institutions designed to provide short-term intensive treatment in a controlled environment. This is generally followed by a system of gradually relaxed controls aimed at helping the offender get reestablished in the community. Once he is so established, the offender is released under parole supervision. Likely to be operated by the state on a regional basis, they are designed to replace large prisons for all but the most dangerous and hardened of offenders.

Probation Subsidy Program

Provides for the state to pay counties for not committing certain types of offenders to state correctional institutions. Counties are then expected to use these state funds to develop their own innovative community-based programs as an alternative to institutional commitment. Only the most dangerous offenders would be sentenced to the state prisons.

Diversion Programs

Refers to all programs in which formal efforts are made to limit the processing of the delinquent or criminal offender into the criminal justice system. Before he is sentenced, formal proceedings are suspended and the offender is assigned to a rehabilitation program. If he completes the program, no further legal action is taken against him, and, in most cases, the offender is allowed to "clear" his record.

Special Intensive Supervision Programs

Selected probationers or parolees are carefully screened and classified and assigned to a specially trained probation/parole officer in the community. The officer then uses a special set of treatment and supervision techniques matched to the offender type. Caseloads of officers in such programs may consist of 5 to 15 offenders compared to 75 to 100 offenders on an average caseload not using these techniques.

Work Release Programs

Permits carefully screened offenders to leave prison or jail each day to go to a job in or near the community and to accept a job that is paid at the going wage rate. At the end of the day, the prisoner returns to the prison or jail. A special feature of this program is that the prisoner uses his earned wages to pay for his room and board while he is in jail or prison. He also is able to pay for the support of his family, and anything in excess of this is put into a savings account for the prisoner until the day of his release.

Training Release Programs

Like the work release program above, training release programs allow carefully screened offenders to leave jail or prison each day to attend vocational or educational programs. At the completion of his classes, the prisoner returns to the jail or prison, generally at night.

Halfway Houses

Small homelike residential programs located in or near the community. They are designed specifically for the offender who needs more control and supervision than he would ordinarily receive in traditional parole programs. Usually operated by private groups, organizations, or foundations, most of them have resident directors or house parents present around the clock, and nearly all of them employ a screening process to select certain individuals for admission. Depending on the nature of the program and type of offender served, various degrees of control and supervision are used.

Stipend Programs

Similar to the unemployment compensation program, this program provides selected parolees with $55 a week for a maximum of 26 weeks so that the parolee, when released, can adequately support himself without turning to crime. As soon as the parolee is financially self-sufficient, the payments are stopped. This program is generally supervised by parole officers and can be terminated at any time if the officer has reason to believe the parolee is not actively looking for work, violating the conditions of his parole, or breaking the law.

Prerelease Guidance Centers

These programs are designed specifically to ease the offender's transition from total confinement in an institution to freedom in the community. The program generally involves education or information sessions conducted by community agency representatives or other citizens in the community. These sessions cover such topics as using community resources, how to obtain a driver's license, legal problems of divorce, how to apply for a job, and so on. These programs were originally located on the grounds of correctional institutions, but many are now located in halfway-houselike facilities in, or near, the community. This program is usually administered by the same unit of government that administers the prison from which the prisoners are to be released on parole.

Furlough Programs

These programs allow selected inmates to be released for a brief period of time from a correctional institution, normally toward the end of their terms. Purpose is to help the inmate establish or reestablish his ties in the community. They may include family visits, interviews with potential employers, and the like, but they are not to be confused with supervised leaves that inmates ordinarily receive for family emergencies.

REFERENCES

Advisory Commission on Intergovernmental Relations
   1971   State-Local Relations in the Criminal Justice System.
           Washington, D.C.: U.S. Government Printing Office.

Alper, B. S.
  1974   Prisons Inside Out. Cambridge, Mass.: Ballinger.

Bailey, W. C.
  1966   Correctional outcome: an evaluation of 100 reports.
          Journal of Criminal Law, Criminology and Police Science
          (June).

Bakal, Y., ed.
  1973   Closing Correctional Institutions. Lexington, Mass.:
          D. C. Heath.

Berk, A., H. Rossi, W. E. Bose, and S. Zulver.
  1973   Corrections reform and state elites: assessing the poten-
          tials for change in state corrections systems. Unpublished
          joint report of the Social and Demographic Research In-
          stitute, University of Massachusetts, Amherst, and the
          Center for Urban Affairs, Northwestern University.

Biderman, A. D., S. S. Oldham, S. K. Ward, and M. A. Ebey
  1972   An Inventory of Surveys of the Public on Crime, Justice
          and Related Topics. Washington, D.C.: National Insti-
          tute of Law Enforcement and Criminal Justice, Law En-
          forcement Assistance Administration.

Boydell, C., and C. Grindstaff.
  1972   Public opinions and the criminal law: an empirical test
          of public opinions toward legal sanctions. In Deviant Be-
          havior and Societal Reaction, ed. C. Boydell, C. Grind-
          staff, and Whitehead. Toronto: Holt, Rinehart and
          Winston.

Clemmer, D.
  1971   The process of prisonization. In The Criminal in Con-
          finement, ed. L. Radzinowicz and M. Wolfgang. New
          York: Basic Books.

Conrad, J.
  1970   Crime and Its Correction: An International Survey of
          Attitudes and Practices. Los Angeles: University of
          California Press.

Cressey, D. R.
  1972   Sources of resistance to innovation in Corrections. In
          Correctional Institutions, ed. R. M. Carter, D. Gloser,
          and L. T. Wilkins. New York: J. B. Lippencott.

Empey, L., and M. Erickson
  1972   The Provo Experiment. Lexington, Mass.: D. C. Heath.

Galtung, J.
  1958   The social functions of a prison. Social Problems 6.

Gibbons, D. C.
  1963   Who knows what about corrections? Crime and Delin-
          quency 9 (April).

Goffman, E.
  1961   Asylums. Garden City, N.Y.: Anchor Books.

Harris, L.
  1969   Volunteers look at corrections. Survey conducted for
          the Joint Commission on Correctional Manpower and
          Training.

  1968a   The public looks at crime and corrections. A survey
          conducted for the Joint Commission on Correctional
          Manpower and Training.

  1968b   Corrections 1968: a climate for change. A survey con-
          ducted for the Joint Commission on Correctional Manpower
          and Training.

  n.d.   Changing public attitudes toward crime and corrections.
          Federal Probation 32 (December).

Irwin, J.
  1970   The Felon. Englewood Cliffs, N.J.: Prentice-Hall.

Menninger, K.
  1966   The Crime of Punishment. New York: Viking Press.

Miller, W. B.
  1973   Ideology and criminal justice policy: some current issues.
          Journal of Criminal Law and Criminology 64 (June).

Mitford, J.
  1971   Kind and Usual Punishment. New York: Vintage.

Morris, N.
  1966   Impediments to penal reform. University of Chicago Law
          Review 33 (Summer).

National Advisory Commission on Criminal Justice Standards and
Goals
    1973   Corrections. Task Force Report, Washington, D. C.

National Institute of Mental Health
    1971   Community Based Correctional Programs: Models and
            Practices. Washington, D. C. : NIMH.

Parker, H.
    1970   Juvenile court actions and public response. In Becoming
            Delinquent, ed. P. Garobedian and D. Gibbons. Chicago:
            Aldine.

Perlstein, G. R. , and T. Phelps, eds.
    1975   Alternatives to Prison: Community Based Corrections.
            Pacific Palisades, Calif. : Goodyear.

Riley, P. J. , and V. L. Rose
    1975   Prison reform and public policy. Paper presented at the
            Annual Meeting of the Pacific Sociological Association,
            Victoria, British Columbia.

Roll, H. W.
    1975   Public Attitudes toward Community Based Correctional
            Programs. Ph.D. dissertation, Washington State Uni-
            versity, Pullman.

Sykes, G.
    1958   Society of Captives. Princeton, N. J. : Princeton Uni-
            versity Press.

Yablonsky, L.
    1967   Synanon: The Tunnel Back. Baltimore: Penguin Books.

ABOUT THE EDITOR AND CONTRIBUTORS

DENIS SZABO received his doctorate in social and political science in 1956 at the University of Louvain, and his degree in criminology at the Sorbonne in 1958. He has lectured at the Universities of Louvain, Lyon, and Paris and since 1958 has been a professor at the University of Montreal. He is the author of many books, in particular works on urban crime, new forms of delinquency, and public reaction to them. Dr. Szabo was the founder of the School of Criminology of the University of Montreal and the International Centre for Comparative Criminology of which he is Director. He is a member of many Canadian, American, and European societies including the Royal Society of Canada, the American Society of Criminology, and the American Sociological Society and he is the vice-president of the International Society of Criminology. Dr. Szabo has been called upon as consultant by a number of commissions of inquiry, among them Le Comite d'etude sur la violence, la criminalite et la delinquance (France), the President's Commission on Law Enforcement and the Administration of Justice, and the Eisenhower Commission on Violence.

SUSAN KATZENELSON received her bachelor's degree from Tel-Aviv University and her master's degree from the University of Pennsylvania. Presently she is a doctoral candidate at the University of Pennsylvania, completing her dissertation with an LEAA fellowship on the "Female Defendant in the Criminal Justice System." She also teaches criminology and methodology at the Center for the Administration of Justice of the American University in Washington, D.C. and is involved in research on the female offender, deterrence, and the processing of cases in the criminal justice system.

RONALD L. AKERS is Professor of Sociology at the University of Iowa, currently on leave as a Visiting Fellow at the Boys Town Center for the Study of Youth Development. He is the author of Deviant Behavior: A Social Learning Approach and Control in Society (with Richard Hawkins). His current research at the Boys Town Center is on adolescent drinking and drug use and on the diffusion of knowledge and opinion about the law.

JOSEPH J. COCOZZA has recently taken the position of Director of the Bureau of Research and Program Evaluation of the New York State Council on Children and Families. For the past five years he has worked with Dr. Henry Steadman in the New York State Department of Mental Hygiene's Special Projects Research Unit. During that period he focused primarily on the collection and analysis of data regarding the psychiatric predictions of dangerous behavior. In addition, he has merged his interest in the relationship between violence and mental illness with his interest in youth in a continuing research project on a special program for violent, mentally disordered juveniles. This research and others related to the provision of child care services will continue in his new position. Dr. Cocozza received his Ph. D. in Sociology from Case Western Reserve University.

DENNIS D. DORIN obtained his undergraduate training in political science at Arizona State University and received the Ph. D. in government from the University of Virginia. He has contributed articles to professional journals on Supreme Court policy making and public policy analysis in criminal justice. Dr. Dorin is currently Assistant Professor of Political Science at the University of North Carolina at Charlotte, North Carolina.

RENÉE GOLDSMITH-KASINSKY has taught criminology and sociology of law courses at both the University of Calgary and the University of British Columbia, Canada. She has also served as a consultant to both the Department of the Attorney General of British Columbia, as part of the Justice Development Commission, and the Health Security Programme of British Columbia during the years 1973-76. Presently, she is a professor of sociology at Utah State University in Logan, Utah.

DON M. GOTTFREDSON is Dean and Professor at the Rutgers University School of Criminal Justice. Formerly Director of the Research Center of the National Council on Crime and Delinquency, Dr. Gottfredson is a Fellow of the National Center for Juvenile Justice, a member of the Advisory Council of the National Institute of Law Enforcement and Criminal Justice, and Vice President of the American Society of Criminology. He has been a consultant or advisor to various national and state criminal justice planning bodies including recent membership on the Task Force on Research and Development, National Criminal Justice Standards and Goals and Chairmanship, New Jersey Correctional Master Plan Policy Council.

WERNER GRUNINGER is an assistant professor of sociology-corrections, and assistant director of a graduate program in corrections, at Oklahoma State University. He has taught criminology in Canada and in the United States for fourteen years. Most of his other publications were in the area of the inmate subculture. He is presently engaged in the study of sentencing disparity, and has submitted a text in corrections for publication. He holds a B.A. from the University of British Columbia, an M.A. from Duke University, and a Ph. D. from the University of Seattle, Washington.

NORMAN S. HAYNER (deceased 1977) was Professor Emeritus of
Sociology of the University of Washington. He was author of Hotel
Life and of numerous articles in sociology and criminology during
the past 55 years. His career included a term as Chairman of the
Washington State Board of Prison Terms and Parole.

ELLEN HANDLER is currently assistant professor at the University
of Illinois School of Social Work in Urbana, Illinois. Her primary
areas of specialization are social policy, program evaluation,
corrections and delinquency. Much of her work has been in social
policy issues related to the field of corrections. The current article
presents evidence to support the expansion of halfway programs and
community based alternatives to the current system whereby offenders
are exiled for lengthy periods of time to isolated, fortress type prison
settings.

ROBERT JOHNSON obtained his undergraduate training in psychology
at Fairfield University and received his Ph. D. in criminal justice from
the State University of New York at Albany. His published works include
Culture and Crisis in Confinement and articles in professional journals on
the social psychology of prison survival. Dr. Johnson is currently Assistant Professor of Administration of Justice at The American University
in Washington, D. C.

PETER B. MEYER, Associate Professor of Economic Planning in the
Division of Community Development at the Pennsylvania State University,
has been conducting research in a broad range of topics associated with
public sector productivity, including issues of public-private interactions and balance. Author of Drug Experiments on Prisoners, as well
as numerous other books and articles, he is currently focusing his
research on community economic development and issues of corporation-
community interactions. His research approaches socioeconomic problems from a socialist perspective and he applies a mix of Marxist and
systems analysis to social problems.

MARTIN B. MILLER is presently Assistant Professor in the Center
for Studies in Criminal Justice, St. Cloud State University, Minnesota.
He is also a doctoral candidate at the University of California, Berkeley
studying illicit check-writers.

HERBERT W. ROLL is presently Assistant Professor of Sociology/
Social Work at Eastern Washington University. He received his B. A.
from E. W. U. in 1963, his M. S. W. from the University of Washington in
1969, and his Ph. D. in Sociology from Washington State University in
1976. He is a past Parole Officer, Supervisor, and Trainer with the

Washington State Division of Adult Corrections and presently acts as a Training and Organizational Consultant for several governmental agencies in the Pacific Northwest.

PETER SCHARF is an Assistant Professor in the Program in Social Ecology at the University of California at Irvine. He is completing a book on the "Just Community Approach to Corrections" to be published in the Fall of 1978. He is currently studying moral decision making by police officers facing discretionary situations.

LORI SCHUETT has a M.S.W. and teaches at the School of Social Work, the University of Illinois-Urbana.

HENRY J. STEADMAN is Director of the Special Projects Research Unit of the New York State Department of Mental Hygiene in Albany. He has been there since receiving his Ph.D. in Sociology from the University of North Carolina, Chapel Hill, in 1970. Much of his work has examined the legal and organizational implications of diversion from the criminal justice system into mental health programs. A particular focus has been on the role of psychiatric predictions of dangerousness in these processes. He is currently directing a project examining situational factors associated with violence in mental patients and offenders. He is also an Adjunct Associate Professor in the Sociology Department of SUNY-Albany.

PETER WICKMAN, author of "Industrial Wages for Prisoners in Finland and Sweden," has conducted research on community based alternatives to incarceration and local corrections. This article is one of several he has written as a result of his study tour of Nordic corrections in 1974. He has published articles on crime, deviance, and delinquency, edited several books on criminology and also social policy, and is senior author of a forthcoming text in criminology. He is currently Professor of Sociology at State University of New York, College at Potsdam.

NANCI KOSER WILSON teaches at Southern Illinois University at Carbondale.

AMERICAN SOCIETY OF CRIMINOLOGY SERIES

THE EFFECTIVENESS OF CORRECTIONAL
TREATMENT: A Survey of Treatment
Evaluation Studies

> Douglas Lipton
> Robert Martinson
> Judith Wilks

PRISONER EDUCATION: Project NewGate and
Other College Programs

> Marjorie J. Seashore
> Steven Haberfeld

REFORM IN CORRECTIONS: Problems and Issues

> edited by Harry E. Allen
> Nancy J. Beran

TREATING THE OFFENDER: Problems and Issues

> edited by Marc Riedel
> Pedro A. Vales

YOUTH CRIME AND JUVENILE JUSTICE:
International Perspectives

> edited by Paul C. Friday
> V. Lorne Stewart